The UN, UNESCO and the Politics of Knowledge

Clare Wells

St. Martin's Press   New York

First published in the United States of America in 1987

Printed in Hong Kong

ISBN 0-312-83277-X

Library of Congress Cataloging-in-Publication Data
Wells, Clare
The UN, UNESCO and the politics of knowledge.
Bibliography: p.
Includes index.
1. Unesco. 2. Freedom of information (International
law) 3. Politics and education. I. Title.
AS4.U83W39 1987   341.7'67   86-6567
ISBN 0-312-83277-X

To Amna

Contents

Contents

Preface

At the beginning of the 1970s, the average member of the Western public was likely to be either oblivious or jokingly dismissive of UNESCO. The Agency was probably best known at the time to Third World countries where it ran operational projects; to professional circles in the fields of education, science and culture; to the populace of the headquarters city of Paris; and of course to its official and former staff, such as this writer.

Between 1974 and 1976 UNESCO achieved sudden notoriety as press coverage on a scale unprecedented in its history alleged, in response to decisions affecting Israel and debates on the mass media, that the Organisation had become 'politicised'.

This study was begun in the late 1970s and completed in mid-1983. Since that time and in line with the general arguments of the study, which has been updated to record subsequent factual developments, the USA and the UK withdrew from membership and further Western pullouts were canvassed.

At the same time, criticism of the Agency came to focus increasingly on the person of its Director-General since 1974, and in particular on allegations of mismanagement and overspending. These more recent accusations may or may not be well-grounded, but in any case do not seem to me to be at the heart of the debate on 'politicisation'.

It is instead to an examination of concepts of 'politicisation' as applied to the UN system and of the deeper issues which gave rise to the original charges that the present study is devoted. If the book serves in some measure to make better known a side of the discussion which to date has received less than its share of coverage, then it will have been worthwhile.

CLARE WELLS

Acknowledgements

I am indebted to all those who have contributed moral, material and intellectual support to the preparation of this book.

In the first place, I thank the Social Science Research Council (now the Economic and Social Research Council), Nuffield College and the Centre National de la Recherche Scientifique for the awards and scholarships which financed the research.

Thanks are due, too, to those at the University of Oxford who helped from the earliest stages of research. Most especially, I wish to thank Mr Wilfred Knapp of St Catherine's College and Dr Laurence Whitehead of Nuffield College for their encouragement and attentive scrutiny of the arguments; and the Warden and Fellows of Nuffield College for their support at all times; and the late Professor Hedley Bull, Montague Burton Professor of International Relations, Balliol College, for the opportunity to present a seminar paper in which some of the ideas were first aired.

Warmest thanks go to Professor Christopher Thorne, to Dr Stuart Holland M.P. and to Dr Michael Leigh whose teaching, enthusiasm and guidance at the University of Sussex encouraged the endeavours which ultimately led to this study.

I wish to express my gratitude to the many officials of UNESCO, present and retired, who gave generously of time and information but who are too numerous to be listed here individually.

I am also grateful to Ambassador John Reinhardt, Head of the United States Delegation to the 20th Session of the General Conference, and to Mr V. D. Dratch, First Secretary of the Permanent Delegation of the USSR to UNESCO for taking the trouble to answer questions.

Thanks go, too, to Mr Charles Hargrove and to Miss Colleen Roach, consultants to UNESCO, for agreeing to answer queries in 1983.

The later stages of research were completed after I took up employment with the European Parliament in Luxembourg. The Grand Duchy has too small a population to support a university and has no depositary library for English-language documentation of the United Nations system. In seeking to overcome the resulting difficulties, I counted myself fortunate in the consistently patient and knowledgeable response of many librarians and archivists to my enquiries. Most particularly, I wish to thank Mr M. Jarvinen, Chief of

UNESCO Archives and Records Management Section; Mr Donald Ross, British Library of Political and Economic Science; Mrs P. Farquhar of the United Nations Information Office in London; Mrs H. Coppolecchia of the European Parliament Library in Luxembourg; Miss Collinet, Library of the Institut Royal des Relations Internationales in Brussels; Mr Jean Onckelinx of the United Nations Information Office in Brussels; Mr Breynzeels of the Bibliothèque Royale Albert in Brussels; Mr Gavilan of the Bibliothèque Nationale du Luxembourg; Mrs Golliez-Meyer of the Council of Europe Library in Strasbourg; Mr van Bellinghen of the United Nations Information Office in Paris; the Distribution and Sales Section of the United Nations in Geneva; and staffs of the Bodleian, British and European Parliament Libraries more generally.

Warm thanks go to former colleagues and friends at UNESCO for smoothing a number of paths, especially Chela Birkas, Jenny Clark, Brenda Paladini, Cynthia Horn, Jane Raïs, Carole Bradley, Joan Budd, Carmen Boisson, and Dinah Winship-Bouteiller.

I also owe sincere gratitude to European Parliament colleagues at all levels, especially Mr Enrico Boaretto, for their support and understanding during completion of the research.

Last, but closest to home, fondest thanks to family and friends who bore with me and volunteered help of every kind: my mother, father and sister Helly; my husband Muawia; Nena and Sue; Maggie; Brigitte and Heidi; Joyce; and Rita.

Finally, let it be stressed that none of those who have helped me with this book are accountable for its arguments or conclusions.

List of Abbreviations

ACC	Allied Control Council
Add.	Addendum
ADG/CC	Assistant Director-General for Culture and Communication
AFL/CIO	American Federation of Labor/Congress of Industrial Organizations
AFP	Agence France-Presse
*ahPC	*ad hoc* Political Committee
AJIL	*American Journal of International Law*
Ann.	Annex
AP	Associated Press
Apartheid Convention	International Convention on the Suppression and Punishment of the Crime of *Apartheid*
App.	Appendix
Art.	Article
AT&T	American Telephones and Telegraphs
Beirut Agreement	Agreement for Facilitating the International Circulation of Visual and Auditory Materials of an Educational, Scientific and Cultural Character
BYIL	*British Yearbook of International Law*
*C.1	First Committee
*C.3	Third Committee
CAME	Conference of Allied Ministers of Education
Ch.	Chapter
CHR	Commission on Human Rights
CIA	Central Intelligence Agency
*CIRC	Convention on the International Right of Correction
COMECON	Council for Mutual Economic Assistance
Corr.	Corrigendum
*CR File	Central Registry File
*(d)CITNRC	(Draft) Convention on the International Transmission of News and Right of Correction

* Abbreviations devised by the author

DDG	Deputy Director-General
Dept	Department
DEVCOM	International Conference for Co-operation on Activities, Needs and Programmes for Communication Development
Doc(s)	Document(s)
DG	Director-General
DNG	Drafting and Negotiation Group
ECOSOC	Economic and Social Council
EEC	European Economic Community
EXB	Executive Board
FAO	Food and Agriculture Organisation
FBI	Federal Bureau of Investigation
Florence Agreement	Agreement on Importation of Educational, Scientific and Cultural Materials
FO	Foreign Office
FT	*The Financial Times*
GATT	General Agreement on Trade and Tariffs
*Gen.C.	General Committee
IAA	International Association of Art
IAAB	Inter-American Association of Broadcasters
IAEA	International Atomic Energy Agency
IAPA	Inter-American Press Association
IBRD	International Bank for Reconstruction and Development
ICCPR	International Covenant on Civil and Political Rights
ICPIW	International Confederation of Professional and Intellectual Workers
ICSU	International Council of Scientific Unions
IFA	International Federation of Actors
IFAC	International Federation of Authors and Composers
IFM	International Federation of Musicians
IFTC	International Film and Television Council
IHT	*International Herald Tribune*
ILET	Instituto Latinoamericano de Estudios Transnacionales
ILO	International Labour Office

* Abbreviations devised by the author

IMF	International Monetary Fund
IOJ	International Organisation of Journalists
IPDC	International Programme for Development of Communication
*IPDC IGC	Intergovernmental Council of the IPDC
IPI	International Press Institute
ITU	International Telecommunications Union
LNTS	*League of Nations Treaty Series*
MacBride Commission	International Commission for the Study of Communication Problems
Media Declaration	Declaration on Fundamental Principles concerning the Contribution of the Mass Media to Strengthening Peace and International Understanding, to the Promotion of Human Rights and to Countering Racialism, *Apartheid* and Incitement to War
mtg(s)	meeting(s)
NGO(s)	Non-governmental organisation(s)
NIEO	New International Economic Order
NIO	New Information Order
NWICO	New World Information and Communication Order
NY	New York
NYT	*New York Times*
OPEC	Organisation of Petroleum-Exporting Countries
Outer Space Treaty	Treaty on Principles Governing the Activities of States in the Exploration and Use of Outer Space including the Moon and other Celestial Bodies
para(s)	paragraph(s)
*Plen	Plenary
PLO	Palestine Liberation Organisation
PRO	Public Record Office
prov.	provisional
Race Convention	International Convention for the Elimination of All Forms of Racial Discrimination
resp.	respectively
rev.	revised

* Abbreviations devised by the author

Rec.	Recommendation
Satellite Declaration	Declaration of Guiding Principles on the Use of Satellite Broadcasting for the Free Flow of Information, the Spread of Education and Greater Cultural Exchanges
SCC	Sub-Commission on Communication
SCE	Sub-Commission on Education
*SCFIP	Sub-Commission on Freedom of Information and the Press
*SCPDPM	Sub-Commission on Prevention of Discrimination and Protection of Minorities
*Soc.C.	Social Committee
ST	*The Sunday Times*
STC	Standard Telephone & Cables Ltd
Supp.	Supplement
TASS	Telegrafnoie Agenstvo Sovietskavo Soyusa
UDHR	Universal Declaration of Human Rights
UK	United Kingdom
UN	United Nations
UNCTAD	United Nations Conference on Trade and Development
UN DPI	United Nations Department of Public Information
UNESCO	United Nations Educational, Scientific and Cultural Organisation
UNRWA	United Nations Relief and Works Agency for Palestine Refugees in the Near East
UNTS	*United Nations Treaty Series*
UPI	United Press International
USA	United States of America
USSR	Union of Soviet Socialist Republics
WFSW	World Federation of Scientific Workers
WPFC	World Press Freedom Committee
WHO	World Health Organisation
YUN	*Yearbook of the United Nations*

* Abbreviations devised by the author

1 Introduction: Concepts of 'Politicisation'

INTRODUCTION

It has become conventional in the United States and in the West more generally to claim that the Specialised Agencies of the United Nations, and particularly the United Nations Educational, Scientific and Cultural Organisation (UNESCO) and the International Labour Office (ILO), have departed from their properly technical mandates and have become 'politicised'.

This chapter will be devoted to analysis of the concept of 'politicisation', and conversely of 'consensus', as applied to the Specialised Agencies. While the empirical part of this work will be concerned with UNESCO and the politics of standard-setting in the sphere of knowledge, the focus of the present chapter will be more broadly comparative.

After setting out representative statements of the prevailing concept of 'politicisation', we shall identify what seem to be its core components, and shall then attempt to place the discussion in a broader perspective.

1. THE PREVAILING CONCEPT OF 'POLITICISATION'

As a basis for analysing the prevailing concept of 'politicisation', let us consider some representative statements of the case. The principal authors of the charge have been American policy-making, academic and media circles, echoed more mildly by their West European counterparts.

The charge was first to be aired in strength during the mid-1970s. Henry Kissinger referred in July 1975 to 'the trend in the Specialised Agencies to focus on political issues' and claimed that UNESCO and the ILO had 'become heavily politicized'.[1] Similarly, the US Congress spoke of UNESCO's 'recent actions of a primarily political character', while George Meany of the AFL/CIO denounced what he described as the 'blatant, outrageous and unconstitutional politicisation of the ILO and UNESCO'.[2]

Meanwhile, in an article in *International Organisation* in 1976, David Kay expressed the view that

> the functional and technical operations of many of the specialized agencies have become more and more politicized through the introduction of issues designed to attain political ends extraneous to the substantive, technical purposes and programs for which [they] were established.[3]

The nature of the political ends in question was outlined by Kay in a description of recent 'shocks' within the UN system as a whole. These included:

> increasingly aggressive challenges and opposition to Israeli legitimacy and policies, including the equating of Zionism with racism . . . and action in UNESCO to exclude Israel from the European group; support for national liberation movements, including a call for the United States to grant full independence to Puerto Rico; demands for the redistribution of global economic wealth, culminating in a call for the establishment of a New International Economic Order; . . . a general conversion of UN forums into platforms for vitriolic attacks on the West in general and the United States specifically. . . .[4]

In a policy-oriented volume edited by Kay, John Holmes referred to 'the excessive politicization' of the Israeli issue and to 'the notorious resolution equating Zionism with racism'.[5]

Most recently, in announcing in December 1983 that the USA intended to withdraw from UNESCO at the end of December 1984, the State Department claimed that 'UNESCO has extraneously politicized virtually every subject it deals with', and specifically denounced the Agency's policies with respect to the press.[6]

Meanwhile Richard Hoggart, a former senior British official of UNESCO, and one not unsympathetic to Third World positions, defined politicisation as 'the distortion of debate by the *irrelevant* introduction of political issues' (Hoggart's emphasis).[7] More specifically, Professor Hoggart held that:

> What came to be known as the 'Israel resolutions' of the 1974 General Conference marked a main moment in this accelerated, planned and strong politicisation of the Organisation at the expense of any serious attempt at objectivity.[8]

(The UNESCO 'Israel resolutions' were three in number. One alleged that Israeli occupation adversely affected Palestinian rights in the spheres of education and culture, and called upon the Director-General to monitor the situation.[9] Another condemned Israeli archaeological excavations in East Jerusalem as altering the historical and cultural nature of occupied territory, and instructed the Director-General to withhold assistance from Israel until it complied with earlier UNESCO resolutions on the subject.[10] The third rejected Israel's application to join the group designated 'Europe' for the purpose of regional activities.[11] The fact that the three resolutions were widely portrayed by Western media as amounting, singly or jointly, to expulsion of Israel from UNESCO led the Director-General, among others, to issue explanations and denials that such had been their effect.[12])

As can be seen from the above statements, the challenge to Israeli legitimacy features prominently in recent charges of 'politicisation'. Indeed, it may fairly be deemed to have become a defining characteristic of the phenomenon as seen from the Western perspective. Not surprisingly, Zionist organisations and spokesmen for Israel have been among the severest critics of recent trends.[13]

The view expressed in several of the above statements that UNESCO and the ILO have become especially 'politicised' was endorsed in a formal 'politicization continuum' drawn up by Lyons, Baldwin and McNemar, which ranks the Specialised Agencies according to the likelihood that they would 'have controversial issues introduced in their governing bodies'.[14] UNESCO, followed by the ILO, is shown as the most politicised agency; the International Atomic Energy Agency (IAEA), the International Monetary Fund (IMF) and the World Bank (IBRD), in that order, feature as the least politicised; and the Food and Agriculture Organisation (FAO) and World Health Organisation (WHO) lie somewhere in between. This rank order, according to the authors, 'closely parallels the relative degree to which the agency has been attacked by the United States on grounds of "politicization"'.[15]

Robert Gregg, too, saw the IMF and IBRD as among the least politicised agencies:

> [In] the World Bank, the IMF, and the GATT . . . bloc politics is much muted. . . . Elsewhere, blocs are much in evidence. . . . UNCTAD has been the most conspicuously confrontational of international organizations. . . . Nowhere else in the UN system are bloc politics more evident.[16]

The extent to which an Agency is 'politicised' is held by certain commentators to correlate inversely with the degree to which its substantive concerns are 'technical, specific and essential' and, by extension, with the professionalism of its staff.[17] 'Technical' subjects are defined as those comprising a body of 'hard' or 'sophisticated' knowledge. Thus if, as is often claimed, Agencies such as the IAEA, the International Telecommunications Union (ITU) and the WHO are in some measure less 'politicised' than UNESCO and the ILO, this is seen to be because the subjects they handle are correspondingly more technical.

A further explanation for the extent of 'politicisation' is seen to lie in the habitual scale of media attention devoted to an Agency, it being assumed that 'politicisation' will be greater where the normal degree of media concern is higher.[18] If, for example, the ITU is seen as comparatively unpoliticised, this tends to be attributed to the disparity, noted by Jacobson as a paradox, between the 'immense commercial and political implications' of the Agency's work and its 'relative obscurity'.[19]

The charge of 'politicisation' is made by implicit or explicit reference to 'consensus', viewed as the opposite and ideal state. 'Consensus' tends not to be defined with precision but to be treated as both a process and an outcome, as in the following statement:

> UN organs have increasingly adopted proposals by consensus rather than by recorded votes. Such a process permits intense negotiation in working groups, while final action is *pro forma* approval in a plenary session. This technique also promotes general consensus on acceptable international action while preventing proposals that produce intense division among the members. The emphasis is on creating documents that command universal assent rather than forcing some nations into negative votes that would jeopardise the consensus for action by the agency.[20]

Meanwhile Robert Gregg, who characterises certain UNCTAD decisions as reflecting an 'artificial consensus',[21] records that 'the minority of developed states has tried to persuade the developing state majority to abjure voting in favour of consultation leading to consensus',[22] while John Holmes notes that 'the Law of the Sea Conference . . . has been remarkably inventive of new procedures to reach consensus'.[23]

Analysis of the 'politicisation' charge as expressed by the observers quoted above, among others, would seem to reveal the following core elements.

A. The intrusion of 'extraneous' politics: challenges to legitimacy arising from altered power relations in the wider environment

This aspect of the charge has its origin in the functionalist approach to international organisation. Classically expounded by David Mitrany,[24] the functionalist approach relies on a dichotomy between the technical and the political, and in particular between 'high politics' (diplomatic and strategic issues) and 'low politics' (welfare issues). The structure of the UN system embodies this distinction, the UN having traditionally been regarded (in Anglo-Saxon circles at least) as the 'political' body of the system, and the Specialised Agencies as its functional or 'apolitical' auxiliaries.

'Politicisation' at this first level is conceived as violation of the technical nature of the Agencies by the introduction of issues in some sense extraneous or irrelevant to their substantive, functional concerns. Issues so characterised prove on inspection to be of two sorts.

First, they include challenges to existing institutional structure, that is, matters of political representation and legitimacy. 'Politicisation' in this sense would include endeavours to delegitimise and isolate certain Member States or régimes: notably, South Africa; Portugal, in its colonial day; and, more recently Israel and Taiwan. Conversely, it would denote attempts to legitimise and support other political entities: hence it would include not only the seating of the People's Republic of China, but also the granting of observer status to African liberation movements and to the Palestine Liberation Organisation (PLO), as well as pledges to publicise the causes of these bodies.

Second, and closely related, is the challenge to established patterns of resource allocation, that is, explicit questioning of the political ends which may be served by ostensibly technical activity. Denunciation of technical co-operation with South Africa and Israel, on the grounds that such co-operation can only serve to reinforce these States and thus the discriminatory policies they pursue, would fall into this category.

Issues of this sort ultimately relate to power relations and change in the wider environment. For the most part, although not exclusively, they have resulted from the changes associated with decolonisation and the emergence of a new anti-colonial majority within the UN system and, since 1973, from changes in the fortunes of the oil-producing States. It is because of the relationship with political change external to the Agencies that questions of this kind are considered 'extraneous'. By concerning themselves with such issues, the Specialised Agencies are deemed by their critics to be trespassing on UN territory.

B. Challenges to established policy and legal standards

At another level, 'politicisation' is understood as a questioning of prevailing Agency policy. More particularly, it is seen as a trend towards State intervention in areas traditionally regarded in the West as lying within the sphere of professional autonomy.

The operational philosophies of the various Specialised Agencies, adopted at the initiative of the founding fathers and broadly adhered to ever since, have for some time come under attack as reflecting Western priorities and interests. Thus, for instance, the priority accorded within the IAEA to nuclear safeguards as against application of nuclear technology to development ends;[25] within the WHO to prevention as against cure;[26] within the IMF and IBRD to stability and creditworthiness rather than need as criteria for loan allocation;[27] and within UNESCO to the 'free' rather than to a 'balanced' flow of information,[28] are all criticised for serving the purposes of Western populations and interests rather than those of Third World peoples.

Challenges of this sort have also been reflected in debates within the various Agencies on the setting of international legal norms and standards.

Standard-setting tends to involve conflict at two levels at least. On the one hand, it raises the distributional question of who benefits from regulation or non-regulation of a given field. The nature and scale of the interests at stake can be illustrated by a few examples of the type of issues debated within the Specialised Agencies: the handling of radioactive materials and waste (IAEA); the standardisation of telecommunications equipment across the globe (ITU); international trading and advertising of pharmaceutical products (WHO); and the uses of communications satellites and mass media (UNESCO and ITU).[29]

In addition, standard-setting involves the ideological question of whether regulation should be entrusted to the State or rather to the profession concerned. The established policies of the Specialised Agencies may be seen as essentially liberal or *laissez-faire*. Thus, for instance, discussion of socialised medical care has traditionally been eschewed within the WHO; ITU philosophy is based on the principle of self-supporting (commercial) telecommunications services; the FAO tends to favour private over collectivised forms of farming; the tripartite structure of the ILO (States, employers and organised labour) is in itself pluralist; while a cardinal tenet of UNESCO policy is 'free flow of information'.[30]

In all these cases, the questions of whether or not to regulate a given field and, if so, the form and content to impart to regulation, have traditionally been treated as matters to be decided by the professions involved.

The 'politicisation' charge at the level of ideological politics refers to challenges by the new majority to established policy and, more specifically, moves towards greater intergovernmental regulation of the fields concerned. At this level of the charge most especially, and not least in respect of the information debate – as will be seen in the next chapter – Third World positions tend to be construed by the West as a front, witting or unwitting, for Soviet viewpoints.

C. Double standard with respect to national sovereignty

A further dimension of the 'politicisation' charge concerns questions of national sovereignty and domestic jurisdiction. These issues overlap with the debate on liberalism versus interventionism where the domestic organisation of social relations in a given sphere affects, or is seen to affect, a State's capacity to fulfil its international obligations at home or abroad. In the area which will concern us, for example, the question may arise of whether a free or rather a regulated press constitutes the surest way of promoting mutual understanding, justice and peace.

The constitutional texts of all the UN Agencies, as is well known, contain provisions designed to safeguard the principle of national sovereignty over matters 'which are essentially within the domestic jurisdiction of any State'.[31] It is also widely recognised that the test of what such matters are, as indeed of what constitutes 'intervention', is likely to be political rather than legal.[32]

The 'politicisation' charge at this level refers to what is seen as a Third World double standard with respect to national sovereignty. Third World countries, it is argued, assert the inviolability of their sovereignties in all spheres of UN activity, be they strategic, economic or cultural, yet simultaneously seek to influence the exercise of

Western sovereignties in these fields.[33] As will be seen in later chapters, for instance, the new majority within UNESCO has been criticised for demanding 'national sovereignty over information', at the same time that it attempts to impose standards of conduct on Western mass media.

D. Exercise of selective morality

A final and closely related component of the 'politicisation' charge concerns what official Western spokesmen describe as selective morality on the part of the new majority. Western critics maintain that, in determining the agenda for debate, Third World countries focus excessive attention on certain issues, e.g. white racism, Zionism, and neo-colonialism, while neglecting such topics as domestic corruption, black racism, and sexism in Muslim States, to say nothing of human rights violations in the Soviet bloc.

As shown earlier, the challenges to Israel, in particular the Agencies' endorsement of the 1975 UN resolution identifying zionism as a form of racism, and their decisions to promote the Palestinian cause by moral and material means, are especially often instanced in this respect. Indeed, the challenge to Israeli legitimacy, unlike earlier attacks on South Africa and other issues defined by the West as political, was to serve as the catalyst for a concerted Western response to long-standing revisionist trends in the UN Agencies (see below).

2. 'POLITICISATION' IN BROADER PERSPECTIVE

The concept of 'politicisation' discussed above may be seen to focus, explicitly or implicitly, on the levels of process (i.e. debate) and formal outcome.

Without stepping outside this particular framework, it would be possible to level counter-charges against leading Western States for past behaviour corresponding to 'politicisation' so defined. American practices during the McCarthy era, notably FBI vetting of the security credentials of American members of the UNESCO staff, and American interest in UNESCO as an instrument of US foreign policy during the Korean War, constitute well-documented examples.[34]

But for the purposes of advancing the debate, it would seem more fruitful to consider whether the focus on process and outcome might not be broadened to encompass additional levels of analysis. Levels which could usefully be investigated in this connection include: power relations in the wider environment (general, specific and symbolic); institutional structure; and implementation.

It will be argued that these levels of analysis and the interaction between them permit more plausible explanations of 'politicisation' at the process level than the nature of an Agency's subject-matter, the relative professionalism of its staff, or the habitual scale of media interest. The discussion should also help to show why what the West currently perceives as politicisation at the process level might appear to the new majority as a salutary response to earlier Western-backed acts and arrangements constituting a more fundamental form of politicisation.

In examining the type of factors involved in these additional levels of analysis, we shall use the conventional three-way classification of States into West, Soviet bloc and Third World. The West, for the purposes of this discussion, comprises the advanced industrial market economies and includes the White Dominions, South Africa, Japan and Israel.

A. Power relations in the wider environment

On almost every standard indicator of power, the West collectively may be seen as leading the rest of the world. Despite significant disparities between and within its component parts, the West and most obviously the USA, West Germany and Japan, may be held to constitute the core of the international market economy: it contains the largest agglomerations of the world's purchasing power or effective consumer demand.

The West leads the field of armaments production and sales, and commands the bulk of the world's economic and financial capabilities. The financial centres of the world are located in Wall Street, the City of London and Zurich; and the West enjoys the highest levels of trained manpower, health, literacy and GNP per head.

The West is also the seat of the largest multinational corporations, which control technological and financial resources greater than those of many nation-states. Those in the field of mass and telecommunications, of particular interest here, are among the most powerful in the world: they include AT&T, General Electric, Philips, Siemens and Sony, to name but a few. The bargaining strength of such companies in international forums derives, as Jacobson has shown, largely from their command not only over material resources but over technical expertise.[35] (For example, some 200 people were employed, full or part time, over a period of two years, in preparing and publicising American positions prior to the 1963 ITU Conference convened to draw up regulations for space communications.[36])

For reasons of this order, even the power of the oil-producing States is not as boundless as it is often portrayed. It is true that these countries succeeded in quadrupling the price of oil in 1973, that they have raised it at intervals since, and that their diplomatic clout has been enhanced as a result. Nonetheless, their power may be seen as narrowly constrained by dependence on Western financial institutions – and hence on the health of Western economies – as well as on the supply of qualified manpower and technology (including armaments). In practice, despite the considerable financial resources that have accrued to them since the early 1970s, the OPEC States are closely integrated into the economic framework upheld by the West, and enjoy much less autonomy of action than bald statistical comparisons might suggest.

The COMECON countries, meanwhile, although classifiable as advanced industrial economies, and although more linked with the West in terms of trade and production in recent years than formerly, may be seen as essentially peripheral to the dominant international market economy.

At the level of symbolic or propaganda resources, too, the four major international news agencies outside the Soviet bloc are based in the USA, France and Britain. The world's telecommunications satellites are controlled principally by Western interests; and the bulk of the films and television programmes screened across the globe are produced in the West. The material capacity to 'mobilise consent' and to reinforce or shift perceptual frameworks – including perceptions of debates in the UN system – may thus be seen as preponderantly Western.

In sum, the pattern of power relations between the West and the rest of the world could be characterised as essentially unequal. From the Third World point of view, the greater power of Western interests, and hence the latter's greater capacity to ensure that their policy preferences prevail, entails correspondingly greater Western accountability. By the same token, it is considered to entitle Third World countries, as parties directly and often dramatically affected by Western decisions, to pronounce upon and share in determining the way in which Western sovereignties are exercised.

B. Institutional structure

The pattern of power relations in the postwar world may be seen to have largely determined, and been reflected in, the initial structure of the UN and its Agencies. In this section, we shall consider questions of membership; weighted representation; and staffing, budgets and location.

(a) Membership

In a number of respects, membership of the UN and its Specialised Agencies may be seen as exclusivist.

In the first place, membership is based on statehood. Only States – or more precisely those polities recognised as such by the prevailing majority – are entitled to full membership. As a result membership in the Agencies, together with such symbolic and material benefits as it confers, has traditionally been confined to central nationalisms, while sub-State nationalisms and refugee populations, for instance, have lacked direct representation. The UK, the USSR and South Africa were represented from the outset; Scots, Kurds and black South Africans, as such, were not. Nor for that matter were Jews as such, until the international community decided in 1947 – over the opposition of the Arab States, then in a minority of 6 – to partition Palestine into Jewish and Arab States and subsequently to admit the State of Israel to membership of the UN system. The Palestinians were only granted a measure of direct political representation in the UN system, as a national liberation movement, in 1974.

Secondly, the Agencies have excluded particular States. Although universal membership is a professed aim of the Agencies, admission is formally selective. The criterion for selection is 'peace-lovingness'; and in the absence of a Soviet veto in the Agencies, the power to determine whether this quality inhered in an applicant polity lay for a decade and in some instances longer with the Western majority. Decisions as to which groups rightfully represented given States, or even as to the boundaries of a State, were also for long a prerogative of the Great Powers and notably of the leading Western States.[37]

Hence 'ex-enemy' States (e.g. Italy, West Germany and Japan), along with Franco Spain, South Vietnam and South Korea, had all been admitted to membership of the Agencies by the early 1950s, while the China seat was to be occupied by the Chiang Kai-Shek régime for some twenty-five years. Equally, at British initiative, India became a full founding member of the Agencies while still formally a British colony.[38]

On the other hand, the socialist halves of the divided States (North Vietnam, North Korea, East Germany) were denied representation until the 1970s, as were the 700 million or so nationals of the People's Republic of China.

Yet although the Agencies are broadly autonomous of the UN with regard to membership policy, the above distinctions and exclusions did not appear to be based on any identifiably 'technical' considerations intrinsic to the nature of their work. On the contrary, they were applied even by Agencies such as the ITU and WHO which, as we saw earlier, several observers have ranked among the more technical and less politicised and where, moreover, the logic of the enterprise is recognised as universalist (e.g. telecommunications and control of epidemics).[39]

On the other hand, certain countries, although not refused admission to the Agencies, opted for non-participation. This was notably the case with the USSR, which did not exercise its right as a founder member of the UN to automatic membership of certain Agencies until 1954, and which has in fact never taken up membership of the FAO, IMF, IBRD or GATT. Several East European countries, too, after some two to three years' membership in certain Agencies, were to withdraw from active participation for several years in line with Soviet policy.

Western efforts to secure the participation of East European countries are often stressed and in some cases were no doubt sincere.[40] But it could nevertheless be argued that the Soviet bloc's choices in the matter were relatively constrained.[41] The philosophy of most of the Agencies, and the statutory requirements of some (e.g. provision of data on agricultural production) were uncongenial to these States which, as a small and effectively marginal minority, could not hope to challenge them successfully from within. The requirements of the IMF, IBRD and GATT, in particular, could be seen as incompatible with the principles of central economic planning.

Moreover, attempts by the then minority to prevent what they saw as Western political manoeuvres tended to produce little impression upon the Agencies concerned. The Soviet walkout of the IAEA General Conference in response to the election of a second Western Director-General in 1961 failed to reverse the appointment.[42] Similarly, at the third session of UNESCO's General Conference in 1948, Jewish bodies describing themselves as non-governmental sought admission as observers. The Arab States objected to admitting bodies which they regarded as branches of the Israeli State; but Lebanon, host to the Conference, ultimately ceded to majority pressure in favour of granting access.[43]

Such moves tended, in addition, to be largely dismissed by Western commentators. Two former American senior officials of UNESCO writing in 1957, for example, relegated discussion of 'politics' in UNESCO's first decade to a footnote in which they implicitly endorsed the following account by Richard McKeon:

> Intrusions of issues arising from political differences in the discussions of Unesco have been few, including little more than attack on 'war-mongering nations' at the Second Session of the General Conference in Mexico, a debate concerning the seating of Observers from International Jewish Organizations . . . at the Third Session in Beirut, a demonstration against a proposal to introduce Unesco's program into Germany at the Fourth Session in Paris, and the withdrawal of the representatives of Hungary and Czechoslovakia in protest against the seating of the delegation from Nationalist China at the Fifth Session in Florence.[44]

This passage says more about the itinerary of the General Conference than it does about the source, scale and rationale of dissent.

In the circumstances, non-participation by East European countries might not too unfairly be considered a case of constructive exclusion.

In the light of the foregoing, it might well appear to the new majority that what are currently termed 'extraneous politics' and 'selective morality' were built into the Agencies at their creation. At the time, the USA and its supporters had the initiative, but commentators on this era seem generally to have overlooked political acts similar to those which are now condemned as wrecking innovations.

(b) Weighted representation[45]

It will be suggested here that the relevant difference between the various Agencies in the context of 'politicisation' lies less in their subject matter than in their voting arrangements. Subject matter may be seen as indirectly rather than directly relevant, in so far as it may be held to have conditioned the initial structure of the Agency in question.

In certain Agencies, institutional provisions were to differentiate between Member States on the basis of control over relevant resources, that is, in a manner which reflected power relations in the specific environment fairly accurately. In others, formal power was distributed according to the principles of 'sovereign equality' (one state, one vote) and majority voting or what might, in that sense, be called 'egalitarian' principles. Even in these Agencies, however, questions deemed 'important' (notably decisions on membership and budget ceilings) required a two-thirds majority for adoption.

In the IMF and IBRD, representing one extreme, there are no egalitarian forums. In the IMF, voting in all organs is weighted in accordance with quotas which also determine veto powers and the level of a State's financial contribution and drawing rights. In the IBRD, votes are apportioned on a similar basis. As a result of such arrangements, the USA until 1970 controlled about one-third of the votes in both these bodies. (It has also recently shown concern not to surrender its current 20 per cent quota in the IMF, the minimum required for a veto.) In 1967, the less developed countries accounted for three-quarters of the membership, but were allocated only one-quarter of the votes.

In other agencies, egalitarian and inegalitarian organs coexist. The General Conference of the IAEA, for instance, is egalitarian, but seating on the formally superior body, the Board of Governors, is based on relative position in the field of nuclear energy. Consequently, the 'establishment' in this Agency includes the Soviet Union, South Africa and India, and excludes several leading Western States such as Japan and the Federal Republic of Germany. Since the advent of nuclear parity and détente between the USA and USSR, the pattern has been described as one of superpower 'atomic condominium'.[46]

Similarly in the ITU, the Third World has a majority both in the Plenipotentiary Conference, which meets irregularly, and in the restricted-membership Administrative Council, which meets yearly. But membership of the standing Consultative Committees and their subordinate study-groups, which act as the major source of policy initiatives, is based on expertise, and is in fact predominantly Western. Moreover, actual control over telecommunications resources is formally acknowledged in the provision which enables private operating agencies to vote in the Consultative Committees on behalf of the State when the latter's representatives are absent.[47]

Finally, in UNESCO, the WHO, FAO and the ILO, at the other extreme, arrangements in the policy-making organs are egalitarian, and relative rank in the specific fields is not institutionalised. Since about the mid-1960s, the Third World has commanded more than a two-thirds majority on the formal policy-making bodies in each of these Agencies. Where Third World interests have overlapped with those of the Soviet bloc, this majority has reached four-fifths.

It can thus be seen that the institutions devised by the postwar founders to deal with certain subjects (e.g. finance, trade and atomic energy, not to mention security) were structured along relatively oligarchic lines, to the disadvantage of States less well endowed in the fields in question.

Challenges of a similar nature have been registered by the new majority in all the Agencies regardless of subject matter. Questions relating to Israeli legitimacy and to Palestinian rights in the occupied territories, for example, have been raised even in the IAEA and the ITU: in the IAEA, awards of nuclear equipment to Israel have been contested, and Israel has so far failed ever to be elected to represent the Middle Eastern region.[48] Israeli credentials have also been challenged and proposals made for the suspension of its membership in both organisations.[49] But it is in the institutionally less stratified Agencies that such challenges have been and are likely in future to be pressed most forcefully.

(c) Staffing, budgets and location

Other dimensions of institutional structure, too, notably staffing, have traditionally favoured Western States.

Posts of a policy-making, managerial and executive nature in the Specialised Agencies are for the most part allocated in accordance with the principle of 'geographical distribution'. But although so termed, the distribution of posts was in fact for long determined far less by considerations of geographical balance than by reference to assessed shares of an Agency's regular budget. The budget shares of the three major groups of States in the different Agencies are, very broadly, apportioned as follows: the West, four-sixths (the USA, singly, usually accounting for between a fifth and a quarter); the Soviet bloc, somewhat over one-sixth; and other countries somewhat under the remaining one-sixth.[50]

It is generally conceded that in all the Agencies the West dominates the staffing structure in numerical, strategic and hierarchical terms.[51] By way of illustration, let us examine the distribution of posts within UNESCO by the late 1970s.[52] In 1978, despite adjustment of quotas in favour of the developing countries under the guidance of the African Director-General elected to office four years earlier, the USA alone was entitled to a mean of one-fifth of the 765 posts subject to geographical distribution. The countries classified in the West European group, comprising one-fifth of the membership, were entitled collectively to one half of these posts. Thus together with the USA these countries could control 70 per cent of the posts in question. On the other hand, 26 developing countries were not represented on the staff at all, and the maximum entitlement of many of those facing chronic problems of 'educated unemployment' (e.g. Egypt and India) was five.

Western predominance becomes more pronounced once posts in particular departments (finance, personnel, think-tanks) and those not subject to geographical distribution (i.e. field, research, language and clerical posts) are included. Hoggart records that, in the programme sector he headed in the early 1970s, 80 per cent of the field posts in one year went to Westerners.[53] It is also more marked in financial Agencies (especially the IMF, where 85 per cent of the senior posts in 1968 were held by the West) and in those where competence in the subject area is concentrated in the West (most notably the ITU).[54]

(Western corridor comment to the effect that, since the election of a Senegalese Director-General in 1974, distribution of posts in UNESCO has become not so much 'geographical' as 'geografrican' perhaps warrant further perspective. When the previous incumbent, a French national, concluded his 2-term (12-year) period of office, the maximum French quota of 50 was exceeded by 36, i.e. by some 70 per cent.)

The nationality of officials of course provides only a crude measure of institutional imbalance; indeed, to the extent that those recruited to UN agencies from the Third World tend to have backgrounds and to acquire orientations which fit in with the tone set by the founders, it may even understate the Western leaning of the Agencies. Conversely, Westerners working for UN bodies may prove keen champions of Third World causes. Nevertheless, nationality affords some indication of the problem of imbalance.

The significance of what the Third World sees as the 'colonisation of secretariats' lies in the capacity of bureaucracies to define problems and shape policy options by influencing flows of information, as well as their ability to promote or obstruct implementation of policy decisions.

Meanwhile the fact that the Headquarters of the various Agencies of the United Nations are all located in Western capitals (New York, Geneva, Paris, Rome, Vienna, . . .) may also be seen to favour

Western interests insofar as quicker and cheaper access to officials, information and meetings, and familiarity with work-styles and in-house *linguae francae* generally reflecting those of the host country, ease the task of Western lobbyists relative to that of their Third World or East European counterparts.

To sum up so far, the established policies of the Agencies discussed earlier may be seen broadly to reflect the preferences of those States and interests best represented institutionally.

C. Implementation and modes of containment

Certain means of containing opposition by the new majority at the level of implementation have always been available to Western powers and, of late, new institutional modes of containment have also been devised.

At the institutional level, new restricted-membership bodies have been created within and/or parallel to a number of Agencies. Operating at top diplomatic level and off the record, bodies of this kind are mandated to achieve 'consensus' on 'controversial' issues (meaning, in practice, issues so defined by the West).

The trend to establishment of such organs is especially visible in the more 'egalitarian' Agencies where challenges have been registered most strongly (viz. the Drafting and Negotiation Group created within UNESCO in 1976; and bodies set up in connection with the World Food Conference and with debates on the Law of the Sea).[55]

But it is discernible, too, even in the case of the more oligarchic Agencies. In the IMF, for instance, challenges from the new majority with respect to development finance led to creation of the Development Committee.[56] At the same time, policy-making on major international monetary issues has been progressively confined to a core group of finance ministers and central bank governors meeting outside the framework of the Agency in shadow bodies such as the 'Group of Ten'.[57] In the process, a financially powerful non-member (Switzerland) may be seen to have been 'extraneously' enfranchised, while States which are members but financially weaker may be seen to have been, in effect, disenfranchised.

The concept and mechanisms of 'consensus' have been criticised by a number of Third World and East European States (and, implicitly at least, by the present Director-General of UNESCO) as having the effect of bypassing the majority and of restricting key decisions to a minority of powerful States and interests.[58]

Where, despite arrangements of this sort, debates nevertheless yield results distasteful to the West, a number of other responses remain available. At one end of the scale are explanations of vote or declarations by delegates serving notice that a given outcome will be construed in a manner compatible with the policies of the States concerned. Statements may also be made dissociating from the text in question and, to that extent, undermining its legitimacy. In the case of legally-binding texts, reservations may be entered upon ratification to provisions considered unacceptable. More radically, Western States may opt not to sign or ratify an instrument as a whole.

Beyond responses by States, the Western interests concerned may be able to limit implementation of majority decisions by simple means of command over relevant resources. It may be noted, in this connection, that Western appeals to 'realism' tend to be made by reference to the hard (and 'extraneous') facts of material inequality.

Meanwhile Western media, whether as directly or as indirectly interested parties, may mobilise to forestall or, alternatively, to discredit certain outcomes. Such, for instance, has been the case with challenges to Israel and Zionism[59] and also, as will be seen later, with respect to the media debates. Conversely, it may be assumed that where Agencies present no significant challenge to, or indeed actively promote Western interests, the fact is unlikely to be advertised unduly. This assumption reverses the prevailing view that it is the coverage which encourages the challenge, rather than the challenge which inspires the coverage. (Jacobson's paradox concerning the obscurity of the ITU may then be resolved by the fact that, as Jacobson himself shows, the latter's policies, so far from damaging Western communications interests, have hitherto tended to advance them positively.)

The specific power of the media in this connection lies in their capacity to focus attention and to set the terms of public discourse on selected issues, and to that extent to shape public perceptions of the topics involved. With regard to current debates on the UN system, the power to organise the 'hue and cry' includes the capacity to generate and sustain perceptions either of 'politicisation', or – where no hue and cry is organised – of 'consensus'.

In fact the mass media occupy a unique dual position in relation to debates on information policy, insofar as they represent both the principal challenged interest and the principal source of public information on the subject. The point has tended to go unremarked, although the potential conflict between the two roles is not without implications for the objectivity of coverage.

Finally, Western States and interests may threaten or actually inflict penalties on an Agency as such, notably in the form of budgetary reprisals and withdrawal from participation. For example, after adoption by UNESCO's General Conference in 1974 of the decisions unfavourable to Israel, the USA withheld its assessed share of the Agency's budget (25 per cent) for two years, while France and Switzerland held back a percentage of theirs.[60] Western States also walked out of subsequent meetings where the question of Zionism was raised.[61] Meanwhile, pro-Zionist and/or pro-Israeli bodies organised meetings in the USA and Europe on UNESCO–Israel relations: one well-publicised colloquium arranged by former Israeli Foreign Minister Abba Eban and others in Paris, shortly before the 19th session of the General Conference in 1976, resulted in the creation of a committee 'against further "politicisation" of UN Specialised Agencies'.[62] Those concerned also ran full-page anti-UNESCO advertisements in leading Western newspapers, notably *Le Monde* and *New York Times*, while intellectuals sympathetic to the Zionist cause boycotted UNESCO activities.[63] Lastly, the USA withdrew from membership of the ILO in 1977 in response to what it identified as politicisation of that Agency with respect both to the Israeli issue and to Soviet bloc policy on labour questions more generally; and pulled out of UNESCO with effect from 1 January 1985, followed by the UK one year later, on account of the Organisation's positions concerning the press and of what it termed extraneous politicisation.

Western withdrawal from active membership may perhaps be seen as especially damaging from the point of view of the new majority. Budgetary shortfalls, if not expertise, could no doubt be made up without undue difficulty by the oil-exporting States. However, Third World countries tend to regard Western consent as crucial to the achievement of 'new orders' in various fields and to treat UN Agencies as the principal forums for articulation of their demands at the global (and thus also Western) level. In the event of Western withdrawal, the already declining legitimacy of the Agencies in Western eyes could be expected to diminish still further, so that the developing countries would be left talking, to all intents and purposes, to themselves.

Unlike similar responses on the part of the postwar minority, tactics such as those outlined above would seem not ineffectual when employed by the present-day minority. Indeed, in the wake of Western sanctions, moves were made within the ILO and UNESCO both to amend rules and procedures and, so far as possible, to keep items likely to displease Western powers off the agenda.[64] As a result, Israel was admitted to membership of UNESCO's 'Europe' group in 1976, while Arab challenges to Israel more broadly were also seen by Western commentators to have been generally toned down.[65]

Nevertheless, it may be assumed that Western States themselves would in general prefer to avoid methods which draw attention too overtly to power differentials, and to concentrate on measures of containment at the milder and more pre-emptive end of the scale.

CONCLUSION

We have shown that the conventional definitions of 'politicisation' in the UN Specialised Agencies focus on the levels of process and formal outcome. At these levels, emphasis is placed on power understood as the capacity to muster voting majorities and as the ability of those majorities, potentially at least, to arrogate to themselves the moral authority of the UN system.

We have also argued that consideration of the factors involved at the levels of extra-institutional power relations, institutional structure and implementation provides a basis for alternative approaches to 'politicisation' and 'consensus'. Specifically, it highlights the role of other dimensions of power and notably of vetoes of varying types not only in determining the initial structure and policies of the Agencies, but also in containing contemporary challenges to existing arrangements.

In so doing, it helps to explain why, as suggested earlier, the new majority might regard 'politicisation' at the level of debates as a necessary and positive corrective to 'politicisation' at other levels. For if from the Western perspective 'politicisation' appears to lie in challenge and change to the existing order, it is the prevailing order itself and failure to change it which appear political from the vantage point of the new majority.

Conversely, it contributes to an understanding of why 'consensus' in the more oligarchically-structured Agencies might be seen from the perspective of the new majority as no less 'artificial' and based on 'bloc politics' than the 'consensus' in UNCTAD appears to Western observers. Indeed, taking account of the above factors, it could be argued that what is presented by the West as an earlier state of consensus was not so much a spontaneous phenomenon, but rather the product of arrangements deliberately designed to reflect the preferences of certain powerful countries and interests by isolating, minimising and/or neutralising the opposition.

To put the point at its most provocative, would not consideration of the additional levels of analysis make it possible to reverse the 'politicization continuum' drawn up on the basis of the process level alone by Lyons, Baldwin and McNemar, so that UNESCO and ILO appear as the least, and the IMF and IAEA as the most political of the Agencies?

It could in any event be argued that the concept of 'consensus' as applied to the Specialised Agencies by Western observers has undergone tacit redefinition in recent years. In the postwar era, 'consensus' could be understood as broadly synonymous with the view of the majority. But a close reading of the statements quoted at the beginning of this chapter would seem to show that it has come, over time, to be identified with what the former majority regards as the original spirit of an Agency or as being in the underlying interests of its survival, regardless of the immediate distribution of opinion as manifested in formal votes. As Western spokesmen proceed further and further down this road, it becomes increasingly difficult to discern the difference between this account of 'consensus' and straightforward assertion of Western policy preferences.

Approached in the broader perspective set out above, 'politicisation' at the process level could be seen as a function less of the number of States or of the subject-matter involved than of the relative strength of the established and challenging interests.

The central proposition we wish to advance is that while the extent to which challenges to the established order are registered by the new majority will vary with the degree of institutional openness, the manner in which such issues are settled – where both sides decide to take a strong stand – will depend upon power relations in the wider environment, including the capacity to shape public perceptions of the particular debate. This proposition will be tested in the empirical body of the research by reference to UNESCO and UN debates on the regulation of knowledge.

Chapter 2 outlines the conceptual issues in debates on freedom and regulation of information as seen from the perspectives of the West, the Soviet bloc and the Third World. Subsequent chapters will examine how far the policy preferences of the three broad groups of States so outlined have been reflected in the outcomes of debate on normative texts in this field, and the ways in which Western States and interests have sought to contain majority proposals for greater regulation over time.

Chapters 3 and 4 are concerned with the postwar information debate. Chapter 3 concentrates on the emergence of a pragmatic division of labour between the United Nations and UNESCO in the field of 'information' (understood as news and the press), in which responsiblity for controversial issues of information policy was in effect ceded to the UN, and considers the reasons for these developments. Chapter 4 examines the substantive postwar debate on freedom of information within the UN and, residually, within UNESCO.

Chapter 5 examines the contemporary information debate, focussing on those instances where Western States and mass media have organized the most intensive resistance to challenges presented by the new majority. Chapters 6 and 7 consider parallel UNESCO debates in the sphere of education, in the postwar era and in the 1970s respectively.

Chapter 8 analyses a little-known decision by the Executive Board of UNESCO to submit to intergovernmentally-sponsored scrutiny the Arab State textbooks used in UNRWA/UNESCO schools for Palestine refugees, to consider how far it might be interpreted as a precedent (in this instance, Western-supported) for 'politicisation' as conventionally defined. Chapter 9 offers further comparison with standard-setting debates in the field of information by examining recent UNESCO discussions on regulation in the areas of science and culture.

Finally, before our conclusions are drawn in Chapter 11, Chapter 10 examines outcomes with respect to regulation of information in contexts where the primary focus is not on mass media, but rather on questions associated with race.

The main sources used for this research were debates in UNESCO and the United Nations through the successive stages of drafting of normative texts, including: preliminary reports and drafts prepared by the Secretariats as bases for discussion by Member States; written comments and observations by Member States thereon; final reports and drafts drawn up by Secretariats in the light of Member States' comments; draft amendments tabled by Member States at intergovernmental expert meetings, at the UNESCO General Conference or at the UN General Assembly, as well as at meetings of subordinate bodies of the two Organisations; and verbatim and summary records of debates in the various arenas.

The above documentary sources were supplemented, where necessary and/or possible, by interviews with Secretariat officials, representatives of non-governmental organisations and delegates; by consultation of internal correspondence files; and, on occasion, by reference to national archives of State.

In considering the role of Western media in the various debates, recourse was had to a further set of sources. For an indication of quantitative levels of media interest, we referred, where these were available, to UNESCO press accreditation registers and to the indexes of major American and British media as those most directly challenged in the media debate. For more qualitative assessments, we considered press articles, UNESCO press reviews, comment by Western journalists in academic journals, comment by Western Secretariat officials and delegates, and secondary accounts of media coverage of debates by Western academics and press councils.

2 Conceptual Issues in the Information Debate

INTRODUCTION

This chapter is concerned with conceptual aspects of debates on information and the press within the UN system, including the different ways in which the policy implications of UNESCO's mandate to 'educate for peace' have been construed.

We shall set out the broad positions of the West, the Soviet bloc and the Third World on these questions as expressed in debate or in major published statements. First, we shall briefly sketch liberal democratic theory with respect to information and the press, as the controlling framework to which the various positions tend all to refer in one way or another.

1. INFORMATION AND LIBERAL DEMOCRATIC THEORY

The liberal model of democracy as classically expounded by J. S. Mill[1] is based on a developmental concept of increasing rationality; it applies equally to the individual, to the group and to society as a whole. Democracy is seen as self-government through reasoned choice, as opposed to guidance by authority or custom. It is also essentially dynamic, in that it builds in the potential of a minority to become a majority by virtue of rational persuasion.

Truth in this model is a self-righting process based on competition between facts and viewpoints. The need for comment and interpretation of facts, and in that sense 'bias', is assumed.[2] The central requirements in this method of approaching truth are continuing entry of new information with which to correct prevailing misconceptions;[3] and roughly equal competition or 'fair play to all sides of the truth'.[4] Further conditions are the need for each interest to speak on its own behalf so that a case may be heard 'in its most plausible and persuasive form';[5] and especial tolerance of minority views as representing 'the neglected interests, the side of human well-being which is in danger of obtaining less than its share'.[6]

The liberal model of reasoned self-guidance may thus be said to assume not only bias, but also effectively competing bias. Monopoly of information by any single set of interests is considered to act as a restriction on rational choice and thus on both individual and social development. As such, it is seen as inefficient and damaging to the general interest of the community.

The role of the press in this model is that of a public intelligence service fulfilling three principal functions.[7] First, it fulfils an information function, keeping the citizenry fully supplied with information on matters of public relevance and identifying the range of options available at any given time. Second, it performs a 'watch dog' function, monitoring the activities of the State (understood as autocratic ruler) and checking against abuse of power by any group. Third, it fulfils a liaison function, ensuring a two-way flow of information between State and citizens. The traditional claim for special status of the press before the law is based on this quasi-constitutional or 'fourth-estate' role.

It may be noted that the classical liberal model of the press has been revised since Mill's day to take account of such changes as the rise of a mass press and the trend to concentration of ownership. Of relevance in this context is the work of Wilbur Schramm, an American scholar who acted as a leading consultant to UNESCO on mass communications in the 1960s and whose study on mass media and national development was to serve as a framework for UNESCO communications policy at the time.[8]

Schramm identifies what he sees as two particularly significant and positive developments since the time of Mill's writings. The first is the conscious distinction which came to be drawn between news and comment, 'objective news' – as distinct from comment – being held to provide only the raw facts of the day's events.[9]

The second is the development around the turn of the century, parallel with the trend to 'one-newspaper cities' in the USA, of what Schramm terms a 'social responsibility theory of communications'.[10] This is understood as the conscious attempt, in a context of press concentration if not monopoly, to provide full and fair representation of different groups in society, as well as to set news items in a context which gives them meaning. In this connection, Schramm notes the 'astonishing steps towards responsible action and responsible thinking', the adoption of codes (including the right of reply), and the contribution of journalism schools to producing professionally-minded employees.[11]

Let us turn now to the formal positions advanced by the three major groups of States in the UN system with respect to information policy.[12]

2. WESTERN POSITIONS

The problem of information at the international level has been defined by the West, and especially by the USA, as essentially that of ensuring the 'free flow of information and ideas' between peoples.

Western spokesmen have worked from the position that, in the words of Clement Attlee as enshrined in UNESCO's Constitution, 'wars begin in the minds of men'.[13] More specifically, war was held by Western Allied leaders and by Western executive heads of the UN and UNESCO in the mid-1940s to result at least in part from lack of mutual knowledge and understanding between peoples which, in turn, was held to result to a large extent from manipulation of information flows by the State both domestically and across national borders.[14] Peace, understanding and freedom of information from State control, nationally and internationally, have thus traditionally been treated as interdependent principles. Indeed, the assumption of interdependence has tended to be reflected in a focus on the latter goal in which the primary end of peace, not explicitly recalled, has tended to become somewhat lost from sight.

Within this broad position, nevertheless, shades of opinion may be distinguished, notably as regards the extent to which the liberal model of a free and pluralist press may be said to prevail in the West. Delegates of leading Western States and owners of private media on the one hand, have been inclined to treat this model as generally achieved in Western societies.

The views of William G. Harley, Senior Communications Adviser to American delegations to the UNESCO General Conference in the 1970s, published in an issue of the UNESCO *Courier* devoted to the subject of communications, may be taken as representative.[15] Describing the functions of a free press in essentially the same terms as the liberal model (information, monitoring and liaison functions), Harley argues that pluralism of opinion is ensured by advertising as a major present-day source of finance for private media. Thus advertising is seen not only as helping the latter to withstand pressure from government and 'private interest groups', but as permitting the establishment of 'an enormous number of newspapers, magazines and, in several nations, broadcasting stations'. 'This multiplicity of free and independent media', in Harley's view, 'guarantees that no single voice or group of voices can ever achieve predominance.'

Harley also sees private media, 'though motivated by profit', as nevertheless believing that they serve a higher function 'as guardians of the rights of people and as constructive critics of government'. Safeguards against abuse of press freedom, meanwhile, are seen to lie in competition with other information organs and in the sovereignty of the consumer. Further protection for consumers, in turn, is held to be afforded by opportunities of air-time to reply to opinions or advertising claims found questionable; in the 'letters to the editor' columns of newspapers; and in the increasing growth and vigour of consumer groups.

As their strongest line of argument in international arenas, spokesmen for leading Western States and media owners have tended to rely on a comparison between the 'free press' of the West and 'state-controlled' systems elsewhere.

The dichotomy perhaps found clearest expression in postwar information debates, when the most developed positions were those advanced by the USA and the USSR, and when the contrast drawn was between the information systems of the liberal democracies and those of 'totalitarian' States (read the defeated Nazi and fascist régimes and, more especially, the Soviet Communist system).[16]

But it remains visible in the contemporary debate,[17] where policies adumbrated by Third World countries have tended to be viewed by Western delegates (notably those of the EEC countries, Australia, Canada, Japan, Switzerland and the USA, and to a lesser extent those of the Nordic countries) and by executives of Western media (especially the Inter-American Association of Broadcasters (IAAB), Reuters, United Press International (UPI) and the *Christian Science Monitor*) if not as designed to enhance State control over information, then at least as conducive to that end. Fears are thus expressed with respect to what is described as 'development journalism' or 'committed journalism' where media are seen to be required to act as fully supportive propagandists for prevailing State policy. Similar reservations are aired regarding Third World talk of 'national communication policies', 'national sovereignty over information' and 'democratisation' of communications at the global level, all seen as entailing too interventionist a role for the State and also as likely to result in the exclusion of foreign journalists, with consequent restriction of information flows.

For while the dangers that could result from concentrated ownership of media in private hands are neither ignored nor denied, they are regarded as, on balance, less great than those involved in State monopolies and bureaucratic control of 'truth'. Moreover, the credibility of many Western media, acknowledged by a number of Third

World spokesmen,[18] is held to be a function of their perceived freedom from State control.

By contrast with private media owners and delegates of countries leading the communications field, Western journalists and spokesmen of Western States less well endowed in this respect have tended to draw the distinction between Western information systems and those prevailing elsewhere less sharply. Thus the International Press Institute (IPI), a research and information centre run by and for editors of privately-operated print media, published surveys in the mid-1950s of pressures brought to bear upon the press by the State not only in 'authoritarian' régimes but also in countries 'which ostensibly accept the traditional democratic principle of freedom of the press'.[19]

The pressures in question were divided into the legal and the 'extra-legal'. Legal pressures included constitutional provisions for press freedom 'within the limits of the law'; press laws proper (e.g. those governing defamation of public personalities; the sources which might legally be used; the reputation of government; and the prestige of the nation); national security legislation, seen as a major and growing source of restriction on press freedom; penal laws dealing with defamation, incitement to disorder, sedition, inaccurate news and disclosure of official secrets; laws governing disclosure of sources; and legislation with respect to protection of public morals and family life.

Some of the most stringent examples of legislation instanced in the IPI survey were those in force not only in the 'younger democracies', where national pride was more sensitive and where many of the laws were in any case remnants of the colonial era, but also those introduced in postwar Germany and Japan by the occupying authorities; in Cold War America; and in South Africa.[20]

The central danger of all legislation bearing upon the press is seen by the IPI to lie in looseness of drafting and in the consequent uncertainties of application and tendencies towards self-censorship.

'Extra-legal' State pressures identified by the IPI included those of an economic nature: government subsidies to friendly papers; selective newsprint distribution and exemption from duties on imported paper; discriminatory distribution of official advertising; imposition of security deposits; and resort to 'old-boy' methods and to such attractions as participation in delegations of journalists sent on assignment abroad at government expense. Again, such pressures were held by the IPI to apply even in 'very developed and very democratic countries', albeit in more gentlemanly form than elsewhere.[21]

Among the additional State-generated constraints on the press, meanwhile, the IPI catalogued administrative restrictions on the right to publish, on distribution, and on access to official sources of information; direct political pressures ranging from informal approaches, through the sending of explicit directives to editorial staffs, to detention, arrest, harassment and physical violence; indirect political pressures, notably in the form of illiberal if not inquisitorial 'climates'; and the requirement of conformity with specified religious doctrines.

Like the IPI, spokesmen for some of the smaller Western States (e.g. the Nordic countries, post-Salazar Portugal, Cyprus and New Zealand, among others), along with journalists of various French media (*Le Figaro*, *Le Monde*, TF-1) and the Vatican press, have cautioned against over simplifying the contrasts between 'free' (Western) and 'controlled' (non-Western) press systems.[22] Indeed, some of these spokesmen, in company with journalists from centre or left-of-centre information organs in Western countries, see a necessary and positive role for the State in guaranteeing structures capable of yielding the depth and range of opinion implied in the liberal model.[23]

But these variations on the nature and incidence of State intervention aside, spokesmen for Western States, media owners and journalists alike have insisted on the principle of practitioner jurisdiction with respect to matters of responsibility and ethical conduct. While treating freedom of expression and of the press as accountable freedoms, Western spokesmen have consistently held the basic requirement to be, in the words of the classic ethical injunction, that the journalist 'tell the truth as he sees it' without outside check or guidance. Spokesmen for Associated Press (AP), UPI, Reuters and the *Christian Science Monitor*, in particular, while granting the need for selection in reporting, have tended to assert the value-free or objective character of the process and the non-prescriptive nature of their role.[24] This is also one of Rosemary Righter's central themes.

Rather than adoption of what, in their view, could only be contested norms of professional conduct, proponents of this position recommend concentration on securing freer movement of newsmen, wider access to sources and improved professional training. Whether or not to draw up codes of ethics and, if so, what content to impart to such codes, have thus traditionally been treated by Western spokesmen within the UN as matters strictly for the profession to decide, neither governments nor, *a fortiori*, intergovernmental agencies being held competent to determine these issues.

In fact, Western spokesmen including such senior news agency executives as Roger Tatarian of UPI, Gerald Long of Reuters, and Mort Rosenblum of AP's Paris Office, have not on the whole sought to deny charges either of structural imbalance in the global distribution of communications resources, or of qualitative imbalance arising from Western 'journalism of exception'. On the other hand, they do vigorously refute any suggestion that either form of imbalance is intentional.

Structural dominance is generally explained in terms of an initial lead in the field combined with the workings of the market. While certain Western spokesmen urge that, just as American news agencies successfully challenged those of Britain and France in an earlier era, so the Third World should rely now on local private enterprise to counter foreign media preponderance, others consider competition with the major Western agencies and media to be 'virtually inconceivable' and hold that large-scale assistance to developing countries will be necessary if their information undertakings are to survive, let alone compete.[25]

On the question of content, a number of explanations are put forward to account for what the new majority regards as unfair coverage. One set of arguments is based on the nature of 'news' as understood in the West and on the operation of market forces. News, it is argued, is not designed to be encyclopaedic, but rather to provide intelligence of 'remarkable new events';[26] hence the tendency to focus on the event rather than the underlying process (e.g. a famine rather than hunger). Meanwhile the Western consumer, seen as the major market and ultimate arbiter of Western newspaper survival, is held in the main to be uninterested in news of the Third World (or in foreign news generally) unless of a striking character.[27] Conversely, the Third World market for news is judged too insignificant in commercial terms to warrant increasing the volume of reporting on the countries in question, even present low levels of coverage being found unprofitable – indeed loss-making – by Western news media.[28]

Representatives of Western media and agencies as well as other commentators also concede that a culturally-determined perspective may operate in the production of information. Although the efforts of news agencies to counter the problem by recourse to indigenous reporting and even editorial staff are stressed, some degree of 'cultural bias' is seen to be unavoidable. But being by definition inherent, it is also seen as unamenable to being legislated out of existence.

On the other hand, spokesmen for the major news agencies and for some other Western media (e.g. Netherlands Radio and the Third World-oriented Italian organ *Politica Internazionale*) contend that what might appear to some as wilful distortion may in fact result from difficulties in access to Third World countries and/or information sources, insofar as hindrance of this sort may compel foreign reporters to fall back on exiles, a régime's opponents, or other potentially unsympathetic sources.[29]

At the same time, and whilst not dismissing the problems involved, Western spokesmen tend to regard claims of 'cultural imperialism' as misleading and on the whole exaggerated. No government, they argue, is obliged to import foreign news or entertainment; equally, no Third World inhabitant is obliged to 'consume' such material. Moreover, in the view of the above commentators, Third World statesmen who allege that their peoples are brainwashed by Western information and cultural products do their citizens an injustice: Third World audiences, according to these observers, are sufficiently sophisticated to judge the worth of information they receive and to discount alien value-loading. In addition, it is argued, research suggests that media seldom change firmly-held convictions, but rather reinforce existing perceptions and values. Hence, if a culture is solidly based in the first place, exposure to alien belief-systems will present no major threat to its survival.

In the Western view, the principal remedy for the many genuine problems confronting the Third World in the information field lies in improvement of domestic communications infrastructure. Any attempt by the State to 'democratise' or 'balance' information flows, whether at the quantitative or the qualitative level, is seen as liable to lead in the shorter or longer term to direct State control over content, irrespective of initial intent. Hence, Western spokesmen urge Third World governments to concentrate on securing enhanced levels of literacy to provide the readership base essential to a viable press, as well as more and better training of journalists. In these as in other areas (supply of equipment, revision of international communications tariffs, increased access to satellites, etc.), the West has proclaimed itself willing to negotiate and to contribute generously.[30]

As will be seen in subsequent chapters, Western strategy on information issues within the UN system has altered with time. In the postwar era, when the principal protagonists were the West and the Soviet bloc, Western (and especially US) diplomacy focussed on the normative level. The object at that time was to secure endorsement of liberal and/or *laissez-faire* principles in the information field as norms of international law and, conversely, to secure condemnation of censorship, jamming of foreign radio broadcasts, and other types of State-imposed restrictions on freedom of information as seen to be practised most notably in the USSR.

More recently, as debates have assumed a North/South rather than an East/West character, and as they themselves have become the minority in UN arenas, Western powers have directed their efforts to promoting technical rather than normative approaches to global communications issues.

At a more tactical level, wherever the prospect of regulation in some form has appeared unavoidable, Western delegates have advocated that any restrictions be kept to a strict minimum and be based on concepts of sufficient legal precision to prevent abusive interpretation. Equally, they have preferred that instruments dealing with restrictions be permissive rather than binding, and that wordings be 'positive' rather than 'prohibitive'. They have also pressed, among other things, for insertion of safeguard clauses based on domestic constitutional provisions with respect to States' rights and/or professional autonomy, and have worked to prevent reference to the 'use', 'responsibilities' or 'duties' of either practitioners, or owners, or the State in relation to media content.

Western media, for their part, have consistently adopted the most strongly *laissez-faire* positions, opposing any proposals for regulation in the information sphere under the auspices of the UN system.

3.   SOVIET BLOC POSITIONS

While also working from the perspective of 'peace', Soviet bloc spokesmen arrive at opposite policy prescriptions with respect to information. The State, in their view, has an ethical duty under the UN Charter and the UNESCO Constitution to ensure the conditions necessary to peace. War, as they see it, does not result from subjective factors alone, but rather from the conflict of objective interests, notably competition between capitalist concerns and the States which serve them. But to the extent that, as Western States claim, information is instrumental to peace, the ethical role of the State in peace-maintenance is seen as extending also to the sphere of information. Indeed, information media are held by virtue of their scale and impact to constitute a major factor for good or evil in international relations.[31]

According to the statutes of the Soviet news agency TASS, 'information should serve the interests of the State, the interests of the whole people'; it should be precise and accurate; it also 'plays an important role in the communist education of workers, in the shaping of public opinion, in the proper orientation of the people on questions of domestic and foreign policy of the Party and of the country and in combating a hostile ideology . . .'[*32]

Society, in the Soviet view, is entitled to demand of journalists a high degree of responsibility given the power they wield. Specifically, the journalist in Soviet society is held to have a duty to educate the public in accordance with socialist principles and to discourage selfish and proprietary values. At the international level, meanwhile, the duty of the journalist is seen as that of contributing positively to the strengthening of peace, friendship and mutual understanding between peoples, and of combating ideas harmful to these goals.

However, ethical codes and individual conscience have tended to be seen by Soviet bloc delegates as insufficient checks on abuse of freedom, and as largely irrelevant in contexts where the production of information is predominantly corporate.[33] Indeed, the moral responsibility of the State in the field of information is considered by Soviet bloc delegates to require active measures, notably legislation, to restrict dissemination of certain types of material ('war propaganda', nazi and fascist ideology, ideas inciting to racism and national hatred, etc.).

Soviet bloc States do not explicitly support State control of information: on the contrary, they object to Western definition of the debate in terms of 'free' versus 'state-controlled' presses. Nor do they take issue directly with liberal ideas in this sphere. Rather, they argue that freedom and pluralism are achieved in the Soviet bloc where, they claim, media are produced by and for the workers; but that such freedom is not ensured in the West where information media are held to be disproportionately concentrated in the hands of a comparatively small section of the population (the business class), whose interests the information purveyed by these media can only be expected to reflect.

This situation is held to be reproduced in still more acute form at the international level, where domination of global information flows by Western news agencies, radio and television concerns is considered detrimental to the cause of peace. Soviet bloc spokesmen claim that, so far from seeking to exclude Western media from other countries and

* Translations from French original by this writer.

thereby restrict global information flows, the aim is instead to expand the qualitative range of such flows. At the same time, the citizen is held to have a right to 'correct' information; the State, accordingly, has a duty to protect the public from inaccuracy, 'misinformation' and distortion, whether intentional or otherwise.

In addition, Western calls for 'free flow' are seen as overlooking the more fundamental international legal principle of national sovereignty by implying an obligation on the State 'to open the doors to any information from abroad, even where unfriendly or hostile . . .'. Referring to the activities of certain Western (and State-supported) broadcasting stations on the borders of Eastern Europe, Soviet bloc spokesmen stress that freedom of information cannot be understood as a right of the stronger to interfere in the affairs of other countries with deliberate intent to destabilise their régimes and disorient their peoples.[34]

Similarly, East European delegates in the postwar era claimed not only that US initiation of the UN debate on 'freedom of information' was designed to serve the interests of American business and press monopolies, but that the latter were already engaged in 'war-mongering' and in slandering the USSR, and that the debate should itself be treated as part of an anti-Soviet campaign led by US Cold Warriors.[35]

Reacting at first to US moves, but later more often acting as initiators, Soviet bloc countries have worked in the UN system for condemnation of private press monopolies and for binding restriction of certain types of expression, either by 'prevention' and 'suppression' (understood by others as censorship) or by legal prohibition. In so doing, they have argued that absolute freedom of expression existed nowhere, but that information was subject to some degree of regulation in every country and indeed had even been regulated internationally.[36] (An important precedent invoked in this connection was the legally binding and prohibitively worded International Convention concerning the Use of Broadcasting in the Cause of Peace, adopted under the League of Nations aegis in 1936 in response to Nazi broadcasting, and which the USSR sought in 1954 to update under UN auspices.[37] Parties to the Convention were for the most part West European and Latin American, and undertook 'to prohibit and, if occasion arises, to stop without delay' the broadcasting from their territories of transmissions detrimental to good international understanding and to the internal order and security of other States Parties.[38])

As a last resort, failing adoption of legal or moral restrictions on 'war propaganda' and other material deemed harmful to peace, Soviet bloc countries have sought support for statements in positive form of the goals to whose achievement they consider that mass media should contribute. Among these, peace and disarmament have been constant; but the list has been adjusted over time to include 'peaceful coexistence between States with differing social and political systems' and (in potential conflict with the goal of peace understood as order, but no doubt with an eye to Third World backing), the elimination of colonialism, racism and related phenomena.

As will be seen, the pattern of Soviet bloc strategy has moved in reverse directions to Western strategy. In the postwar era, ill-placed as they were to influence the outcomes of standard-setting activities, the preference of Soviet bloc States was for technical rather than normative approaches to information issues (e.g. reconstruction of war-damaged communications facilities). More recently, as the West has been reduced to minority status, the Soviet bloc has pursued normative initiatives of its own in this field, seeking in the process to harness the discontent of the Third World majority with the existing information order.

4. THIRD WORLD POSITIONS

In addition to Soviet bloc opposition, some resistance to *laissez-faire* proposals in the information field has always been registered by Third World countries, although the latter were not to advance a fully-developed communications platform of their own until the mid-1970s.

It should be noted at the outset that the 'Third World' represents the most heterogeneous of the three broad groupings considered here: not only does it bracket régimes based on private enterprise with those of more socialist persuasion, but it includes countries at very different levels of development. The basic justification for considering such disparate entities jointly lies in the shared condition of communications-poverty.

Third World countries, in the postwar as in the contemporary era, have tended to view information as a means to achieving a 'just peace'. For spokesmen from developing countries in the postwar years, the major threat to peace lay in inequality and injustice generally, and in racial discrimination more especially. Delegates of India, Ecuador and Mexico, in particular, intimating that Nazism had been an extreme manifestation of tendencies endemic in Western society, held it necessary at the time to rehabilitate all mankind and to work for a just peace.[39] To this end, they considered it necessary to distinguish the concept of a 'free flow' from licence to direct propaganda against other peoples and racial groups, and to take measures against the latter phenomenon.

Among the specific categories of material deemed offending, singly or in some combination, by these countries together with Argentina, China, Egypt, the Lebanon, Pakistan, Saudi Arabia and Syria, were those damaging to 'friendly relations between peoples'; affronts to 'national dignity or prestige'; and incitement to racial, ethnic, religious or other forms of violence, discrimination, hatred or intolerance. Also regarded as harmful to peace were 'Soviet propaganda', 'Western propaganda', and/or 'rival superpower propaganda', as well as what was seen (not least by the Arab States with respect to Palestine) as partisan reporting of conflicts.[40]

At the narrower level of communications as such, a number of Third World countries with newly-launched news agencies, especially China, India, Mexico and Pakistan, pleaded the case for protection of 'infant' industries.[41] Even the UK and France, in the postwar era, were directly affected by what amounted to a challenge to the global position of their own news agencies. French spokesmen in particular were to stress the rights of journalists vis-à-vis centres of political or financial power – including media institutions.[42] Countries with no indigenous news agencies expressed apprehension at the prospect of being over-whelmed by foreign and/or commercial information and cultural products, while Latin American spokesmen within UNESCO sought to qualify the principle of unlimited free flow by reference to respect for the values of cultural pluralism.[43]

At the level of policy prescription, the positions of Third World countries at this time were largely uncoordinated: some States advocated legally binding restrictions; others permissive limits; and yet others moral codes. It was only in the 1970s, after a period of some twenty years during which information was treated by Third World countries chiefly as a technical adjunct to development, that this group of States, led by the Non-Aligned Movement, began to handle information as a policy area in its own right and to present concerted alternative positions of its own. In the two intervening decades, the global information environment had undergone major technological change, most dramatically illustrated by the appearance of communications satellites and computerised information systems.

The Non-Aligned Movement formally concerned itself with information policy from a series of meetings in 1973 onward when, building on research conducted in other arenas, it was to develop earlier scattered Third World questioning of the doctrine of 'free flow' into a more systematic critique explicitly concerned with both the means and the content of communications. While the ultimate goals of Third World and Soviet bloc communications policies may be seen to differ, the critiques of 'free flow' are in many respects similar. Third World analyses hold in essence that, given existing global communications structures, traditional rights and freedoms in this sphere have served mainly to advance the interests of a few well-endowed countries and groups, but are virtually meaningless for the larger part of the world's population.[44]

First, it is argued, present information relationships are structurally imbalanced. The West, and especially the USA, spearhead technological advance in the communications sector and produce the bulk of the hardware traded internationally. Global flows of software or 'messages' (a term used to overcome what are viewed as overdrawn distinctions between news, entertainment and advertising) are also seen to be dominated by the West.

This is held to result, in part, from the resources available to the 'Big Four' news agencies based in the West, namely Associated Press (AP), United Press International (UPI), Agence France-Presse (AFP) and Reuters, and from the 'packages' of programming and commercial sponsorship by which poorer countries (as indeed a number of Western States with small domestic markets such as the Scandinavian countries and Israel[45]) finance acquisition of the hardware. Given the cost of worldwide news coverage, the effective choice for Third World countries and their national agencies is described by some delegates (e.g. those of Guyana, Yugoslavia, Niger and the Congo) as being between dependence on the Big Four or isolation.[46]

In addition, postal and telecommunications tariff structures are seen to discriminate against smaller countries in the periphery and against non-bulk producers, so that South–South and South–North communications tend to cost more than those from North to South. To the communications-poor, in consequence, the doctrine of 'free flow' appears to have promoted not so much a balanced exchange as a 'one-way flow' of messages moving vertically from 'dominating' to 'dominated', with peoples in the South being reduced to the role of passive consumers. In the eyes of some, the scale of West-to-South flows amounts to little less than 'permanent cultural aggression'.[47]

Secondly, imbalance in structure is considered to have produced imbalance in content, in that information tailored primarily to Western markets is seen to reflect particular (Western) rather than universal relevance and values, even where the reporters used are native to the region covered. This situation, whether intentional or unintentional, is held to be best evidenced in the selection of items (quantitatively insufficient; qualitatively ethnocentric and overly focussed on the sensational, the exceptional, the conflictual, the event rather than the process, and on the 'negative' generally), and in the definition of problems (e.g. the time-honoured 'freedom fighter'/'terrorist' dichotomy). The processes of selection and definition are seen as undermining the conventional news/comment distinction and, hence, the objectivity of coverage.

The existing information order has also come in for more radical criticism, held to apply not only at the global level but also within Western society. Encompassing policy studies from research bodies like the Latin American Institute of Transnational Studies (ILET)[48] (a body in which many supporters of Allende Chile have found refuge), and pronouncements by delegates of certain Non-Aligned countries, most prominently Algeria, Cuba, the Congo, Ethiopia, Guinea, Guyana, Jamaica and Yugoslavia,[49] such analyses in fact echo long-standing domestic critiques of the 'free' press in the West[50] and show points of convergence with the works of academics of the smaller Western States.[51]

The arguments of radical critics run broadly as follows. Technological advance in the communications sphere has been largely controlled by a few private enterprises including some of the most powerful corporations in the world (AT & T, Siemens, General Electric, Plessey, Standard Telephones and Cables, and others), often moreover supported by the State (defence) sector. Ownership and control of the media have become increasingly concentrated and linked to big business, including the communications industry, with commercially-run media serving as the cutting edge for penetration of foreign markets. Meanwhile big business as advertiser and thus as major source of media finance is held in practice to have largely usurped the sovereignty of the consumer. Such trends are held to be reinforced by the nature of contemporary news gathering methods ('news management' by means of ministerial press releases, press conferences and related techniques as an integral part of the 'management of capitalist crisis'), as well as by recruitment processes (selection of staff on the basis of conforming outlook).

The range of interests and interpretations of truth is thus seen to be inadequately matched by the range of information institutions. The interests of the under-privileged, in particular, at national and international level are held to have been marginalised in minority presses, so that the scale and form of competition between dominant and dissenting views along such dimensions as frequency, intensity, accessibility and cost is considered to be wholly unequal.

In terms of content, this structural situation is seen by radical critics as generating not only a commercial bias but a bias towards the 'maintenance of consensus' on an order based on private profit and thus inherently unequal. These biases (seen as differing in content rather than kind from 'committed' or 'development journalism') are held to be reflected in a focus on the sensational and the trivial, in propagation of values supportive of the private enterprise system, in avoidance of attention to long-term trends in concentration of power, and in a tendency to publicise the failures rather than the successes of socialist experiments, whether in the Third World or elsewhere.

Radical critics would doubtless not allege all manifestations of media 'bias' to be intentional, and indeed may well regard the unwitting but entrenched forms as the more tenacious problem. But in the early 1970s they were able – in company with many Western liberals – to point to the role played in the overthrow of Allende, and well documented since, by the 'free', CIA-financed Chilean press.[52] These activities must, for a time at least, have undermined in Third World eyes generally the claims made in the name of liberal ideals of the press.

As a result of the various factors discussed above, it is claimed, information media increasingly assume the format of entertainment rather than of the public intelligence service adumbrated in the liberal model: people are supplied with the information they are assumed to 'want' rather than that which they may be deemed to 'need'. On the radical view, in other words, the scale of reinforcement for Western life-styles and capitalist values at the level of mass publics is such as to render the claim of pluralism of Western media valid more at the quantitative than at the qualitative level.

Whatever their ideological perspective, the less well-endowed concur in regarding the existing information order as a third dimension of colonialism (after the political and the economic), and as unfavourable to them at more than one level. At the level of communications as such, Third World countries see present arrangements as a threat to survival of traditional forms of communication and culture, and as discouraging local creativity.

At a deeper level, they regard the present order as inimical to achievement of a 'just peace'. As they see it, peace cannot be stable where based on order alone (armed peace) but only where also founded on justice as envisaged in their calls for a New International Economic Order. Establishment of a juster world order is seen to depend upon the consent of Western publics, which in turn is seen as a function of Western perceptions of Third World realities. But Western perceptions of remote and unfamiliar societies, where the individual cannot test reality directly, are held to be shaped chiefly by Western media. As Third World spokesmen see it, so long as they are unable to reach Western publics direct and to correct what they view as misconceptions regarding Third World realities, they will be unable to recruit support for fundamental change.

On the contrary, they contend, incoming flows to their own peoples create expectations which cannot be fulfilled and which may thus prove destabilising. Present arrangements are seen as not even catering adequately for exchanges of experience on matters of shared Southern relevance, but rather as helping to perpetuate the old atomisation of the South, with further adverse consequences for peace. From the point of view of the less well-endowed, in short, the present information order may be seen as precluding new entry at the international and/or national levels, and as failing to deliver the 'effectively competing biases' required by the liberal model, not least at the level of Western audiences.

The challenge to the existing state of affairs has been variously expressed as a call for 'decolonisation of information', for 'democratisation of communications' at the global level, and for a 'new world information and communication order' (NWICO). The new order is framed as a participatory model of communication, the latter term being harnessed to underline the ideally two- or multi-way nature of the process.

The NWICO proclaims a number of new rights. These include a 'right to inform' (i.e. a right of self-interpretation to others) and a right to be heard; as well as 'the right [of every developing country] to exercise full sovereignty over information, both that concerning its day-to-day realities and that diffused to its people', 'to be objectively informed about outside events' and 'to publicise widely its national reality'.[53] Also enunciated are rights to a 'balanced flow' of news and cultural products; and to preservation of a way of life (cultural integrity).

These rights may be seen as new in that they are held to have relevance at the societal as well as at the individual level and to constitute a dimension of national sovereignty and self-determination. While, as we have seen, Western critics tend to regard rights expressed in collective or 'national' form as a cloak for reinforcement of actual or would-be state control, spokesmen from such varying countries as Cyprus, Ethiopia, Honduras, Sudan and Yugoslavia present them as complementing rather than supplanting existing channels and as necessary conditions for domestic information democracy.[54]

The rights at issue may also be regarded as new insofar as they deal less with freedom from political control than with the material conditions for communication. Indeed, so far from proscribing State intervention in information processes, the information rights asserted by the new majority require that States intervene actively at local, national, regional and global levels to rectify market distortions and ensure greater balance in the allocation of relevant resources. In the terms of the liberal model, State intervention with respect to structure is thus seen as necessary to guarantee the requirements of 'new entry' and 'effectively competing bias' at the various levels.

Concrete realisation of such rights is seen as involving both enhanced cooperation between Non-Aligned countries (e.g. creation of regional news agencies and pools; exchange of news on matters of mutual relevance, including media issues; joint moves towards acquisition of communications satellites; etc.); and structural reordering at the North–South level (e.g. through revision of tariff rates, redistribution of the electromagnetic spectrum, allocation of greater space to Third World news and views in Western media, increased aid in developing local infrastructures, etc.).

It is also seen to require explicit regulation of content and codification of duties in the information sphere. Non-Aligned spokesmen (e.g. from Algeria, Togo and Yugoslavia) have argued that technical cooperation in this field should not simply prepare their societies the better to receive more of the same type of information as in the past, and that a code of conduct would provide the necessary framework for such cooperation.[55] Anticipating, moreover, that existing disequilibria will persist for some time to come, successive meetings of the Non-Aligned Movement have urged the formulation of principles and/or legislation to govern the functioning and use of satellite communications and the activities of multinational news agencies as well as, more generally, a code to regulate the 'direct and objective dissemination and the free circulation of news in the different countries'.[56]

Within a general commitment to development and to achievement of the goals of a new international economic order, Non-Aligned countries hold that mass media (domestic and foreign) should contribute among other things to 'abolishing the dependence of Non-Aligned economies' and to eliminating racism and *apartheid*.[57]

Insofar as the call for regulation is directed towards Western mass media, it tends to be perceived by Western critics as involving a double standard on the part of the Third World with respect to national sovereignty in this sphere. But from the Third World point of view, the superior power of Western media and the likely persistence of major differentials in capability for the foreseeable future entail correspondingly greater accountability. To the extent thay they are affected by the kind of coverage devoted (or not devoted) to them in Western media, Third World States consider themselves justified in pronouncing on the latter's standards of conduct. (Indeed, the reaction of Western media to the media debates of the 1970s and 1980s has itself been taken by some – for instance the delegates of Algeria, India, the Congo and Syria – as proof of the need for both regulation and fundamental change.)[58]

In the following chapters, we shall examine the extent to which the outcomes of standard-setting debates in the UN system with respect to the regulation of information have reflected the policy preferences of the West, the Soviet bloc and the Third World as outlined above.

We shall begin, in Chapter 3, by looking at the impact of the postwar debate on the inter-institutional division of labour within the UN system in the sphere of information.

3 The UN/UNESCO Division of Labour in the Postwar Information Debate: UNESCO 'Technicised'?

INTRODUCTION

The researcher interested in providing a historical perspective to the contemporary information debate at UNESCO will need to look beyond the records of UNESCO alone to those of the United Nations. Indeed, during the postwar era, an informal division of labour was to emerge between the UN and UNESCO with respect to information policy. The basis for the division of labour was the distinction which came to be drawn between aspects of the subject deemed to be 'political' ('news' and the press; freedom of information as a human right, including the responsibilities inherent in such a right), and aspects considered non-political or at any rate less political (free flow of information of an educational, scientific and cultural nature). The UN was to assume responsibility for the former, UNESCO for the latter.

Although the fact of a division of labour has been mentioned by a number of observers at the time and since, the developments in question do not appear to have been examined in any depth. On the contrary, commentators on the contemporary information debate within UNESCO tend to treat a division of labour along the above lines as not only given but proper, alleging that UNESCO has encroached on the competence of the UN and politicised a previously consensual area.[1]

This chapter will begin by considering the constitutional basis for competence of UNESCO and the UN respectively in the information field. It will then examine the emergence of the division of labour, the reasons which would seem to have given rise to it, the problems involved and the decline of the arrangement. Finally, setting these

43

developments in the context of the debate on 'politicisation' of UNESCO, it will consider whether they might not be regarded as having constituted 'technicisation' of UNESCO in the sphere of information policy.

1.   THE CONSTITUTIONAL POSITION

A.   The UNESCO Constitution

1.   UNESCO policy autonomy

As was suggested in Chapter 1, the orthodox characterisation of the UN as a 'political' organisation and of its Specialised Agencies as 'apolitical' or 'technical' bodies is somewhat misleading.

UNESCO, like the other Specialised Agencies of the United Nations, was established on an intergovernmental basis and endowed with its own policy-making organs. Chief among these is the General Conference, a full-membership body composed of plenipotentiary representatives of States. Among other things, the General Conference is empowered under UNESCO's Constitution 'to determine the policies and main lines of work of the Organisation'.[2]

The policy autonomy of UNESCO within its fields of competence relative to the UN, meanwhile, is explicitly spelt out in Article X of its Constitution[3] and in Article I of the agreement by which UNESCO was 'brought into relation' with the UN as a Specialised Agency.[4]

It follows from their structure and powers that the Specialised Agencies of the UN, and thus UNESCO, may reasonably be regarded not merely as technical adjuncts to the UN or as executors of policies determined by the latter, but as 'political' bodies in their own right. While provisions exist for wide-ranging consultation with the UN, these may be seen as qualifying rather than vitiating the policy autonomy of UNESCO as of the other Agencies in relation to the United Nations.

2.   UNESCO's realm of competence

UNESCO's tasks were founded on the proposition that 'it is in the minds of men that the defences of peace must be constructed'.[5]

The Preamble to UNESCO's Constitution speaks of the 'education of humanity for justice and liberty and peace' and holds that 'the peace must be founded . . . upon the intellectual and moral solidarity of mankind'. It goes on to declare that the States Parties

> are agreed and determined . . . to increase the means of communication between their peoples and to employ these means for the purposes of mutual understanding and a truer and more perfect knowledge of each other's lives.[6]

The purpose of the Agency, under Article I of its Constitution, is

> to contribute to peace and security by promoting collaboration among the nations through education, science and culture in order to further universal respect for justice, for the rule of law and for the human rights and fundamental freedoms affirmed . . . by the Charter of the United Nations.[7]

To realise this purpose, Article I continues, the Organisation will

> collaborate in the work of advancing mutual knowledge and understanding of peoples, through all means of mass communication;

to that end, it will also 'recommend such international agreements as may be necessary to promote the free flow of ideas by word and image'.[8]

UNESCO's prime task was thus to be promotion of peace at the level of intellect and conscience, or what could be termed mental and moral disarmament. The ethical role of the future agency, which would set it apart from organisations already active internationally in the fields of education, science, culture and communications, was in fact the central theme of debates leading up to and immediately following its creation. Speaker after distinguished speaker at the founding Conference and first session of the General Conference, held in the wake of the war against nazism and fascism, was to warn against the dangers of 'knowledge without morality'.[9] Such was the alarm sounded by Léon Blum, René Cassin and Julian Huxley among others, while William Benton, a senior US delegate, stressed that UNESCO was not designed to promote the various branches of knowledge as ends in themselves but as means to peace.[10] The dissemination and exchange of knowledge in all fields were thus conceived instrumentally, as means to peace.

It should nevertheless be noted in this connection that the relationship between the goals enunciated in UNESCO's Constitution, and in particular the instrumental nature of the goal of free flow, have traditionally given rise to heated debate.[11] For those who, like the founding majority, believed peace to be a function of understanding, and understanding a function of free flow, the instrumentalism could remain implicit. But for those who, at the time and since, questioned these interdependencies, the primary goal of peace involved explicit responsibility for content and could be held to justify regulation of information flows in one form or another.[12] But although political in the ideological or policy sense, such basic issues as whether or not to regulate information flows and, if so, what form and content to impart to regulation could only be regarded as germane to UNESCO's substantive concerns and therefore as legitimate subjects for debate in that arena.

Meanwhile, as can also be seen from the wording of the Constitution, the founders intended neither to compartmentalise the mind nor to exclude from the Agency's remit any major channel for reaching it. Reference was to 'knowledge', 'intellect' and 'understanding' quite generally; and to 'all means of communication'. As used at the time by such senior British and US representatives as Clement Attlee, Ellen Wilkinson and William Benton, as well as by Western Secretariat officials, the terms 'mass education' and 'mass information' were in fact virtually interchangeable.[13] US delegate Benton, for instance, held that 'mass education of the peoples of the world', and especially of adults beyond the reach of formal education, could only be achieved through 'the modern instruments of mass communication, the modern press, the radio and motion pictures'.[14]

To summarise, UNESCO's central mandate under its Constitution could be described as 'knowledge for peace' understood as concern with the goals of knowledge in all fields, at all levels, and by whatever means communicated.

B.   The UN Charter

The Charter of the United Nations, for its part, does not refer specifically to freedom of information or to mass communications.

Under Article I, the UN has general competence 'to take all measures appropriate to consolidating the peace' and to promote 'respect for human rights and fundamental freedoms for all . . .'. Meanwhile, the General Assembly may initiate studies and make recommendations with a view to 'developing international cooperation' in the fields of 'intellectual culture and education' among others. Similar provisions appear in Chapter IX of the Charter, governing international cooperation in the economic and social spheres, and in Chapter X devoted to the Economic and Social Council (ECOSOC).[15]

While these provisions confer upon the UN general powers in the spheres of peace and human rights, it would seem difficult to interpret them as endowing that Organisation with greater legal competence than UNESCO, let alone with exclusive jurisdiction, for information as a policy area.

The absence of an explicit mandate for information policy in the UN Charter may well explain why documents dealing with the division of labour in this field were to cite as legal authority for UN competence not only the Charter but also subsequent General Assembly resolutions, thus providing the UN with an evolving juridical base in this field, while in the case of UNESCO the Constitution alone was to be instanced.[16]

Comparison of the relevant texts thus shows that the division of labour which emerged between the UN and UNESCO with respect to information policy lacked any particularly solid constitutional grounds. That the arrangements arrived at (to which we turn below) were essentially pragmatic can be inferred from references according to which the division of labour was 'practical', 'logical', 'empirical', and 'had gradually emerged'; and according to which the United Nations 'have taken the initiative and responsibility' for certain aspects of the subject.[17]

Let us now consider the stages in the process.

2.   EMERGENCE OF THE DIVISION OF LABOUR

During 1945–6, the USA argued for a privileged position for freedom of information among the human rights and fundamental freedoms for which the UN was to have general responsibility.[18] During 1946, it was decided within the UN to call upon the Commission on Human Rights to consider the question of freedom of information; to convene a conference on the subject under the aegis of the UN; and to set up a Sub-Commission on Freedom of Information and of the Press (SCFIP) with a mandate to prepare the conference and to examine the concept of freedom of information from a human rights perspective. As is shown in Chapter 4, these initiatives quickly led to calls for consideration of the obligations and responsibilities inherent in freedom of information, and of the content and goals of communication.

Such concerns overlapped with UNESCO's sphere of competence as described above. The result, not surprisingly, was the tabling of a number of broadly parallel proposals in the information field within the two institutions at this time, as for instance French proposals within UNESCO[19] and American and Philippine initiatives within the UN[20] for a world conference on the press and for an international broadcasting network.

At these earliest stages, some concern to preserve UNESCO prerogatives was visible. For example, although UNESCO decided to accept an invitation to help prepare the UN Conference rather than convening a separate meeting, the importance of joint official patronage was stressed both by the relevant organ of the UNESCO General Conference and by senior UNESCO officials.[21] (In the event, however, the title of the Conference made no mention of UNESCO.) Similarly, it was resolved at the first session of the General Conference, at the suggestion of the Australian, British, US and French delegations, that any agreement regarding a division of responsibilities with respect to freedom of information between the two organisations would require approval by the Executive Board of UNESCO.[22] Representatives of France and New Zealand also expressed regret in the early years at what they saw as a loss of ground in this field to the UN.[23] So, too, adopting a somewhat maverick stance within her delegation, did US representative Anne O'Hare McCormick.[24]

UN activity in the sphere of information policy was increasingly to be invoked as grounds for non-involvement of UNESCO. This was especially true in the case of attempts by India, Poland and Yugoslavia to raise questions within UNESCO concerning 'false news', press and media content as they bore on matters of war and peace, and the possibly harmful effects of commercial media.[25]

The practical division of labour was largely to crystallise by the close of the Conference on Freedom of Information held under UN auspices in March–April 1948. Interested circles in the USA and UK considered the outcome of the Conference (many of whose participants had been newsmen) sufficiently encouraging to urge consideration by official UN organs of the Final Act of the Conference and, in particular, UN adoption of the conventions drafted by the latter.[26] The USA also moved the establishment of continuing UN machinery in this field, including additional funds and full-time expert staff.[27]

René Maheu, an official representing UNESCO at the Conference (and later Director-General of UNESCO) reported that a demarcation of terms of reference between the UN and UNESCO in the information field had been proposed during the conference by the USA and 'finally agreed to' by the UK and France.[28] (The grounds for the implied reluctance of the latter were not explained and neither UNESCO nor British archives of State provide much enlightenment.[29]) The content of the proposed division of effort was summarised by the Secretariat in a document prepared for the General Conference some months later:

> The UN would have the initiative and main responsibility as regards *news* proper, in view of the essentially *political* character of the factors conditioning it, and of the measures for improving its international circulation; UNESCO would concentrate on promoting the free flow of material . . . in respect of educational, scientific and cultural information.[30] (Emphases added.)

UNESCO would also be competent, in the field of 'news', for improving technical conditions for production and exchange.[31]

In line with American proposals, the 1948 Conference recommended extension of the existence of the UN SCFIP for a further three years as well as expansion of its terms of reference.[32] The broader mandate approved by ECOSOC in 1949 empowered the Sub-Commission not only, as previously, to consider freedom of information from a human rights perspective, including the obligations and responsibilities involved; but also, among other things, to study: the problems involved in dissemination of information by newspapers, radio and newsreels; political, economic and other barriers to free flow of information; the adequacy of news available to peoples; problems of 'false news'; professional standards of conduct; the degree of freedom of information prevailing around the world; the operation of intergovernmental agreements on the subject; and ways of promoting a wider degree of freedom of information and of reducing obstacles thereto.[33]

Meanwhile, as compared with the programme adopted for 1947,[34] UNESCO's programme in the information field gradually came to reflect a more auxiliary or technical role relative to the UN. Under the programmes adopted for 1949 and 1950, UNESCO would offer its services to the United Nations 'in matters concerning freedom of information, and particularly by the publication of reports and the conduct of studies which will assist the work of the Sub-Commission on

Freedom of Information'.[35] Certain delegates, notably Mr Guéhenno of France, Mrs McCormick of the USA and Mr Sutch of New Zealand, took exception to arrangements which seemed to them to reduce the role of UNESCO (an intergovernmental agency) in the information field to that of a research institute, while leaving it to the UN Sub-Commission (a body of experts sitting in personal capacity) to secure action by Member States.[36]

The significance of the arrangement was that policy debates on the goals and quality of information would be left to the UN, while UNESCO would work for implementation of the principle of free flow, treated as given, in respect of education, science and culture. To characterise the situation in the starkest form, UNESCO would implement the rights and the UN would debate the responsibilities. In the process, the 'minds of men' would be compartmentalised in a manner not intended by UNESCO's founders, and UNESCO would in fact relinquish to the UN that part of its mandate bearing on 'information for peace' as distinct from 'education for peace' narrowly understood.

3. SOME DIFFICULTIES WITH THE DIVISION OF LABOUR

The division of labour was thus based on a distinction between the 'political' and the 'technical'. But it can be seen from the debates, as well as from the constantly shifting descriptions of the division of labour, and from the attribution of items as between organs within the UN itself, that the 'political'/'technical' dichotomy was not always easy to apply in practice.

In accounts[37] of the proposed or actual division of labour, the distinction sometimes referred to the type of information ('news proper' and 'topical information', versus information of an educational, scientific and cultural nature), and sometimes to the vehicles for its transmission (the press, versus those means of communication judged more suitable for treatment of the latter type of subject, e.g. books, documentary and feature films, recreational broadcasts, etc.).

Meanwhile, the distinction between 'news' and other types of knowledge implied that education, science and culture were in some sense non-political. In this connection, it should be noted that UNESCO was to retain unchallenged jurisdiction within the UN system with respect to 'education for peace' where education was understood in the narrow sense. It may thus be assumed that 'education for peace' (which might reasonably be termed 'peace propaganda') was regarded as somehow less political than 'war propaganda', for which the UN was to be competent, although the reasons for the differentiation were never made explicit. Similarly, the difficulty of attempting to define scientific information as non-political found topical illustration in the question of 'atomic information', the free flow of which was deemed by US delegate Archibald MacLeish in 1945 to fall outside UNESCO's purview.[38]

The classification of economic obstacles to free flow, too, was to remain unsettled. While different in kind from such 'political' obstacles as censorship, obstacles in the form of trade and tariff barriers could nevertheless be regarded as elements of national economic policy and in that sense political. Consequently, UNESCO's 'technical' role was on occasion taken to involve efforts to reduce economic obstacles,[39] but on others was understood (notably by Sir John Maud of the UK) simply as improvement of exchanges within existing limitations.[40] More ambiguously still, US spokesman Lloyd Free suggested that the 'stubborn' economic obstacles should be the responsibility of the UN.[41]

The allocation of items to the different organs of the UN was also revealing. As we have seen, UN competence for questions of freedom, responsibility and content in the information field had been justified largely on the grounds that these issues were politically sensitive. Yet most of the debates on the subject within the UN were in fact referred to organs with a 'non-political' brief: the Third Committee of the General Assembly (Social, Cultural and Humanitarian Affairs), ECOSOC, the Commission on Human Rights, and the SCFIP.[42] (It may be noted, though, that the SCFIP was itself viewed alternately as 'political' – by virtue of its subject-matter – and as 'technical' – on account of the non-State basis of membership.[43])

However, when the word 'war' appeared in the title of a motion, it was referred to a 'political' organ. So it was that, in 1947, a Yugoslav proposal for regulation with respect to 'slanderous statements' concerning foreign States was referred to the Third Committee of the General Assembly, while a draft on the subject of 'war propaganda' tabled by the USSR, also in 1947, was referred to the First Committee (Political and Security Questions).[44] Thus at one and the same session of the General Assembly, texts both concerned in essence with the permissible limits to freedom of information were handled respectively by 'technical' and 'political' organs of the UN.

4.   THE DIVISION OF LABOUR: AN ADMINISTRATIVE ARRANGEMENT

No decision was in fact ever taken by UNESCO's governing bodies on an inter-institutional division of labour in the information field, this division being instead worked out, on the UNESCO side at least, by the Secretariat. Indeed, at the 1948 Conference where the division of labour was made explicit, UNESCO was represented only by officials; and the latter were subsequently to remark on the lack of prior guidance received from UNESCO's policy organs.[45] Although the question of a division of labour was touched upon in a number of documents prepared for the General Conference,[46] as well as in the course of discussions both in that arena and in the Executive Board,[47] it was never tabled as a formal item for debate in UNESCO's policy-making bodies.

This may have been in part because staff members were careful regularly to recall UNESCO's overall and unlimited constitutional responsibility for 'free flow of ideas by word and image' as well as for the 'quality and quantity' of information flows, and to stress that such divisions of labour as might be arrived at could be regarded as no more than working arrangements between the two Secretariats.[48] If held to apply only at the administrative and not at the policy level, arrangements of this sort would not call for policy decisions.

The scrupulousness with which the Secretariat entered the formal reminders of UNESCO's constitutional jurisdiction may itself have been due more to concern to avoid awkward discussions in policy-making bodies than to any desire for active involvement in what, by 1948, they had come to regard as highly sensitive issues. During the 1948 UN Conference, the UNESCO Secretariat had had ample opportunity to witness debates in which Soviet bloc delegates, although systematically outvoted, had taken a prominent part. In addition, as Maheu was to report, the positions advanced by UNESCO representatives, led by the then Director-General, Julian Huxley, which stressed the responsibilities inherent in freedom of information and the need for equalisation of the concrete means to make it effective, had been widely interpreted by the US press as showing that the Agency inclined towards Soviet views.[49] Conversely, UNESCO staff were aware of very positive press coverage with regard to the Agency's efforts to implement a policy of 'free flow' where this was treated as given.[50]

Following the Conference, Maheu dubbed the division of labour agreed to on that occasion 'reasonable and practical',[51] and the Secretariat ceased to insist on high-profile UNESCO involvement in the policy issues.

5. DECLINE AND CONSEQUENCES OF THE DIVISION OF LABOUR

Within three years, however, circumstances had changed again and the arrangements described above had begun no longer to hold.

In 1951, on British initiative,[52] the question of overlapping between the UN and UNESCO in the information sphere was to be discussed in the UN Economic and Social Council by the Council itself, by an *ad hoc* Committee, and by a Working Group on the Delimitation of the Activities of the UN and UNESCO in the Field of Freedom of Information. The document prepared for the purpose jointly by the two Secretariats purported to show that, while the responsibilities of both organisations in this field were wide, they were also complementary and that the division of labour was working satisfactorily.[53]

But by this time it had already become plain that the positions of the USA and its supporters on questions of information policy would not prevail in the major organs of the UN itself (see Chapter 4). As can be seen from the statements of US members of ECOSOC[54] and the views of Carroll Binder, erstwhile American member of the SCFIP,[55] the United States had also become dissatisfied with the record of the latter body, several of whose later members were not as intended experts sitting in a personal capacity, but instructed delegates. Moreover, it was likely that SCFIP initiatives would be deadlocked in the General Assembly as had been the case with most of the output of the 1948 UN Conference.

The US Government had already suggested in 1950 that the SCFIP devote itself more to technical questions.[56] By 1951, encouraged by the US press, the USA could be seen during debates on the future work of the UN in the field of freedom of information to be aiming both at removal of the subject from the UN agenda and at discontinuation of the SCFIP.[57] British records of State show that the UK supported overtures made to it in this sense by the USA[58] and sought to rally Commonwealth governments to the same line.[59] In so doing, the UK was also heeding the British and Commonwealth press (notably the Empire Press Union, Commonwealth Press Union, Guild of Newspaper Editors, Reuters and the Newspaper Society), whose disapproval of the trend of debate in the UN had been persistently and forcefully brought to bear on the Foreign Office.[60] A serviceable device for achievement of US and UK aims in this respect could be seen to lie in reassertion of UNESCO competence, not least given non-participation in UNESCO during this period by the Soviet bloc.

Further grounds for asserting equal if not superior UNESCO competence for policy aspects of the problem were supplied by the Korean War. On this occasion, as has been well documented, the USA was to stress what it described as UNESCO's ethical mission in the information field. UNESCO's role in this context was understood by the USA as that not so much of autonomous agent, but rather of supportive publicist for UN policy.[61] Again, the absence of the Soviet bloc within UNESCO at the time made reaffirmation of the Agency's competence for information policy propitious.

These various developments may help to account for the positions adopted in ECOSOC by the USA and UK. Interpreting the joint Secretariat document mentioned earlier as revealing less complementarity than competition between the functions of the two institutions in the information field, American and British delegates were to stress the broader constitutional responsibilities of UNESCO and to advocate winding up the SCFIP.[62] Similarly, in separate discussions within ECOSOC on the annual UNESCO report to the UN, the USA explicitly urged that UNESCO pay more attention to political dimensions of the subject:

> UNESCO should in future devote more attention to problems connected with freedom of information, ceasing to concern itself with purely technical aspects and reaching out towards the political causes of restrictions on freedom of information.[63]

The Working Group on Delimitation referred to above consisted of delegates from the UK, Brazil and India. Its conclusions, to the drafting of which the USA contributed unofficially, broadly reflected US and UK positions and formed the basis of those of the *Ad Hoc* Committee.[64] In the latter's findings, the wording of the distinction between UN and UNESCO roles is more tentative than in earlier texts. 'It might be said', the Committee ventured, 'that UNESCO is essentially concerned with the technical aspects of Freedom of Information . . .' and 'by contrast that the UN should be essentially concerned with political aspects . . .'[65] But such generalisations, the Committee pursued, might be misleading. The point was illustrated by a rather curiously-drafted statement which, in the circumstances, could only be taken to refer to the Korean War:

The responsibility of UNESCO to promote education concerning the United Nations may require the dissemination of information concerning matters which form the subject of propaganda of aggression. It is evident that while such a course of action may be considered primarily political, it is one which UNESCO cannot escape.[66]

(The point was less evident to the USSR which voted against the text.[67])

Even so, the fact that UNESCO's role was not defined still more broadly was due to Secretariat efforts to tone down the wording. The words 'education concerning the United Nations', for instance, were substituted at the suggestion of a UNESCO official for the words 'propagation of the truth' initially favoured by the UK and USA.[68] Similarly, Secretariat initiative ensured that UNESCO's responsibility was defined only as 'education', not as 'education and information concerning the UN'.[69] Ostensibly this wording aimed to avoid confusion with the role of the UN Public Information Department; but an equally plausible motive would seem to have been Secretariat concern to limit the extent of any direct campaigning which might be required of UNESCO in relation to Korea.

The overall conclusion of the *Ad Hoc* Committee, subsequently endorsed by the Economic and Social Council, was that any detailed delimitation of activities between the two institutions 'can only be achieved on an *ad hoc* and pragmatic basis'.[70]

On a recommendation by ECOSOC, the General Assembly decided to dissolve the SCFIP in 1952.[71] Meanwhile, with the tacit consent of the Soviet bloc, the USA was also soon to secure systematic postponement of debates within the UN on questions of information policy. However, no formal decision was ever taken on the respective terms of reference of the UN and UNESCO in this field after the SCFIP was discontinued.

The most obvious course, in the absence of any formal decision to the contrary, might simply have been to revert to the *status quo ante* and to reactivate UNESCO concern with the policy issues on the basis of its constitutional responsibilities in the information field. As it happened, however, no particular moves were made in this direction. Instead, UNESCO continued to confine itself to implementing the policy of free flow treated as given, and later to administering the UN Technical Assistance programme in the communications field.

It should be noted in this connection that it was only within UN arenas that the US and UK were to proclaim UNESCO jurisdiction for information policy, not within the confines of UNESCO itself. This would seem to reinforce the hypothesis that the essential purpose of such affirmations was to remove information policy from the agenda of the UN system as a whole.

The initiative for reassertion on UNESCO's part of competence for the policy issues might in fact have been expected to come from the Secretariat as the body most closely involved up to that point with the division of labour between the UN and UNESCO.

The fact that no such initiative was forthcoming might, at a passive level, be taken to indicate that the Secretariat had simply become accustomed to an arrangement which left the policy issues to the UN; and, in addition, that a division of labour always presented as applying only to the Secretariat had in practice (as might well have been foreseen) come to apply to the Organisation as a whole. In any event, references to respective jurisdictions in certain documents prepared by the UNESCO Secretariat as late as the 1970s make no distinction between the administrative and the policy levels.[72]

On the other hand, more active deterrents to renewed UNESCO concern with the policy issues could be seen to lie in the experience of several years' debate on such matters in the UN, as well as in adverse press coverage both of those debates and of what were seen in some US quarters as UNESCO moves to regulate other branches of knowledge in un-American ways (notably textbook revision: see Chapter 6 below, p. 118).

In the circumstances, abandonment for practical purposes of a portion of UNESCO's constitutional mandate which seemed unlikely to yield any significant area of agreement may have seemed to the Secretariat a small price to pay if it ensured a favourable climate in which to pursue more constructive work not only in other spheres, but in the information field itself. Internal correspondence advocating avoidance of 'political' issues and urging concentration on practical means of increasing exchanges of information would seem to provide support for this view.[73] So, too, would an article by the Norwegian Director of the UNESCO Department of Mass Communication in 1960 remarking that the UN's assumption of responsibility for the political issues had made UNESCO's work easier.[74] Interviews with senior Western UNESCO officials involved with the subject at the time confirm that the Secretariat was less than enthusiastic to see UNESCO resume the debate where the UN left off.[75]

These preoccupations on the part of the Secretariat are only too understandable. The net result, nevertheless, was that the basic questions of information policy, disappearing from the agenda of the UN but finding no place on that of UNESCO, were to enter an effective jurisdictional vacuum for the better part of the next twenty years.

Indeed, debate within UNESCO on the goals and responsibilities of information was not to resume on any scale until the 1970s. By that time, the potential power of communications satellites had given rise among many Western observers, including René Maheu,[76] then Director-General of UNESCO, to a greater sense of the relationship between the means and the ends of communication – i.e. the 'political' and the 'technical' aspects of the subject. Starting with the question of satellite communication in the mid-1960s, as will be seen in Chapter 5, UNESCO was gradually to involve itself more explicitly with the goals of communication and as such with content.

SUMMARY AND CONCLUSIONS

In this chapter, we have shown that under its Constitution UNESCO has competence in the sphere of 'education for peace', where this is taken to refer to the whole intellect and to all means of communication. We also argued that the mandate to educate for peace entailed competence for such policy issues as regulation or non-regulation of information flows.

We then showed that a division of labour had emerged in the postwar years in which UNESCO concentrated on promoting free flow in certain branches of knowledge and on improving the technical means of communication, while policy debates on the goals and quality of communication, and concern with the press in particular, were left to the UN. While retaining unquestioned jurisdiction with respect to 'education for peace', narrowly understood, UNESCO could thus be said to have surrendered that portion of its constitutional mandate and policy autonomy bearing on 'information for peace' more broadly defined.

It has been seen, in addition, that the division of labour was agreed to by a UNESCO Secretariat concerned primarily to distance the Organisation from debates which, through the adverse publicity they attracted, might jeopardise public support for the Agency as a whole. It was shown, furthermore, that the arrangement purported to prevail only at the administrative level, and was never formally endorsed by

UNESCO's governing bodies; but that it was to become customary and that it also came, in practice, to apply to the Organisation as a whole.

Meanwhile, we showed that although from the early 1950s onward the UN in turn effectively ceased to debate the policy issues, the latter failed to be reinstated on UNESCO's agenda and were for all practical purposes relegated to a jurisdictional limbo. This situation persisted until UNESCO's concern was revived in connection with satellite communication some two decades later. But by that time it had become conventional to regard UNESCO as having no competence with respect to information content.

These developments may serve to set the contemporary debate on 'politicisation' of UNESCO in some perspective. The evidence reviewed points to the conclusion that the consensus which was broadly to prevail for some twenty years within UNESCO in the information sphere was the result not so much of an absence of controversy, but rather of its referral to other arenas. In this sense, the developments in question may fairly be deemed to have constituted 'technicisation' of UNESCO in the information field.

If this interpretation of events is accepted, then later developments would need to be understood not so much as 'politicisation', but rather as 'de-technicisation' through active resumption by UNESCO of concern with a neglected portion of its constitutional mandate.

4 The Postwar Information Debate: A Consensus?

INTRODUCTION

The UNESCO debates of the 1970s were thoroughly rehearsed in the United Nations in the postwar era, and to a lesser extent within UNESCO itself, in discussions ranging across the spectrum of information policy.

Contemporary allegations that UNESCO has been 'politicised' by the media debates of the 1970s and 1980s imply a prior state of 'consensus' on the subject. By examining the postwar debates more closely than has been done to date, the aim of the present chapter is to establish the extent to which such a consensus may reasonably be held to have existed at the time. In so doing, it will provide a basis for reassessing certain accounts and for setting the contemporary debate in historical perspective.

This chapter will concentrate on the questions which occasioned greatest controversy, in the 1940s as thirty years later, namely attempts to draft legally binding instruments and codes of practitioner ethics in this field. Before analysing the outcomes of the substantive debates, we briefly summarise the postwar setting, examine the process by which 'freedom of information' was initially placed on the agenda of the UN system, and consider the structure of bodies involved in the question.

1. THE POSTWAR SETTING

The debate on freedom of information first arose within the UN in the mid-1940s, as the Cold War took clearer shape. Given the postwar dependence of the larger part of the world on its military, economic and/or technological support, the USA emerged at the time as both the foremost world power and the unquestioned leader of the Western camp.

The founding membership of the UN, meanwhile, was preponderantly Western or Western-controlled. The fifty or so founder Members included twenty Latin American States, barely beginning to assert

59

their independence of the USA; six Arab States, under British or American control; Chiang Kai-shek's China, reliant on the USA for its seat at the UN, especially after 1949; and the Philippines, a virtual American dependency. Greece, Turkey, Iran and Ethiopia, too, in one way or another, were passing under American control at this time.

The UK and France, despite left-wing postwar governments, were militarily and economically dependent on the USA with which, as superpower relations chilled, they were generally to close ranks. Britain, in particular, was later to opt for transatlantic rather than European links. The Soviet bloc, for its part, accounted for six of the founding Members: the USSR; Byelorussia and Ukraine (both of course part of the USSR); Czechoslovakia and Poland; and, until the Titoist breakaway, Yugoslavia.

Information policy constituted a crucial dimension of the Cold War, both as an instrument in the conflict and as an aspect of the discourse. In the circumstances of the time, the extent of dissent from American policy in the information field, which will be illustrated below, was in fact remarkable.

2. 'FREEDOM OF INFORMATION' ON THE AGENDA

As has rather tended to be overlooked in comment on recent debates,[1] but as is established both in the documentary record and in academic comment of varying political persuasion[2] and in accounts by the UN Secretariat,[3] the USA took the initiative in placing the topic of 'freedom of information' on the agenda of the United Nations system.

The Charter of the UN, drafted in the early 1940s, contains no explicit reference to freedom of information. This formal gap notwithstanding, US delegates moved during 1945 and 1946 to place the subject on the agenda of the UN and UNESCO in response to promptings from Congress. Congress in turn had been lobbied to this effect during 1944–5 by the American Society of Newspaper Editors (ASNE) as is recorded among others by Carroll Binder, a member of ASNE who was also to become US member of the UN Sub-Commission on Freedom of Information and of the Press (see below).[4]

An immediate achievement of note was a General Assembly resolution of 1946 calling on the Economic and Social Council (ECOSOC) to convene a UN Conference on Freedom of Information. The formal proposals were tabled by the Philippines[5] (later elected to preside the conference); but it would seem not unreasonable in the circumstances to assume that the initiative came from the USA*, whose delegates in any event seconded the motions.[7]

Backed also by several Latin American States, the proposal was adopted despite reservations expressed by Chile, India and the USSR among others regarding the mandate and structure of the conference, and regarding the implications of the *laissez-faire* concept of freedom of information.[8]

These misgivings found some expression in the relevant General Assembly resolution, as well as in a toned-down agenda which referred not only to the rights but also to the obligations to be included in the concept.[9] But these concessions may be considered to have been somewhat overshadowed in the scales of history by the solemn proclamation contained in the opening words of the resolution, and regularly invoked since by supporters of 'free flow', to the effect that

> Freedom of information is a fundamental human right and is the touchstone of all the freedoms to which the United Nations is consecrated.[10]

The Soviet bloc sponsored a subsequent debate in an unsuccessful endeavour to revise the conference agenda further.[11]

The Conference took place in Geneva for one month in 1948 and was attended by delegations from 54 States, it having been specified at the initiative of the UK[12] that the meeting be held independently of official UN machinery and that delegations should include practising newsmen.[13] The Final Act of the Conference,[14] although not wholly satisfactory from the American point of view, was generally welcomed in the USA. Carroll Binder commented in an academic journal that 'our initial attempts to commit the United Nations to [the US concept of freedom of information] were successful beyond expectation',[15] and recorded that the USA had formally moved referral of the Conference output to official UN organs with a view to its adoption by the latter.[16] (However, as will be seen below, debate in these arenas was to be deadlocked.)

Other bodies were also brought into being during these years to deal with freedom of information. In 1947, for instance, the Sub-

---

* The following views expressed by a Philippines spokesman at UNESCO in 1946 do not suggest a highly developed sense of cultural integrity at the time: '. . . perhaps there was a blessing in disguise in [this] almost total destruction of Philippines culture, and that we were able to receive, on a clean slate, as it were, a new culture and civilisation at the end of the Spanish–American war. Thus we received with enthusiasm American culture and American ideas of democracy and government . . .'[6]

Commission on Freedom of Information and the Press (SCFIP) of the Commission on Human Rights, to be composed of uninstructed experts, had been set up to deliberate on the concept of freedom of information and to prepare the 1948 Conference,[17] and was in fact kept in existence with a revised mandate until 1952.[18]

The International Press Institute (IPI) was also set up at this time, as a by-product of debates within UNESCO.[19] UNESCO moves toward creation of a research centre on the problems of journalists had seemed to Western practitioners to entail too great a risk of political control. The IPI was therefore set up, pre-emptively, by an American newspaperman as an editorial institute 'run by and for the press'.[20] In pursuit of its prime purpose – 'the furtherance and safeguarding of freedom of the press'[21] – the Institute publishes the monthly *IPI Report* on the state of the press around the world.

Meanwhile, as former senior American UNESCO officials record, both UNESCO's Constitution as a whole and explicit reference to the 'media of mass communication' were largely based on American drafts, including a US proposal stressing the 'paramount importance' of such media and the need to identify 'opportunities of UNESCO furthering [their] use for the ends of peace'.[22] An American official of UNESCO, Howard Wilson, also suggested that staff in the mass communication section receive salaries higher than those of officials in other sections and aligned more closely with 'those paid in corresponding spheres of private enterprise'.[23]

While the whole of UNESCO's programme was to be conceived in the spirit of 'free flow', a separate division was also created for purposes of coordination and to handle technical aspects of the subject (study of obstacles to free flow and of means to their removal). The resolution embodying the division's first annual programme, it may be noted, was to make only token preambular reference to respect for the 'independence, integrity and fruitful diversity of the cultures and educational systems of Member States'.[24]

A further American project envisaged a worldwide radio network be run under UNESCO auspices.[25] Some US delegates, at least, would seem to have been guided by motives other than the purely cultural in putting forward this plan. William Benton, Head of the US delegation to the first and second sessions of the General Conference where the project was first discussed, and who was to advocate for this project alone a yearly budget of US$1–2 billion (a level never attained by UNESCO for the whole of its biennial programme), addressed Congress on the need for a 'Marshall Plan for Ideas' in order to 'bridge 'the mental gap between ourselves and the rest of the world' and canvassed the possibility of 'piercing the iron curtain' by broadcasts from Germany.[26]

The USA also tabled motions recommending that Member States 'make more radio time available for UN and UNESCO news . . .' and 'make increased use of radio to promote international understanding'; and that UNESCO's programme give priority to preparing radio materials 'and to promotion of their use by . . . governments and private broadcasting organisations'.[27]

However, as former US officials record, many smaller countries feared that 'the nations most expert in using these powerful media, and especially the USA, would employ them for "cultural imperialism" . . .'[28] According to one observer, it was failure to win majority support for certain of the above mass communications projects which before long led the USA to 'disengage' from UNESCO.[29]

Indeed, the vigour of American diplomacy on behalf of 'free flow' was to provoke comment on possible ulterior (Cold War, commercial and/or cultural–supremacist) motives, not least on the part of one US delegate.[30] The records of the British Foreign Office, for instance, disclose initial reluctance based on just such suspicions to follow the US lead,[31] although British misgivings were later on the whole dispelled.[32] At the first session of the General Conference, the UK in particular repeatedly cautioned against moves liable to appear to the majority with weaker means of communication as a bid for cultural overlordship on the part of those (including the UK) better equipped.[33]

The fact that reservations to US proposals on mass media were voiced more clearly on the latter occasion than at the Founding Conference the previous year suggests that the USA may have taken the majority unawares. Whitehall files, in any event, reveal a strong sense of unpreparedness relative to US initiatives in this field.[34]

The attitude of the USSR, meanwhile, may perhaps best be gauged by its failure to take up active membership of UNESCO until 1954 despite entreaties, some undoubtedly sincere, that it contribute to the Agency's work.[35] If initial Soviet aloofness was dictated by a prudent concern to ascertain the direction in which UNESCO's mandate and programme were likely to evolve, the developments described above were not such as to encourage Soviet participation. Given that the USSR was certain to occupy a minority position in UNESCO's policy-making councils and secretariat, these trends doubtless served to confirm the Soviet Union in its 'empty seat' stance.

Ill-placed as they were to influence standard-setting activities, the

East European countries in fact consistently urged both within ECOSOC and within UNESCO that the latter concentrate on concrete programmes of reconstruction and eschew normative undertakings.[36] This preference was best expressed by Poland, which appealed from the founding conference of UNESCO in 1945 onward for help in rebuilding its own war-damaged facilities.[37] In 1945, Poland abstained in the vote on the Final Act of the founding conference on the grounds that UNESCO was not to be constituted sufficiently along the lines of a relief organisation;[38] and in 1947 it abstained on the same basis in the vote on the budget.[39] Not long after Stalinisation, Poland and Czechoslovakia withdrew to all intents and purposes from participation in the Agency's work until after the entry of the USSR in 1954.

Yugoslavia, for its part, voiced strong doubts at insertion in UNESCO's Constitution of the concept of free flow, seeking in vain to qualify the principle by explicit reference to 'democratic ideas' and to the need to 'combat doctrines glorifying violence and racial inequality'.[40] Yugoslav spokesmen were also to raise within UNESCO the question of 'war propaganda' in terms identical to those used at the UN by the USSR (see pp. 66–8).[41]

However, these objections on the part of the East European States were to be overruled and, in all, between 1947 and 1952, the concept of 'free flow' was to be placed on the agenda or written into the mandate of over a dozen UN bodies, either existing or created for the purpose.

Nevertheless, it would seem unjustified to assert that initial US success at the level of the agenda was due wholly to underlying consensus and not at least in some measures to tactics. The delayed reaction to American proposals mentioned above, and the unpreparedness of at least one major West European State, as well as the impasse which, as we shall see, was rapidly to be reached in attempts thereafter to draft legally binding instruments on the subject, suggest that the victory of US delegates might better be interpreted as that of the prepared over the unprepared.

3.   THE STRUCTURE OF THE UN BODIES INVOLVED

The United Nations bodies dealing with freedom of information varied widely in structure and powers. At one extreme were full-membership arenas composed of plenipotentiary representatives of States, such as organs of the General Assembly (e.g. the plenary, the First Committee, the Third Committee and the 1954 *ad hoc* Political Committee), as well as those of the General Conference of UNESCO. At the other end of the scale were rapporteurs acting in a personal capacity, as for example Salvador López of the Philippines, appointed in 1952.

Between these extremes came limited-membership bodies such as the 18-member Economic and Social Council (ECOSOC) (plenary, Social Committee and Human Rights Committee); the 15-member Commission on Human Rights (plenary and 1957 *ad hoc* Committee); the 12-member Sub-Commission on Freedom of Information and the Press (SCFIP), composed in theory if not always in practice of experts sitting in an individual capacity (1947–52);[42] and the 1951 *ad hoc* Committee, composed of 5 representatives of States.

As in the case of the 1948 UN Conference, it will be seen that US policy fared best in limited-membership bodies and/or those based on personal or mixed official/personal representation, notably ECOSOC, the SCFIP and rapporteurs. Indeed, ballots to constitute smaller bodies representing States sometimes failed to yield American membership, as happened, for instance, with the 1957 *ad hoc* Committee discussed below.

Thus, among the arenas most regularly seized of the subject, the USA and its supporters were on the whole better able to control outcomes in ECOSOC organs than in those of the General Assembly where the opposition was numerically stronger. Conversely the opposition, disposing of a wider margin of manoeuvre in Assembly forums, seemed prepared on occasion to accommodate US positions at the subordinate level of ECOSOC.

Moving now to the debates, we shall examine first the responses to Soviet bloc positions, and then the outcomes of discussions between supporters of 'free flow' and non-Soviet bloc proponents of regulation.

4. RESPONSES TO SOVIET BLOC POSITIONS

Having failed to exclude normative aspects of information policy from the agenda, East European countries found themselves in an essentially 'responsive' position. Thus, as the USA moved in the name of peace to secure adoption of the principle of free international flow of information as formal UN policy, so the Soviet Union and its allies responded, also in the name of peace, with calls for regulation.

But the position of this group of countries in all the UN bodies dealing with information policy in the postwar era was that of a small and virtually permanent minority, accounting for between 9 per cent of the votes in full-membership organs of the General Assembly and 20 per cent of those in the Commission on Human Rights.* This structural position of itself sufficed to doom most Soviet motions to defeat.

Moreover, with the tightening of Cold War lines, the fact of Soviet sponsorship tended to deprive motions of any support which might otherwise have been forthcoming.

Hence from the beginning, as we shall see, Soviet bloc motions proposing limits to international 'free flow' were systematically emasculated. To be specific, references to practices in named Western countries were deleted; criticism of private media monopolies was deleted or diluted; proposals to classify 'war propaganda' (equated by the Soviet bloc with 'nazi or fascist ideology') as a crime and to punish it accordingly were defeated; all calls for 'prevention' (taken by Western Members to imply censorship) of particular types of expression were rejected, as were those aimed at prohibiting and legislating against such expressions; and constitutional safeguard clauses were regularly inserted at Western initiative. In some instances the original motion was transformed into its very opposite – a vehicle for promotion of free flow – leaving the Soviet bloc, by way of sole comfort, that of having authored the initial motion. The fate of the following motions illustrates the pattern.

A. The Resolution on Measures to be taken against Propaganda and the Promoters of a New War (UN, 1947)

The above resolution arose out of a Soviet draft by which the United Nations would have condemned

> the criminal propaganda for a new war carried on by reactionary circles . . . in particular, in the United States of America, Turkey and Greece, by the dissemination of all types of fabrications through the press, radio, cinema and public speeches . . .[43]

According to what was widely seen as the 'censorship clause' of the draft,

* The *Yearbook of the United Nations* provides membership lists of all UN bodies.

The United Nations deem it essential that the Governments of all countries be called upon to prohibit, on pain of criminal penalties, the carrying on of war propaganda in any form, and to take measures with a view to the prevention and suppression of war propaganda as anti-social activity endangering the vital interests and well-being of the peace-loving nations.[44]

The General Committee of the General Assembly referred the proposal to the First Committee (Political and Security Questions).[45] In the text as revised by that Committee and adopted by the Assembly in plenary, reference to any given country is eliminated; warlike propaganda in general – not of any particular variety – is condemned; governments are simply 'requested' to take steps to promote friendly relations between nations; and this request is qualified by a constitutional safeguard clause (inserted at US initiative) to ensure that steps are only taken 'within constitutional limits'. All that remains of the Soviet original is the title and a general condemnation of war propaganda.[46] The 'censorship clause' was defeated by an unambiguous majority of 42:6:6.[47]

The fact that at one stage a passage sponsored by Poland was rejected in favour of almost identically-worded amendments tabled by Australia, Canada and France[48] led the USSR to remark that the real issue seemed to be not so much the substance as the sponsor.[49]

B. The Resolution on False and Distorted Reports (UN, 1947)

This resolution originated in a Yugoslav motion on the subject of 'slanderous statements' which invited States

> to take urgent legislative and other measures to establish the responsibility of the owners of media of information and their directors or contributors who publish or spread false and tendentious reports calculated to aggrave [sic] relations between nations, provoke conflicts and incite to war,

and

> to take measures to prevent the publication and dissemination through governmental or semi-governmental bodies of reports or news which have not been carefully and conscientiously checked.[50]

The Yugoslav delegation ultimately withdrew its draft in favour of a French text, amended by Belgium, Luxembourg and Mexico (to delete the words 'legislative or other') and by the USA (to insert the words 'within the limits of constitutional procedures').[51] As adopted by the Third Committee and the plenary of the General Assembly after lively debate,[52] the resolution confined itself to inviting governments, among other things,

> to study such measures as might with advantage be taken on the national plane to combat, within the limits of constitutional procedures, the diffusion of false or distorted reports likely to injure friendly relations between States.[53]

Heavily outnumbered as they were, the USSR and Yugoslavia joined in the unanimous votes on these resolutions and announced, of necessity rather than choice, that they did so in a spirit of conciliation.[54] Soviet bloc attempts in the General Assembly[55] and ECOSOC[56] over the next few years to put teeth into the two resolutions as adopted were no more successful.

Nevertheless, for reasons to be analysed below, agreement on formulae to substitute for Soviet wordings in these debates was not easily achieved. In one extreme case, votes on portions of a Soviet motion[57] in the plenary of the Assembly yielded results of 6:5:43 and 5:5:45, that is, an abstention rate of some 80 per cent.[58] Votes on amendments to an identical Soviet draft[59] in Third Committee also produced high rates of abstention (e.g. 21:5:27, 18:6:29, 16:6:29, 17:10:23, and 9:9:30.)[60]

We should note, moreover, to balance the picture, that motions challenging the USSR by name and emanating notably from the USA or the SCFIP also tended almost invariably to be diluted in the course of debate.[61]

C.   The Universal Declaration of Human Rights (UN, 1948), Article 19

The Universal Declaration of Human Rights adopted by the General Assembly in 1948, whose moral weight as a statement of principles and as a 'common standard of achievement for all peoples' is historic, refers to freedom of information in Article 19. This article expresses the rights involved in *laissez-faire* form:

> Everyone has the right to freedom of opinion and expression; this right includes freedom to hold opinions without interference and to seek, receive and impart information and ideas through any media and regardless of frontiers.[62]

Soviet draft amendments designed to prohibit propaganda for fascism, aggression and hatred between nations were rejected by the Third Committee of the General Assembly, but not out-of-hand, by votes of 20:6:10 and 22:9:5.[63] Article 19 was then adopted by the Third Committee by a vote of 36:6 and in plenary by 44:7:2, the Soviet bloc (which unsuccessfully tabled amendments in plenary[64]) opposing on both occasions. The negative vote in plenary was higher than for any other article of the Declaration.[65]

The duties implied in this as in the other rights proclaimed by the Declaration are referred to in a separate part of the text in minimalist form.[66] It may be noted that, in urging UNESCO in 1948 to publicise the Declaration, the USA called attention to Article 19 but not to the latter provision.[67]

D.   Polish proposals regarding 'war propaganda' (UNESCO, 1947)

During the second session of the UNESCO General Conference in November 1947, Poland tabled two proposals on war propaganda and promotion of peace, one a draft resolution addressed to governments and the other an appeal to intellectuals.[68] However, a coalition of Australia, France and China, and Latin and North American States ensured, by skilful use of procedure, that alternative appeals to intellectuals[69] were adopted[70] and that the text addressed to governments was never put to the vote.[71]

As can be judged from these outcomes and as will be seen further below, the Soviet bloc was regularly marginalised in the postwar era in debates both on its own motions and on other texts. At most, the USSR might find itself tactically allied with the USA in opposition to a given text, as in the case of codes of ethics for journalists, or in support of such texts as those condemning incitement to changes of régime by violent means.[72]

5.   'FREE-FLOW' AND NON-SOVIET BLOC OPPOSITION

In support of its policy in the postwar era, the USA was generally able to count on the Scandinavian States, the Low Countries, the White Dominions, the Philippines, the UK – once its initial misgivings had been overcome – and, intermittently, on other countries. Meanwhile the Soviet bloc, as we have seen, was easily marginalised in this period. But opposition to *laissez-faire* proposals was also to be registered in the 1940s and early 1950s by a loose coalition of States favouring some limits on the international flow of information, whose views could not be so lightly dismissed.

Generally led by France, Mexico, India and Saudi Arabia, the opposition included certain West European States, a number of the 'banana republics', other States traditionally regarded as US satellites or 'faggot votes', and most of the then politically independent colonial or developing countries.

Taken together, these States formed a majority of the fifty or so founding members. But whilst agreed on the risks of abuse of freedom, their ranks were regularly divided both over what precisely constituted such an abuse and over the appropriate form of regulation (see Chapter 2).

As will now be shown, these differences added to Cold War cleavages were to generate a record of tied votes, roll-calls, abstentions, postponements and overall stalemate.

A. UN Draft Conventions on Freedom of Information

Controversy was greatest over those instruments intended to be legally binding and precise, namely draft conventions on freedom of information.

The 1948 UN Conference mentioned earlier had prepared drafts of three conventions concerned with (i) the gathering and international transmission of news, sponsored by the USA; (ii) the institution of an international right of correction, sponsored by France; and (iii) freedom of information, sponsored by the UK.[73] The Final Act of the Conference embodying the drafts along with 40-odd resolutions had been adopted by some 30 votes in favour, over Soviet bloc opposition.[74] But subsequent debates in official organs of the UN, although frequent and of great length, were to prove ultimately inconclusive.

At French instigation, the Third Committee of the General Assembly decided in 1949 to amalgamate draft conventions (i) and (ii). Debate on the two instruments, together with more than 60 related resolutions, proposals and amendments, and over 20 Secretariat documents, lasted 36 days.[75]

Indicative of the lack of consensus were votes in which opponents and abstainers combined typically numbered more than supporters (e.g. 22:17:7, 24:15:10, 20:13:15, 6:28:13, 24:12:14, . . .).[76] The draft convention as a whole was eventually adopted by the Third Committee in 1949 by a roll-call vote of 27:4:12, and by the plenary three days later by a roll-call vote of 33:6:11, the Soviet bloc opposing in both cases.[77]

As such votes would suggest, the final text was a compromise; however, its adoption may on the whole be judged a qualified success for the USA. True, the right of correction – not an American priority – was now formally linked to the transmission of news. The convention also contained certain provisions which, although diluted, remained uncongenial to American eyes,[78] for instance: greater emphasis on the 'responsibilities' of correspondents;[79] restriction of the term 'foreign correspondent' to 'correspondent of another Contracting State';[80] extension of 'national military defence' as grounds for controls to 'national defence';[81] inclusion of ethical considerations;[82] and reference to 'national prestige and dignity'[83] as well as to monopolistic practices.[84] Not popular, either, with the USA any more than with West European States or Australia, was the clause governing applicability of the convention to colonies and Trust Territories:[85] the article as redrafted by the USA was adopted by a roll-call vote of 24:12:14.[86]

On balance, however, the draft reflected the priorities of the USA as sponsor with regard to improving the gathering and transmission of news, while the provisions governing correction were minimalist: contracting States would be bound to make available to the information enterprises concerned the corrections sought by other States Parties, but neither the State nor the news organ would be compelled to publish them. The acceptability of the draft to the UK, meanwhile, was evidenced by a British motion in Third Committee urging that it be submitted for adoption to the plenary of the General Assembly at the session then under way.[87]

This move was opposed by France, several other States and the Soviet bloc, which considered that it would have the effect of divorcing that convention wholly from the convention on freedom of information.[88] Indeed, the States in question treated the latter text, in which they aimed to codify not only the right to freedom of information but also the concomitant duties, but on which negotiations were blocked, as forming a single unit with the previous instrument.[89]

The Netherlands, UK and USA succeeded in Third Committee in May 1949 in securing referral of the first draft convention to the plenary,[90] but only with the French-backed proviso that, if adopted, it should not be opened for signature until 'definite action' had been taken on the second text.[91] The Assembly duly adopted the Convention on International Transmission of News and the Right of Correction by 33:6:11 and the resolution to hold over the opening for signature by 40:6:6, the Soviet bloc opposing both times.[92]

However, work on the crucial section of the draft convention on freedom of information designed to specify the permissible limits to 'free flow' (Article 2, paragraph 1) was deadlocked. Successive debates on both form (mandatory or permissive) and content (the specific categories of expression warranting restriction) of this article failed to elicit any consensus. Thus, despite much prior debate, the vote in Third Committee in May 1949 yielded a result of only 18:12:12.[93]

In 1951, an *ad hoc* Committee was set up by the Commission on Human Rights at the initiative of Egypt and France, among others, and over US abstention, to examine the draft yet again.[94] The USA was overruled in this forum, which comprised most of its leading opponents, on several points it considered crucial:[95] Article 2 of the draft Convention as revised by the Committee,[96] in particular, was adopted by 7:2:5:1 with the USA opposing.[97]

As a result, the USA was to back motions for postponement or referral of debate[98] on this and related issues which were carried for the next eight years, sometimes narrowly, by the Assembly and ECOSOC.[99]

But by the same token, the first convention was still not open for signature. In 1952, prompted by the prospect of indefinite postponement of debate on the second convention, France, Egypt, Lebanon, Uruguay and Yugoslavia urged the opening for signature of a separate convention on the right of correction comprising the relevant articles of the Convention on International Transmission of News and the Right of Correction – those least acceptable to the USA.[100] The Third Committee adopted the proposal by a roll-call vote of 25:19:10,[101] and so in turn did the plenary of the Assembly by a vote of 25:22:10 over American opposition.[102]

In fact, however, the Convention was to remain largely inoperative on account both of the cumbersomeness of the procedures involved[103] and of non-ratification by those States in which the major media were located. By 1982, only seventeen States had signed or ratified the Convention, and of these the only major Western State was France.[104]

The outcome may thus be judged on balance a stalemate.

B.   UN Draft Codes of Ethics

Alongside legally binding texts, codes of ethics for practitioners were frequently discussed, from the standpoint both of substance and of jurisdiction.[105]

On the question of substance, the USA, the UK and several other Western or pro-Western countries would countenance only the classic injunction that the journalist 'tell the truth as he sees it'.[106] The USSR meanwhile generally adhered to the view that what it termed 'moral and platonic statements' were ineffectual.[107] Many Third World spokesmen, however, treated codes of ethics as another avenue by which the duties of the media might be approached, seeking to provide in such codes more specific guidance as to the concrete content of ethics and 'truth'.

In 1950, for example, the Lebanese, Egyptian and Chinese members of the SCFIP tabled a draft code of ethics, of which Articles 4 and 5 ran thus:

> In the exercise of their professional duties, it is the obligation of everyone engaged in the gathering, transmission and dissemination of information to work for the peaceful solution of all disputes and problems, whether international or national, and whether political, social, economic, racial or cultural . . .
>
> Everyone engaged in the gathering, transmission and dissemination of information shall foster understanding and cooperation between peoples, and help maintain peace and security. They shall discourage the view that there may be disputes between states which could be solved only by violent means. They shall not disseminate information which is likely to cause prejudice, mistrust, hatred or contempt for other peoples or states, or convey a false impression concerning their civilisation or culture . . .[108]

The SCFIP which, as mentioned earlier, was composed primarily of practising newsmen, rejected these draft articles by 3:5:1.[109]

Similarly, the draft code adopted by the SCFIP in 1952 reflects no trace of the resolution adopted by the 1948 UN Conference advocating that future journalists be inculcated with

> a keen sense of the moral and social responsibility of their profession stressing the undesirability of commercialism, and racial and religious intolerance . . .[110]

although it stipulated a more abstract duty to acquire the knowledge necessary to 'fair and accurate comment' on any given country.[111]

The SCFIP draft code was referred to ECOSOC in 1952. The USA and its supporters were still broadly able to control proceedings in ECOSOC at this stage, although partial re-election had reduced their share of representation somewhat, but majorities on the subject of 'free flow' were slender. Votes in the ECOSOC plenary on a Soviet bloc draft[112] were as follows: 8:3:5, 7:7:4, 8:6:4, 8:5:5, and 7:7:4.[113]

Controversy also centred on the question of UN jurisdiction for ethical codes, and the appropriateness or otherwise of including ethical considerations in legally binding texts. The record reveals discord between the West and the Third World, and tactical super-power alliance.

The 1948 Conference had declared that 'prior discussion' with the profession was a 'principal condition' for drafting and enforcement of an international code of ethics for information personnel.[114] But the SCFIP, reflecting the liberal position more fully, held in 1952 that the drafting of a code should be left to the profession without interference by governments.[115] The final text of the SCFIP draft code of ethics reasserts this principle in an unequivocal concluding article:

> . . . Nothing herein may therefore be interpreted as implying any justification for intervention by a government in any manner whatsoever to enforce observance of the moral obligations set forth in this code. [116]

Further discussion focussed on whether the Secretary-General of the UN should transmit the various drafts adopted to information enterprises direct or through governments; and on whether or not the Secretariat should call an international professional conference to finalise the text. Several countries (notably Egypt, India, Iraq, the Lebanon, Pakistan, Saudi Arabia, Syria and Yugoslavia) felt that the UN could properly adopt a stimulative and advisory role, and successfully sponsored motions to this effect in the Assembly.[117]

In 1954, however, at the initiative of the Philippines backed by both superpowers and the UK, the General Assembly decided unanimously not to organise a conference, but instead to transmit the draft code to information enterprises for such action as they might deem fit.[118]

But although work on a draft code of ethics as such was effectively shelved at this point, ethical considerations were inserted into other texts over superpower objections both before and after that time, as, for instance, in the case of the 1949 Convention cited above.[119]

C. UNESCO Agreements on Free Flow

In pursuit of its mandate, and with the continuing encouragement of the USA, UNESCO was to draw up two agreements designed to free the flow between States of certain types of material. The texts in question were the Agreement for Facilitating the Circulation of Visual and Auditory Materials of an Educational, Scientific and Cultural Character, adopted in Beirut in 1948 and often referred to as the Beirut Agreement; and the Agreement on Importation of Educational, Scientific and Cultural Materials, adopted in Florence in 1950 and known as the Florence Agreement.

These agreements, in fact the first to be drawn up by UNESCO, could be regarded as 'technical' instruments insofar as they were designed to promote implementation of the policy of free flow, treated as given. However, as with the more avowedly normative texts discussed above, debates and votes reveal not so much a harmony as a conflict of interest based on differing levels of endowment in communications resources.

Under the Beirut Agreement, Contracting States agree to exempt visual and auditory materials (e.g. films, film-strips, sound recordings, etc.) of an 'educational, scientific and cultural character' not only from customs duties and related charges, but also from quantitative import restrictions and from the necessity of securing import licences. Certification that materials are of the required character is made by the exporting State or by UNESCO, the final decision in this respect being left to the importing State.[120]

Misgivings were expressed from the earliest stages of preparation of the Beirut Agreement, notably by India whose spokesman invoked what he saw as the problem of distortion of truth in Hollywood films and the dangers of commercialism; France (whose delegate, Sedar Senghor, feared the impact of certain films on South West African society); Canada, Italy, Poland and Yugoslavia.[121]

The French delegation argued forcefully that not all countries were able to contribute to exchanges of such materials on an equal footing and that many faced acute postwar currency problems.[122] Concerned lest ostensibly cultural accords serve as a front for private business interests, French delegates stressed that 'UNESCO does not exist to facilitate commercial conventions'.[123]

France failed narrowly in its endeavour to secure insertion in the definition of the materials at issue the fact that their use should be non-profit-making: its amendments to this effect were rejected in committee by 5:4 and in plenary by 11:8.[124] Instead, a clause was added entitling importing States to regulate on an optional basis against use of such imports for profit-making purposes. In France's view, however, States applying such an optional provision would be placed in an invidious position. Meanwhile Poland's call at an earlier stage of drafting for a clause to protect national film production was also rejected.[125]

The Agreement was adopted by only a relative majority of 15:5:11:13 (=15:29) with Colombia, France, Egypt, Greece and Luxembourg opposing; and the UK, Austria , Italy, 5 Latin American and 3 Arab States abstaining.[126] (The UK's abstention was ostensibly procedural; nevertheless at the same session of the General Conference, the UK was obliged to defend its import policy against New Zealand charges of restrictionism.[127]) Had Soviet bloc States been active Members of UNESCO at this time, it may be assumed that the negative vote would have been higher.

The USA, the first country to sign the Agreement, and the UNESCO Secretariat exhorted other States to follow suit.[128] But over thirty years later, the Agreement had been signed and/or ratified by only 34 States.[129]

The Florence Agreement,[130] by contrast, contained greater safeguards for importing States and consequently met with less opposition. The Agreement applies to a wider range of materials, including books and other printed materials, but its provisions are narrower. Exemptions relate only to customs tariffs and related charges, not to import quotas; the items in question must be consigned to institutions approved as non-profit-making and licensed for the purpose by the importing State; and the latter is required to make foreign exchange available only 'as far as possible'.

These provisions hepled to calm the fears of dumping and of pressure on national currencies voiced by France, Italy, Mexico, Pakistan, Norway, Iraq and Austria.[131] The USA, possibly sensing that most of the resistance related to its own market position, secured the addition of a Protocol to apply in the event of discriminatory restrictions. The Agreement was then adopted by 19 in favour (about one-third of the then membership), none against, and 9 abstaining.[132]

By 1982, the Florence Agreement had been signed and/or ratified by 83 States, about half of UNESCO's membership at the time.[133]

6. THE CONSENSUS ON TECHNICAL ASSISTANCE

Unlike debates on normative aspects of information, those on technical assistance for development of indigenous communications facilities were to yield agreement.

The concern manifested by Third World delegates from the earliest stages of the 'free flow' debate for protection of domestic information undertakings against powerful foreign competition had been translated by the late 1940s into requests from several States (notably Afghanistan, Chile, India, Lebanon, Liberia, Mexico and the Philippines, soon followed by others) for aid in this field under multilateral auspices.[134]

At first, such calls aroused apprehension on the part of United States spokesmen lest official aid result in the creation or strengthening of government-run media.[135] Early resolutions, in the event, often amounted to little more than decisions to study the problem.[136]

However, these initial hesitations were fairly soon overcome. A report prepared by UNESCO at the initiative of Third World members of the Commission on Human Rights and its 1957 *ad hoc* Committee, and presented to the UN in 1961, marked the turning-point.[137]

The UNESCO study, after laying down desirable minimum levels of provision in the information sphere and stressing the importance of broadcasting services, reported that nearly 70 per cent of the world's population lacked even these minimum facilities. The report concluded that development of information media should be considered an integral part of development more generally and thus eligible as of right for inclusion in the UN Technical Assistance programme (which, up to that point, had not catered for communications).[138]

Motions to this effect and calling for increased assistance to the Third World in this field, both multilaterally and bilaterally, were carried unanimously that year and next.[139] The principal form of assistance envisaged consisted in the training of technicians and media practitioners, the expertise to be supplied for the most part by information enterprises and professional associations.

Further impetus for aid to Third World information structures came in 1964 from a study effected by Wilbur Schramm, US consultant to UNESCO, entitled *Mass Communications and National Development*. Concerned essentially with ways of changing traditional values in order to mobilise populations for development, Schramm's study endorsed the use of mass media to enlist public support for change.[140]

Technical assistance for development of Third World media was thus to become the one area of agreement in the UN information debate.

7.   'FREEDOM OF INFORMATION' OFF THE AGENDA

'Freedom of information', as we have seen, had been placed on the agenda of the UN system in the mid-1940s at US initiative. The peak year for debate on the subject in the UN was 1949: 46 meetings (or 23 full days, in the General Assembly (plenary and Third Committee) in the part-session following the 1948 UN Conference.[141] But from then onward, as it became clear that no easy agreement on the policies advocated by the USA would be forthcoming, American delegations pressed with equal insistence for removal of the topic from the UN agenda.[142]

In the process, direct attempts at persuading other Member States to follow suit, press coverage denouncing the 'restrictionist' majority in the UN, and Brickerite trends in the Eisenhower Administration urging withdrawal from or infliction of penalties on those bodies and States not actively 'with' the USA on these (and other) issues, were all brought to bear.[143]

The outcome was that, for the larger part of the 1950s, at the instigation of the United States, the General Assembly and ECOSOC either carried over the subject of information policy for 'debate with priority' at each other's future sessions or else referred it to subordinate organs, sometimes created for the purpose.[144] A number of Western States, notably the UK and the Netherlands, tended actively to support the USA in this course.[145] Nevertheless, opposition to what France deplored as the 'politics of referral' and 'priority for burial' continued to be registered by States interested in codifying limits to free flow.[146]

Two major political developments restored information policy to short-lived prominence on the UN agenda towards the late 1950s: the launching of the Non-Aligned Movement in 1955 and, around the turn of the decade, the large-scale accession of developing countries to membership of the United Nations.

Thus in 1957 Egypt, India and Yugoslavia, leaders of the Non-Aligned Movement, successfully sponsored motions in the Commission on Human Rights to set up a 5-member Committee to report on the work of the UN system in the field of information.[147] The *ad hoc* Committee, composed of France, India, Lebanon, Mexico and

Poland, in due course recommended adoption of one or more international conventions on freedom of information,[148] which implied a re-opening of earlier debates.

Thereupon, the USA and three Latin American States successfully moved adoption by ECOSOC and referral to the General Assembly of a draft Declaration on the same topic containing a minimalist restrictions clause.[149] Egypt, Afghanistan and the USSR in particular opposed this move in ECOSOC as liable to prejudice General Assembly adoption of a legally binding text based on earlier drafts,[150] but were overruled.[151]

In the Assembly, however, Western States were unable to secure approval of the draft Declaration.[152] At the instigation of the newer members of the UN, substantial debates also took place in 1959, 1960 and 1961 on the draft Convention left pending since the early 1950s.[153] But the views of governments on the draft Convention as expressed in debate as well as in writing[154] were still split, and thereafter the Third Committee of the Assembly reverted to a pattern of systematic postponement of debate.[155]

As will be seen in the next chapter, it was not until the mid-1970s (aside from developments bearing on information in 'race' contexts) that the Third World was able to muster a clear majority behind a distinctive information platform of its own.

SUMMARY AND CONCLUSIONS

The findings of this review of the postwar debate on 'freedom of information' in the UN and UNESCO may be summarised as follows.

First, the USA was the principal initiator of the information debate in UN arenas where, for reasons which were seen by many as not always wholly germane to the topic, it sought to write the *laissez-faire* concept of freedom of information into international law. Conversely, other States were placed in the position of reacting to US initiatives.

Secondly, even in the 1940s, only a minority of the UN membership supported US positions fully. Despite prevailing Cold War tensions, the opposition to *laissez-faire* policies, which included some West European States, proved to be in a majority. However, the opposition was also sufficiently heterogeneous in source and nature, and sufficiently dependent on the USA in other respects, to ensure that liberal tenets were not supplanted as UN policy by more interventionist concepts.

The mark of postwar efforts at standard-setting in this field was in fact lack of consensus, as witnessed by repeated resort to roll-call votes, and majorities so slender as to render outcomes almost arbitrary. The Soviet bloc, meanwhile, was to manifest its disapproval of normative/political undertakings which it was poorly placed to direct, as distinct from technical activities, by vigorous opposition in the UN and several years' non-participation in UNESCO, in what may perhaps not unfairly be considered a case of constructive exclusion.

Thirdly, American success was confined largely to the level of agendas and mandates. The accomplishment at this level should not be dismissed as negligible, since it was to set the controlling framework for future discourse and practical work in the information field for the bodies concerned. Nevertheless, the USA was to prove unable to consolidate these achievements through adoption of legally binding instruments of any weight. Moreover, US success at this level may be attributed, in part at least, to an initial element of surprise rather than to deep-seated consensus.

Finally, confronted with a majority opposed to American policy and which it could not fully control, the USA was to move and secure effective closure of the debate it had initiated.

By the early 1960s, 'consensus' could in effect only fairly be held to prevail in the information field at the technical level of assistance for development of Third World communications facilities.

5 The Contemporary Information Debate

INTRODUCTION

Clear majorities within the UN system in favour of international regulation of communication did not emerge until the mid-1970s, discussions in full-membership arenas of the UN and UNESCO during the 1960s and early 1970s issuing,[1] with a few notable exceptions,[2] in stalemate.

But by the mid-1970s, under the leadership of the Non-Aligned Movement, the Third World was advancing calls for a 'new information order' – later renamed 'new world information and communication order' (NWICO) – seen as integrally linked with achievement of a New International Economic Order and addressing questions of both form and content.

In the meantime, the Third World had increased its majority in full-membership organs to over two-thirds and had also secured enlarged shares of representation on restricted-membership bodies. In addition, for those aspects of their policy limited to reducing Western 'information dominance', and thus overlapping with Soviet bloc interests, the Third World could generally count upon the latter's support. Where united, the new majority had thus come to account for some four-fifths of the membership.

This chapter examines the outcomes of contemporary UNESCO information debates and, in particular, the ways in which Western States and media have responded to the altered political structure of the UN system. In so doing, it will confine itself to the most salient debates, namely: the regional Conference in Latin America in 1976 where press interest in UNESCO involvement in mass communications policy was first aroused; the Media Declaration of 1978 (a Soviet-bloc initiative treated by Western media as a test-case of UNESCO involvement in this field); and debates on Third World proposals for a NWICO.

81

1.   THE 'DECLARATION OF SAN JOSÉ' AND RECOMMENDATIONS OF THE INTERGOVERNMENTAL CONFERENCE ON COMMUNICATIONS POLICIES IN LATIN AMERICA AND THE CARIBBEAN (UNESCO, 1976)

The above texts have neither binding legal force nor global backing. Their significance lies in the fact that the San José Conference was the first intergovernmental meeting in the field of communications policy to be organised by UNESCO; that the participants were not the newer or more radical régimes of Africa and Asia, but Latin American countries comprising a preponderance of right-wing governments and located in the 'Monroe' area; and that it marked the start of widespread Western media concern with UNESCO activities in the mass communications field. (Subsequent regional ministerial conferences on communications policies in Asia (Kuala Lumpur, 1978) and Africa (Yaoundé, 1980) are less significant in these respects, and will therefore not be discussed here.)

Two small-scale expert meetings were held to prepare for the ministerial conference, one in Bogotá in 1974, the other in Quito in 1975. For an account of these two meetings, it proved necessary to turn to secondary sources, specifically a study by *Sunday Times* journalist Rosemary Righter, funded by the Ford Foundation;[3] and a less well known work based on class analysis by Roger Heacock.[4] Indeed, as Righter records, the reports of both meetings have since been removed from UNESCO files.[5] This fact is itself not without significance for our argument, as we hope to make clear below.

According to Heacock, organisations representing owners of private media in the region, notably the Inter-American Association of Broadcasters (IAAB) and the Inter-American Press Association (IAPA), were alerted to the proceedings of the Bogotá meeting by a Western staff member of UNESCO.[6] From that point onward, intensive coverage emanating mostly from these two bodies was to be devoted to the preparatory meetings and to the ministerial conference. American media, and especially UPI (as the news agency with most extensive interests in the area), were soon to follow suit.

Neither Righter nor Heacock judged the content of reporting to have been especially favourable. Righter, although not unsympathetic to the response of the media, referred to a 'campaign' against UNESCO's policies and the San José meeting, and noted that 'contrary to some Western press reports' the conclusions of the Quito meeting had been 'surprisingly moderate'.[7]

Heacock provides more detailed analysis of the coverage.[8] With a few exceptions in the presses of Peru, Cuba and Venezuela (i.e. the more centre or left-of-centre régimes in the region) and later Costa Rica (host to the ministerial conference), Heacock found the debate to have been reduced to the terms of a simple conflict between 'free' and 'state-controlled' media systems. The meetings were portrayed as part of a Soviet plan to promote and legitimise government censorship of the media in the region. The conclusions of the expert meetings were depicted as unrepresentative of the positions of governments in the area, doubts being cast in the process (by Righter among others[9]) on the credentials of the experts. Soviet influence was also the dominant *leitmotiv* of the coverage which built up in anticipation of the intergovernmental meeting.

These themes were relayed by UPI to its North and Latin American subscribers and reproduced, with varying moderation of tone, by such leading organs as the *Wall Street Journal*, the *New York Times* and the *Christian Science Monitor*, the most extreme versions being circulated by the US-wide Hearst chain. Headlines such as 'World-Wide Plot against the Free Press', 'A Russian Threat to the International Press' and 'Free Press Braces for Attack by UNESCO' were found to be representative.

Certain developments, recorded by both Righter and Heacock albeit from different value perspectives, followed upon this coverage. At the level of States, Ecuador withdrew its offer to host the intergovernmental Conference.[10] The output of the Bogotá meeting was also held by one Western reporter to have been toned down as a result of efforts by 'American free enterprise press delegates'.[11] At the level of the Secretariat, meanwhile, the issuing of statements purporting to dissociate the Organisation from the conclusions of the Bogotá meeting, the reshuffling of staff and the 'laundering' of archives (removal of the reports mentioned above) suggested publicity-induced defensiveness.[12]

The San José Conference itself brought together the Ministers of twenty Latin American and Caribbean countries.[13] A number of Western States leading the communications field (France, Germany, Japan, the UK and the USA) as well as Spain and the USSR were represented but, as non-regional powers, had only observer status and no voting rights. Also represented by observer delegations were the IAAB and IAPA.

The Director-General opened the meeting with what Righter describes as a 'spirited attack' on the latter two organisations (which, she notes, were 'ensconced in campaign headquarters across the street')[14] and was later echoed by other delegates in his criticism of press coverage 'tending to misrepresent the purposes of the Conference and the concept of communications policies'.[15]

The formal output of the Conference (this time not withdrawn from the public record) consisted of a Declaration and some thirty Recommendations. The San José Declaration,[16] adopted by acclamation and serving as an all-purpose statement of areas of agreement reached, speaks of the 'responsibilities' and 'use' of communications media and links these to the needs of development but is otherwise, as Righter remarks, 'diplomatically bland'.[17]

The challenge to prevailing concepts and interests emerges more clearly from the Recommendations.[18] While acknowledging the existence of differing media ideologies among States of the region, the Recommendations equally explicitly question the implications of the 'free flow of information' in a context of unequal technological and political power as between generators of flows.[19] The challenge is expressed – by reference to dependence on 'information channels representing interests alien to the region' and to what are seen as the shortcomings of private media with respect to public access and participation – as a call for a 'balanced flow' and a 'right to communicate' at national and international levels.[20] Recommendations are also made concerning the 'duties' and 'legal and social responsibilities' of professional communicators.[21] The Recommendations were addressed to States, and legislation was envisaged as a possible remedy for some of the problems involved.[22]

However, as Righter records, the Conference also asserted the value of pluralism and the need for the continued existence of privately-run-media, and sought to 'reassure the Western opposition' on certain points.[23] Heacock, meanwhile, identified a trend to progressive obliqueness in the challenge to the established information order as expressed in the output of the Bogotá, Quito and San José meetings respectively.[24]

Following unanimous adoption of the Final Report of the conference, US and Latin American media ceased to claim that the positions in question were endorsed by only a handful of leftist governments. Coverage instead tended increasingly to allege the responsibility of the Secretariat, not least through its choice of advisers, for the interventionist and/or 'Marxist' positions adopted by the meeting and more generally for leading rather than following Member States in the sphere of communications policy.[25] Righter, too, was to expand on this theme at length in her study.[26]

It would therefore seem that, as a consequence of what was considered by commentators of differing political persuasion to be an adverse publicity campaign, the conclusions of the San José Conference in July 1976 were diluted relative to those of earlier meetings, while the UNESCO Secretariat was placed on the defensive.

Nevertheless the San José results remained prescriptive and in many respects objectionable from the Western point of view. This in turn may have been due to the fact that the Western States had no formal power, as observers, to influence proceedings, and that the full strength of the Western media had yet to be brought to bear on UNESCO communications debates.

2. THE MEDIA DECLARATION (UNESCO, 1978)

The Media Declaration of 1978 (the full title of which is Declaration of Fundamental Principles concerning the Contribution of the Mass Media to Strengthening Peace and International Understanding, to the Promotion of Human Rights and to Countering Racialism, *Apartheid* and Incitement to War) was the first instrument to be specifically devoted by UNESCO to the goals of information. As such, the Declaration addressed communications interests more centrally than isolated references to mass media scattered through instruments bearing primarily on education, race or other subjects. Moreover, its drafting history overlapped with the San José Conference where, as we have just seen, Western media had been alerted to UNESCO activities in relation to mass communication.

The Declaration was an initiative of the Soviet bloc minority and, in this sense, its significance as compared with broader pressures for structural reform of global communications could have been seen as marginal. But, in the event, it came to be treated by mass media for all practical purposes as a test-case of UNESCO involvement in the sphere of mass communication. For this reason, its drafting will be considered at some length.

The origins of the text go back to a number of resolutions adopted by the General Conference from the mid-1960s onward, mostly at East European initiative, and concerned to set standards of conduct for mass media.[27] Like the resolution of 1972 instructing the Director-General to draft a Declaration of principles 'governing the use of the mass information media', these referred to the 'use' of information media 'against propaganda on behalf of war, racialism and hatred among nations' and 'to strengthen peace and international

understanding'.[28] Despite their instrumentalism, however, these resolutions were to occasion little press interest or comment.

Early drafts of a declaration drawn up between 1972 and 1975
successively by Hilding Eek, a Swedish lawyer familiar with earlier UN
debates on information policy (with comments from Swiss and
Yugoslav consultants),[29] by a meeting of experts sitting in personal
capacity,[30] and by an intergovernmental expert meeting,[31] also spoke
of the 'use', 'duties' and 'responsibilities' of mass media and of the
State in relation to the latter.[32]

When the first official draft was tabled at the 18th session of the
General Conference in 1974, Western States took exception to such
terminology and in particular to an article according to which

> The responsibility of the State in the international sphere for the
> activities of mass media under its jurisdiction is governed by
> customary   international   law   and   relevant   international
> agreements.[33]

At Western initiative it was decided, quite exceptionally, to refer the
question to a further intergovernmental meeting of experts.[34]

A meeting was duly held in December 1975 and attended by 85
Member States.[35] The text of the draft Declaration as reworked by the
meeting[36] for submission to the 19th session of the General Conference
was adopted by 41:8:3.[37] Subsequent references by Canada, the USA
and Australia[38] to what they saw as the small majority involved suggest
that opposing votes would have been more numerous had Western
States been present at the time the text was adopted. In fact, however,
they had walked out of the meeting in protest at the insertion of a
preambular reference to the UN resolution identifying zionism with
racism.[39]

Up to this point, as the Director-General was later to observe,[40] the
draft was still the subject of little if any publicity: Western press
coverage of the 1974 General Conference, in particular, was to focus
essentially on developments relating to Israel and to the election of a
new Director-General.

Indeed, it may be noted that press coverage of UNESCO prior to
1974 had in the main been characterised by scarcity rather than surfeit.
An indicator of the evolution of interest can be found in *The Times
Index*, which contains a guide to *The Times*, *The Sunday Times*, *The
Times Educational Supplement*, *The Times Higher Educational Supplement* and *The Daily Telegraph*. For the 1972 General Conference as
a whole (at which the Director-General was instructed to begin work

on a declaration), the Index contains four entries, none concerned with communications issues. For the 1974 Conference, 13 items are recorded, of which ten relate to Israel and three are of a general nature, but still none are concerned with the media draft. By contrast, the *Index* contains 31 items for the 1976 General Conference, 40 items for the 1978 session and 36 items for the 1980 session, of which 8, 24 and 18 respectively are on communications topics.[41]

The situation had in fact changed by the 19th session of the General Conference in Nairobi in 1976, which followed shortly upon the San José meeting. At this juncture, the draft Declaration was to meet with publicity and opposition from Western States and media on a scale hitherto unprecedented.

The circumstances of the Nairobi Conference were, in themselves, such as to render the Third World unusually vulnerable to Western pressure. The 19th session of the General Conference was not only the first to be held in black Africa, but also the first under the stewardship of an African Director-General (Amadou-Mahtar M'Bow of Senegal). African States thus had a clear interest in the smooth running of the Conference.

The Director-General was in addition personally vulnerable, as a black African and a Muslim, having taken office at the height of the crisis in UNESCO–Israeli relations. Moreover, the Organisation had by that time experienced two years' exposure to reprisals by Western Member States (notably US budgetary withholding) consequent upon decisions taken at the 18th session, and was thus unlikely to dismiss as bluff any threat of further chastisement, however oblique.[42]

UNESCO had also, in the interval, been the subject of more than customary Western press coverage which was to intensify prior to the opening of the Conference and which was characterised by forecasts of confrontation.[43] Advance dispatches from Nairobi were to state that the crucial issue on that occasion would be 'press freedom'. UPI, for instance, taking as its source Western delegates, signalled that 'the issues of press freedom and Arab–Israeli conflict could produce the most controversial General Conference in UNESCO history'.[44]

A leading French commentator suggested that the scale of attendance by Western journalists in Nairobi had contributed to raising the level of tension.[45] To several African and Arab States, too (e.g. Egypt, the Gambia, Guyana, Nigeria, Sierra Leone and Zambia), the volume and tone of Western coverage subjected the new majority and the Secretariat to unwarranted pressure.[46] The Director-General, for his part, referred to 'the campaign mobilised against UNESCO by powerful interests'.[47] However, appealing again for moderation on all sides, he took the precaution of warning that aspects of the draft Declaration might be seen by some (implicitly, Western States) as conflicting with certain basic international texts.[48]

In the general policy debate most leading Western States were to dwell at length on information matters, references to the draft Declaration being more or less thinly veiled. In a strongly-worded statement, the USA held the draft to be in conflict with UNESCO's Constitution and in 'flat contradiction' to the Universal Declaration on Human Rights.[49]

Warning against 'politicisation', spokesmen of several Western countries (e.g. Finland, Austria, Italy, Canada and the Netherlands) also appealed for 'consensus'.[50] The term was not defined with any precision, but a number of statements made it clear that something other than a majority, even a large majority, was involved. The American delegate, after alluding to 'that golden consensus that UNESCO traditionally has sought', argued that the requirements to make UNESCO an effective Organisation 'through which we can cooperate' included

> a political consensus among Member States that reflects a sense of community and rejects confrontation over narrow and disrupting interests . . . we should perhaps avoid even the adoption of resolutions, *no matter how strong the majority behind them*, that leave profound bitterness among some of us.[51] (Emphasis added)

(This statement echoed almost word for word the Director-General's appeal for consensus at the close of the previous session.[52]) In the same way, the Finnish delegate declared

> I do not think it is wise to try to decide complex issues which involve ideological and philosophical questions by a majority vote. [In such matters] I should therefore recommend the slow and difficult method of working by consensus . . .[53]

Proceeding one step further, statements by the UK, Switzerland, Italy, Canada and the Netherlands went on to question the value of UNESCO's standard-setting role more generally.[54] In the immediate, Western powers as well as Western officials and news executives pressed for postponement of debate and 'fuller consultation' with professional organisations.[55]

Soviet bloc delegates, backed by representatives of a number of

Non-Aligned governments (Cuba, Algeria, Sudan, Yugoslavia, Ethiopia, Niger, Iraq, the Congo, Guinea, Mozambique and Zambia), spoke strongly in the Programme Commission in support of the draft, opposing postponement of debate and holding that the response of the mass media provided the best proof of the need for regulation.[56]

However, most Third World countries either made no reference to the declaration or took no clear stand on the subject.[57] With the support of several African delegates (notably Senegal, Nigeria, Benin, Togo and Ghana), the Programme Commission ultimately decided to refer the question to a newly-created UNESCO body, the Drafting and Negotiation Group (DNG).[58]

The DNG had been set up by the Director-General in response to the open confrontations of the 18th session. It consisted of the representatives of twenty-five States, meeting at a plenipotentiary level and off the record, with a mandate to achieve 'consensus' on subjects deemed sensitive by the steering committee of the Conference.[59] (The fact that the need to include the draft Declaration among the subjects so classified had been anticipated neither by the Executive Board nor by the Secretariat, as witness the provisional list of topics drawn up a few weeks before the opening of the Nairobi Conference,[60] provides evidence that the intensity of Western opposition on that occasion was unexpected.)

The composition of the DNG gave the Third World a majority: five Western, three East European and seventeen Third World countries,[61] the chairmanship in Nairobi being held by an African State (Benin).[62] Nevertheless, it reduced considerably the absolute numerical advantage enjoyed by the Third World in full-membership organs. Moreover, the draft was also referred to a sub-group of the DNG where this advantage was further diminished.[63]

In the event, the Western preference for postponement of debate prevailed: failing to agree on a text, the DNG and its sub-group advised referral to the 20th session of the General Conference.[64] The majority in plenary subsequently endorsed the DNG's recommendation, instructing the Director-General to rework the draft Declaration on the basis of 'broad consultations'.[65]

After a first round of soundings, a revised text[66] was drawn up with the help of three consultants representing a cross-section of political opinion.[67] The text was then submitted for comment to some 100 individuals and institutions, a preponderance in the Third World.[68] The majority approved the text as it stood or subject to some amendment.[69]

But a small minority continued to oppose the principle of a Declaration on the mass media as such.[70] William Harley, Communications Adviser to the US National Commission for UNESCO, pronounced the latest draft an 'undoubted improvement' on earlier versions and, while stating plainly that he preferred there to be no Declaration, put forward an alternative draft in which reference was in fact made to the 'responsibilities' of the media and to legislative action.[71] On the other hand, the IPI, Freedom House, the World Press Freedom Committee, the Inter-American Association of Broadcasters, Reuters and *The Times* were more categorical in their opposition.

A further text[72] emerged from the various consultations in which no mention was made of the 'use' of the media ('contribution' being substituted), of State responsibility for media activities in the international sphere, or of legislative measures, permissive or otherwise. On the other hand, the new text repeatedly stressed the 'responsibilities' of media institutions and practitioners, including explicitly (on account of the 'international nature' of their activities) news and press agencies as well as radio and television organisations. It also emphasised the requirement that information be accurate; spoke of a 'balanced flow' of information; introduced into the concept of freedom of expression the dimensions of public access and participation; and included a preambular reference to the prohibitively worded 1936 League of Nations Convention on the Use of Broadcasting (see p. 34).[73]

The Director-General judged the prospects for 'consensus' on the text at the 20th session of the General Conference to be slight.[74] Seemingly tempted to abandon the task, M'Bow turned to the Executive Board for guidance as to whether, in the circumstances, he should pursue work on the draft. But although thus effectively calling into question the instructions of the General Conference, he refrained from indicating the exact distribution of support for the various positions and, specifically, from indicating that opponents to the principle of a Declaration were few.[75]

Western members of the Board, notably those from Norway, the USA, Switzerland and France, took the opportunity to express again their doubts as to the value of UNESCO's normative activities, especially in a field where 'diversity was so extensive and so vigorously asserted', on the grounds that the authority of an instrument would depend on its being adopted by 'consensus'.[76] However the Board ascertained, in response to queries and comments from Indian, Jordanian and Venezuelan members,[77] that opposition to a Declaration constituted a small minority. Thereupon the Board, on which the Third World by then held a majority, confirmed the General Conference mandate to prepare a revised text.[78]

The new draft, slightly reworked once more in the direction of Western preferences, was submitted to the 20th session of the General Conference in 1978,[79] where the importance attached to the subject by Western powers was again reflected in the space devoted to it, explicitly or implicitly, in their speeches.

However, the tone adopted by Western delegates was not unconciliatory. Drawing a clear distinction between Third World and Soviet bloc positions, most Western powers were by then conceding the former's contention of a structural imbalance and even of a concomitant qualitative imbalance (albeit not intentional) in global information flows.

The Head of the US delegation, in particular, making only occasional references to 'extraneous political elements' and to the draft Declaration, concentrated on conveying a sense of heightened American awareness since Nairobi of what were now described as legitimate Third World grievances and aspirations, and of the range of practical measures undertaken in the USA as a result.[80] Sympathy was also strongly expressed by Judith Hart MP, leader of the UK delegation (who, in the process, invoked media treatment of socialists in the Western World),[81] and by Nordic countries which evoked their own experience as small and relatively communications-poor peoples.[82] Nevertheless, Western States and media organisations were unanimous in urging that attempts at standard-setting be shelved in favour of enhanced aid programmes for development of the Third World's own communications facilities.[83]

On the Third World side, as in 1976, certain factors encouraged accommodation to Western positions. Not only was the post-1973 confidence of these countries evaporating rapidly, but elections to the office of Director-General were approaching. Failure to achieve a consensus on the Declaration, together with the tendency of Western commentators to identify M'Bow with the instrument, either personally, as Head of the Secretariat, or via the selection and recruitment of advisers, would not be conducive to the latter's re-election.*[84] The Director-General appealed in his opening speech to what had become known as the 'spirit of Nairobi' and to the need for consensus.[85] Meanwhile statements on the draft Declaration by African and

---

* Mr M'Bow was in fact re-elected in 1980.

Muslim delegations, M'Bow's main sources of electoral support, were as scarce and generally bland at the 20th as during the 19th session of the General Conference.[86]

The position of Western media, on the other hand, was expressed in somewhat blunter and more categorical terms than that of Western delegates. Representation of media interests on this occasion was powerful. Official delegations of observers from media organisations attended in greater numbers at the 20th than at the 19th and earlier sessions of the General Conference: the IAAB and IAPA, in particular, increased their representation from five to twelve and from nil to four respectively, while five observers from media bodies having no formal consultative status with UNESCO (including the European Broadcasting Union and the World Press Freedom Committee) were admitted by special decision of the Conference.[87] Media interests, public and private, were in addition represented on the delegations of certain Western States (in particular France, West Germany and Sweden) in greater strength than in previous years.[88]

The 20th session in 1978 was also attended by journalists in considerable numbers: the UNESCO press accreditation register shows a total of 392,* of whom at least 245 were Western.†[89] (The only register available, covering the years 1976–81 (but not the 1976 General Conference) does not permit comparison with attendance at earlier sessions of the General Conference before press interest in UNESCO information debates was aroused. But accreditation to intergovernmental meetings on subjects other than communications during the same period may provide a yardstick of sorts. The register shows that meetings on youth, seismology, science information systems, the biosphere, and artists attracted 11, 13, 4, 6 and 2 journalists respectively.[90] It may meanwhile be noted that the 1976–81 register was only located and made available after some dozen calls on the Press Room in the course of three separate visits to UNESCO Headquarters in early 1983. This was no doubt due at least in part to changes in the top staff and in the premises of the Press Room, but in part may also be seen as further indication of Secretariat defensiveness following the publicity of the previous few years. The fact that, to secure access to the register, this writer was required to obtain

---

* The last number in the register is 391 but two entries are numbered 176.
† The latter figure is necessarily approximate. In fact, the press register proved a somewhat disappointing research tool. Entries not infrequently indicate a journalist's name without that of the press organ, or an obscure acronym without country of origin; nor is the item of interest to the particular journalist shown.

clearance from the highest levels lends support to this view.)

Western journalists would seem, moreover, to have devoted most of their attention on this occasion to the communications debate. Representatives of leading Western print and broadcast media, complete with visual and sound recording equipment, were observed by this writer and by certain delegates to be present in strength at the proceedings of the Culture and Communication Commission where at times, packed into the standing space at the back of the room, they outnumbered representatives of States.[91]

The assumption that Western reporters were interested primarily in communications issues is borne out in surveys by Western observers of press coverage of recent sessions of the UNESCO General Conference. Perhaps the most significant for our purposes is a study carried out by the National News Council in the USA on American press coverage.[92] Although confined to reporting on the 21st session in Belgrade in 1980, there is no reason to assume that the findings do not apply equally – if not more so – to the session of 1978. Indeed, in 1978 the draft Declaration had still to be adopted and Western journalists were three times more numerous than in Belgrade.[93]

The American study (to whose qualitative findings we turn later) was based on 448 news clippings and 206 editorials from newspapers around the USA, some 80 per cent of the stories being derived from AP or UPI material. Quantitatively, the study found US coverage to have centred disproportionately on communications:

> Not one story emanating from the six-week conference dealt with . . . UNESCO's basic activities in [education, science and culture]. By contrast, there were 173 news and feature stories dealing with the debate over communications policy. This was also the central topic for 181 editorials.[94]

The head of AP's world service for his part was quoted as declaring that 'if it were not for the controversy over the "new communications order", nobody from the press would be there at all'.[95]

In terms of general tenor, coverage prior to and during the opening stages of the Conference predicted tension. True, some reporters forecast that the Conference as a whole would be 'less controversial' than the Nairobi session;[96] and a number suggested that even the debate on the draft Declaration has been defused (a fact attributed by some, significantly, to media lobbying[97]).

Others, however, identified the draft Declaration as chief among the few likely 'flashpoints' and prophesied confrontation. AP, for example, signalled 'stormy confrontations expected over the issue of international news coverage' and quoted George Beebe, publisher of the *Miami Herald* and Chairman of the World Press Freedom Committee, as considering that there was 'little chance of avoiding a bitter confrontation over the draft declaration which several Western journalistic groups have come to fight'.[98] An article in *The Sunday Times* heralded a 'Third World threat to the right to the Truth',[99] while another in *The Times* predicted 'Clashes over Press Freedom and Israel likely to dominate UNESCO meeting'.[100]

In what might well have seemed an attempt to raise the stakes in the debate, the US delegate was questioned at a news conference on the likely American response to adoption of an unacceptable text. While some reported the US spokesman as having simply suggested, when pressed, that Congress would doubtless 'be affected by all Conference outcomes' when voting funds, others described him as having actually threatened major US reprisals or, again, as having 'obliquely vowed' that these would be forthcoming and as 'relying on Western pressure to head off a confrontation'.[101]

Headlines still reflecting an unmoderated East–West view of media questions predicted the imminent replacement of press freedom by State-controlled media, with the active support of the Director-General. A UPI dispatch relayed by the *International Herald Tribune* announced that 'Unesco Head backs Media-Control Draft', while an article in *The Times* pointed 'The Way to a Captive Press'.[102] Articles and headlines in *Le Monde* and the *Guardian*, drafted in more dispassionate style and avoiding the balder dichotomies, were the exception.[103] Meanwhile Righter's study, referred to above and published in time for the 20th session of the General Conference, advised that if UNESCO wished to withdraw from 'the ideological front line', it should revert to 'its role of technical assistant'.[104]

Western media coverage of the early stages of the Conference was to be described not only by the Director-General[105] but by a number of Western delegates (notably from Norway, Sweden and the UK) as based on misunderstanding where not deliberately biased.[106] The British Chairman of the Executive Board personally appealed to the press to report the work of the Conference 'accurately, fairly and objectively', while the Head of the UK delegation was to quote a sample of the many headlines she had noticed in the Anglo-Saxon press stressing the dimension of conflict.[107]

The American study of US press coverage of the 21st session in Belgrade referred to above may again be taken as relevant and is therefore worth quoting at some length. In addition to the finding of quantitative imbalance, the study identified what it saw as qualitative imbalance:

> Without exception, the editorials expressed apprehension about UNESCO's involvement in attempts to establish policy in matters affecting the worldwide flow of information. In 158 cases the editorials were strongly hostile, to the point in 27 papers of suggesting United States withdrawal from UNESCO if it persisted in moves deemed destructive of press freedom. . . . The news events that got the widest press use and the greatest prominence tended to be those that reinforced the fears expressed on editorial pages. . . . News analysis and feature stories concentrated almost exclusively on Western worries about the UNESCO initiative, with little presentation of opposing viewpoints.[108]

This finding was corroborated by citations and analyses of press content. It also drew support from complaints by senior US delegates and spokesmen for press interests (notably Leonard Sussman, a leading critic of UNESCO media debates and representative of both Freedom House and the Inter-American Press Association) to the effect that their own positions had been misrepresented and that US reporting on the subject was 'monolithic' and 'astigmatic'.[109] The main conclusion of the American News Council was that

> The imbalance that characterises most of the Belgrade news coverage in this country provided an inadequate foundation for independent judgement by Americans of the correctness of the editorial positions their newspapers were taking on the communications issue.[110]

Other studies of coverage of UNESCO communications debates, including some commissioned by the UNESCO Secretariat, came to similar conclusions; European coverage, however, was in general found to be somewhat more balanced.*[111]

During the course of the 20th session of the General Conference, a

---

* At a more anecdotal level J. Behrstock, a retired US official with nearly thirty years' experience in the UNESCO Mass Communications sector, told this writer during interview on 21 March 1983 of the failure of the *International Herald Tribune* to publish an article in which he sought to balance a set of three articles critical of the Agency and of Director-General M'Bow. Not long after the article was refused – on the grounds that to print it would mean giving too much space to UNESCO – the *IHT* published a further article on the Agency in the same spirit as the original three.[112]

final draft of the Media Declaration (sub-titled 'Compromise text proposed by the Director-General with a view to consensus'[113]) was put together. But on this occasion, unlike the 19th session, even the Drafting and Negotiation Group (DNG) was not involved. The text which emerged was the product not only of off-the-record negotiations between the Director-General, official delegates and non-governmental bodies, but also of the views of an 'informal reflexion group' meeting around the Peruvian Chairman of the relevant programme commission.[114]

The group consisted of representatives of five countries: the USA and the USSR, Italy (for the EEC), Sri Lanka (as having the ear of the People's Republic of China), and Tunisia (elected Co-ordinator for the Non-Aligned countries on information issues). Detailed work on the Declaration was confined to this core group which met, as the press reported, behind the scenes.[115] Evidence of any pressures brought to bear was, more than ever, limited to hearsay.

The final draft was placed before the programme commission on 21 November 1978, for adoption the following day.[116] As with texts tabled by the DNG, the plenary and full-membership programme commission had little time and still less political margin for manoeuvre. (In response to an oral Portuguese proposal for amendment of a DNG text on another topic, the latter's Chairman, Gunnar Garbo of Norway, was to pronounce himself 'extremely reluctant' to accept any change.[117]) At the suggestion of Tunisia, seconded by spokesmen for both East and West, the Declaration in its reworked form was adopted by acclamation in the programme commission, whose decision was endorsed shortly after, without debate, by the plenary.[118]

The text as approved[119] is based on the following compromise.[120] At Western insistence and over Soviet opposition, reference to human rights was inserted in the title and in the text; every reference to the 'responsibilities' or 'duties' of States, of media organisations and of individual practitioners with regard to media content was deleted; and the prescriptive mode was replaced throughout by the descriptive.

In exchange, at Third World behest, the Declaration refers explicitly to a 'new world information and communication order', but not to the principle of establishing it, and only in the preamble. It also refers to 'more' or 'better' balanced dissemination of information and, again in the preamble, mentions the UN Race and *Apartheid* Conventions. In a separate statement, but still as part of the bargain, the USA declared its general support for the interim report of the MacBride Commission (see below). It also agreed to the convening in early 1979 of a planning conference of States, as initially proposed by the

Group of 77 countries,[121] to pursue the question of improving media facilities in communications-poor countries (see p. 102).

The Soviet bloc, meanwhile, failed to secure reference to 'peaceful coexistence' or to the Helsinki Conference, but was able to draw solace from its sponsorship of the original motion.

What, then, was the outcome of a drafting process which, all told, had lasted six years? The very adoption by UNESCO of a Declaration on the mass media could, of itself, be seen as a defeat for the West. The Soviet bloc and several Third World States in any event were to claim it as a victory, since this was the first time the notion of a 'contribution' by the media to achievement of specified goals appeared as the subject of a UNESCO declaration.[122]

Nevertheless, the text as adopted is scarcely recognisable as a statement of principles, given its descriptive form. The following extracts, which are typical of the text as a whole,* may be seen as unobjectionable from the Western point of view even where not tautological:

> . . . mass media . . . contribute to promoting human rights . . . by giving expression to oppressed peoples . . .
> The mass media have an important contribution to make to [specified goals] . . .
> . . . the mass media, by disseminating information . . . contribute to eliminate [sic] ignorance and misunderstanding . . .[123]

The Declaration may in fact be seen as more *laissez-faire* in content than either the Constitution of UNESCO (which speaks of 'employing' the means of mass communication for the ends of peace) or the Universal Declaration of Human Rights (which contains a general clause on the responsibilities inherent in freedom), not to mention the 1936 League of Nations Convention.

The content of the text would seem to deprive any defeat for the West of much of its force. So, too, does the fact that delegates of 59 States and the observers of three non-governmental organisations commented on the text after its adoption, expressing in the process radically contrasting constructions of the Declaration.[124]

Several Third World States (e.g. the Philippines, Algeria, Ecuador, Jamaica, Indonesia, Benin, Ethiopia, Guinea and Nepal) declared that they would have preferred a more normative text.[125] But although Switzerland, Austria and Denmark continued to voice reservations,[126] the USA, echoed by France and the UK, concluded that 'the

---

*For full text of the Declaration, see Appendix I.

declaration contained ideals to which we can all subscribe while imposing no ideological or mandatory constraints'.[127]

The outcome of the drafting process was sufficiently compatible with minority positions to be described by Western journalists, including Rosemary Righter, as a 'turn-around' and as a victory for Western views.[128] In the circumstances, it might not be an exaggeration to suggest that Western media, by the pressure they brought to bear, had for practical purposes been enfranchised on this occasion.

3. UNESCO, THE NWICO, THE MACBRIDE COMMISSION AND THE IPDC

More significant than the Media Declaration, not least in breadth of support, was the Third World call for a New Information Order (NIO) later rebaptised New World Information and Communication Order (NWICO). Where the Media Declaration could be discredited as the initiative of a marginal minority (the Soviet bloc), the Non-Aligned demand for structural change in global communications was, by 1976, solidly backed by the majority of UNESCO's membership.

Western powers have reacted with little enthusiasm to the concept of a NWICO which they rightly see as addressing not only the quantitative but also the qualitative aspects of information, i.e. content.[129]

Western members secured support at the 19th session of the General Conference in 1976 for a review of 'the totality of the problems of communication in modern society' which, subsuming the NWICO, had the effect of postponing decisions on the latter.[130] At the Director-General's initiative, it was agreed to entrust the task to a 'panel of counsellors' rather than to the Secretariat, and M'Bow duly set up an International Commission for the Study of Communication Problems composed of sixteen eminent persons.

Known after its Chairman as the 'MacBride Commission', this body on balance reflected Non-Aligned views,[131] and the concluding portions of its interim report, submitted to the 20th session of the General Conference in 1978,[132] were to occasion Western criticism.

The penultimate section of the report contended that the doctrine of 'free flow', however generous an aspiration, had in practice served the purposes of a few vested interests, nationally and internationally.[133] The final part of the report questioned how best not only to strengthen communication capabilities in developing countries, but also to redress qualitative imbalance, to increase the accountability of controllers of the media, to democratise communication, and to move towards a NWICO. It also canvassed the possibility of legal protection of journalists, of instituting an effective international right of reply or correction, of formulating principles governing use of communications satellites, and of distributing more equitably such limited natural resources as the electromagnetic frequency spectrum and geostation-ary orbits.[134]

The USA described these closing pages and prescriptions as 'less balanced and less well grounded' than earlier parts of the report.[135] At American initiative,[136] the Commission was asked, when drafting its final report, to propose 'concrete and practical measures' that could lead – in the words of a Group of 77 amendment[137] – to a new, more just and more effective world information order.[138]

The Commission's Final Report was, from the Western point of view, an improvement on the interim report. Published by UNESCO in 1980 in book form under the title *Many Voices, One World*, the report was presented by MacBride as a starting point for debate rather than as the last word.[139] It was generally toned down thanks, according to one press report, to the efforts of a minority of (Western) Commission members,[140] and went back on a number of earlier proposals concerning, for instance, the need for an international right of reply and for protection of journalists.[141] Moreover, although sub-titled 'Towards a new, more just and more efficient world information and communication order', and although explaining that the basic considerations expounded in the Report were intended as a frame-work for development of the new order, the study advanced neither a hard-and-fast definition of the new order nor a clear strategy for its establishment.[142]

Nevertheless, the Report still constituted a challenge to prevailing Western concepts and interests. Certain recommendations had, in fact, been the subject of formal dissent on the part of Western members of the MacBride Commission. The recommendations in question concerned most notably: the reduction of commercialisation of communication[143] and of concentration of control over relevant technology;[144] the regulation of advertising content and influence;[145] the responsibilities of journalists;[146] the contribution of mass media to certain goals;[147] and acquisition by the UN of a broadcast capability of its own, possibly including access to a satellite system.[148] The Commis-sion had also suggested that the texts of international instruments, including certain drafts long deadlocked in the UN, be reviewed in order to promote further international legislation in this area.[149]

The Soviet bloc view of the Final Report as revealed in a draft resolution tabled by East Germany and the USSR[150] proved somewhat warmer than the Western response to be discussed below. Nevertheless, in a section of General Comments appended to the Report, the USSR member of the Commission held that the report was 'too westernized', over-emphasised the 'right to communicate', and played down the need for international law.[151] The Non-Aligned spokesman on information, meanwhile, regretted that the Commission had failed to propose the text of a declaration and draft charter on a NWICO.[152] Western members appended no general remarks but were to make their views known during discussion at the 21st session of the General Conference in 1980.

In fact the Final Report as such was not submitted to the Conference. Instead the Director-General, to whom the Commission reported directly, presented an account of the latter's findings which was both to distance the Secretariat from the Commission's work and to set the tone of debate.[153] The Director-General concluded that the Final Report constituted a 'valuable contribution' to the continuing international debate, but sought no endorsement of the Commission's findings by the General Conference and counselled, in addition, that no firm decisions on the principle of a NWICO be taken at that stage.

The Director-General's position, perhaps not fortuitously, accurately anticipated those of Western States and media organisations. Western press coverage of communications issues at the 21st session, discussed above, was generally apprehensive of the outcome of debate on the work of the MacBride Commission and on the NWICO.[154] Western delegates, meanwhile, although themselves speaking of a more just (if not a 'new') information order, espoused an essentially technical definition of the concept.

Paying guarded tribute to the MacBride Report as a contribution to the debate, delegates of the Netherlands, UK, West Germany, Australia, the USA, the IAAB and the IAPA expressed pleasure that General Conference approval of the latter was not sought.[155] In particular, they opposed the Report's proposals for normative action with respect to the responsibilities of journalists and objected to what they saw as insufficient recognition of the benefits of commercially-run media systems. They also expressed concern at the 'ambiguities' in the Report, as well as at what the UK saw as the overall impression it conveyed that existing imbalances should be corrected by increased State intervention or by international directives. Above all, they advocated avoidance of what they termed 'politicisation' and 'ideological politics' in favour of 'practical' remedies on which all could agree.[156]

At the close of the session, the Director-General registered what he identified as unanimity on the priority to be accorded henceforward to 'practical measures of an operational nature designed to strengthen the communication capacities of countries lacking them'.[157]

The resolution adopted by the General Conference on the work of the MacBride Commission pronounced the Final Report a valuable contribution to the study of the problems of communication, urged that it be widely circulated, and called for the comments of Member States.[158] The outcome of the debate thus amounted to a diplomatic shelving of the report, in line with Secretariat proposals and Western preferences.

But the resolution also called for further steps to be taken towards establishment of a NWICO. Although laying far less stress on the NWICO than had the draft resolution tabled by the Third World,[159] it set out considerations on which the new order 'could be based'.[160] Along with plurality of sources and freedom of the press and information, the bases in question included 'elimination of the imbalances and inequalities which characterise the present situation' and of 'the negative effects of certain monopolies, public and private, and excessive concentrations'.* West Germany, the UK and Canada denounced these aspects of the resolution as running counter to the Director-General's advice that no position be adopted at that stage on the question of a NWICO, and declared that as a result they had joined in adoption of the resolution by consensus only with the greatest reluctance.[161]

This result could be considered at least a partial success for the Third World. However, as a programme resolution, the text in question enjoyed only minimal normative status; in addition, the introductory section on the NWICO was worded in only tentative fashion. In the circumstances, the achievement should perhaps not be overrated.

The principal outcome of debate on the NWICO by the early 1980s, as will be seen below, was to mirror closely the preferred Western approach to international communications problems.

* For the text of the resolution, see Appendix II.

Pursuant to the bargain struck with regard to the Media Declaration, the General Conference of UNESCO had decided in 1978, upon a formal proposal by the USA and others,[162] to call a planning meeting to develop a proposal for 'institutional arrangements to systematize collaborative consultation on communications development activities, needs, and plans'.[163] After a preparatory meeting hosted by the USA, the Intergovernmental Conference for Cooperation on Activities, Needs and Programmes for Communication Development (DEVCOM for short) took place in Paris in April 1980 and was attended by 122 States, a majority from the Third World.[164]

The central point of agreement, reflected in a Recommendation adopted by consensus both by DEVCOM[165] and later by the General Conference,[166] concerned the creation of an International Programme for Development of Communication (IPDC).

The aim of the IPDC was essentially operational. As approved by the General Conference by consensus, its task was 'to increase cooperation and assistance for the development of communication infrastructures and reduce the gap between various countries in the communication field'.[167] This practical focus was stressed by the Director-General[168] and repeatedly commended by spokesmen of the leading Western countries (e.g. the UK, West Germany, Australia, Switzerland and Italy),[169] while the USA expressed its 'special pleasure' at the launching of this 'unique new programme'.[170]

The institutional arrangements approved by the General Conference, on a recommendation by DEVCOM, provided that the IPDC would be coordinated by an Intergovernmental Council with a restricted membership of 35 members, elected by the General Conference on the basis of rotation. While this provision reflected Western preferences for non-majoritarian procedures, voting arrangements were somewhat less satisfactory from the Western point of view. Western delegates had proposed that decision making by 'consensus' be made mandatory;[171] but although the relevant draft rule was amended by the Council at its first session to stipulate that 'in its deliberations, the Council should give priority to the seeking of a consensus', majority voting was not ruled out.[172]

Differences with regard to financing of the IPDC were to prove sharper still, especially following adoption of the above procedural provisions. Third World countries wished to see the IPDC develop as a multilateral funding source and, although they failed in an initial bid for creation of a Special Fund, a Special Account to be fed by voluntary contributions was opened by a subsequent decision.[173]

Western States, by contrast, preferred to treat the IPDC as a clearing house or improved source of data for aid programmes of an essentially bilateral character. Rather than a funding body in its own right, they regard the IPDC as a means of ascertaining Third World requirements more precisely and of matching the needs so identified with aid available from government or private sources in the developed countries.[174]

The US position on financial commitments under the Reagan Administration, which sought to keep the IPDC wholly independent of UNESCO,[175] was to prove especially reticent.[176] However, other Western powers too, notably the UK, were to declare that they did not intend to contribute to the IPDC as such, but rather to continue awarding aid on a bilateral basis.[177] Meanwhile, among those Western countries which agreed to donate financially, a tendency was to emerge from the start to tie aid to specified projects.[178]

Delegates of Denmark and Sweden also moved the transfer to the IPDC of certain appropriations earmarked for studies under UNESCO's regular programme.[179] Indeed, in discussions[180] on UNESCO's draft programme and budget for 1981–3,[181] several Western States had objected strongly to proposals for research into subjects such as, among others: advertising content and management of national media; the activities of transnational communications industries; education of the public with regard to mass media; and 'the concentrated industrialised production of messages'.[182] It may be assumed that it was from studies such as these – whose inclusion in the work programme was nevertheless approved by the General Conference[183] – that Western spokesmen wished to withdraw funding.

The level of contributions to the IPDC Special Account some two years after its establishment was not high. Aside from launch credits of US$1.75 million under UNESCO's regular budget, sums received or pledged by December 1982 stood at just over US$5 million, including contributions from a number of the poorest Third World countries.[184] Western offers totalled just under US$3 million, of which US$450,000 was from the USA and nearly US$2 million from Norway, at the time holding the chairmanship of the Council. Offers of services in kind (experts, fellowships, etc.) were also made, notably by the USA (to a value of US$100,000) and by the Soviet bloc.

Third World members were prompt to remark on what they regarded as the meagreness of the Western response.[185] The Norwegian Chairman of the IPDC Council was also to declare that, when visiting Third World countries, he had 'found it difficult to explain why the richer countries were contributing so little to IPDC'.[186]

Western reluctance to fund the IPDC may seem surprising when one considers that the latter constitutes not only the 'show-piece' outcome of the NWICO debate to date, but also the principal multilateral instrument by which Western States aim to defuse pressure for more normative remedies to global communications problems. The central concern of Western States, as recorded in press interviews and domestic parliamentary debates, would seem to be that resources allocated on the basis of decisions by the IPDC Council, on which they can be outvoted, might not be usefully spent and more specifically might be used to create or reinforce government-run information systems.[187]

At the same time, it is not inconceivable that the intention may also be to use the tight financial rein and the tying of donations as a means of rewarding 'good behaviour' in the normative sphere and/or to encourage reallocation of funds away from types of research objectionable to the West.

4. THE RESOLUTION ON INTERNATIONAL RELATIONS IN THE SPHERE OF INFORMATION AND MASS COMMUNICATIONS (UN, 1978), AND THE NWICO

The United Nations, too, had by this time begun to debate the NWICO. In the first paragraph of the above resolution, the General Assembly

> affirms the need to establish a new, more just and more effective world information and communication order, intended to strengthen peace and international understanding, and based on the free circulation and wider and better balanced flow of information[188]

Debate in the UN centered on a Tunisian draft resolution tabled on behalf of the Group of 77.[189] Tunisia had also, separately, submitted a study entitled *The New World Order for Information*.[190] Like the introductory statement by the Tunisian delegate,[191] the study showed that the sponsors of the new order were explicitly concerned with content as well as with the forms of communication, and envisaged among the means of establishing a new order a range of political and legal measures.[192]

The Third World majority on the General Committee of the General Assembly having determined that the matter could no longer be handled at a purely technical level,[193] these texts were referred to the full-membership Special Political Committee of the General Assembly. During debates in this arena,[194] Western members nevertheless pressed for technical approaches to the problem. West Germany, France, the Netherlands and the USA, in particular, stressing the importance of 'concrete', 'practical' measures, announced their intention of continuing if not increasing material aid to the Third World and reiterated their opposition to any suggestion that the media be regulated.[195]

The USA for its part addressed the Tunisian study directly on two occasions. In a first statement, the US delegation pronounced certain of the concepts it contained to be 'totally unacceptable', referring in addition to 'political manifestos' and 'extremist prescriptions'.[196] Later, the USA explicitly stated that its participation in the consensus on a revised Tunisian draft resolution should not be regarded as agreement in principle with the Tunisian study.[197]

Indeed Tunisia had, after lengthy negotiations, submitted a revised draft[198] which was to be adopted by consensus.[199] To Western satisfaction, the final text left the definition of a NWICO relatively open: the USA described the resolution as an important step 'towards' defining the concept, while West Germany considered the process of definition to have 'barely begun'.[200] At the same time, the concluding words inserted in the first paragraph cited above, 'basing' the new order on the principle of free flow, reflected Western concerns; without this link, the USA declared, it would not have joined the consensus.[201] Even so, Canada effectively dissociated from the resolution, considering it premature to assert the necessity of a new information order and declaring that, had there been a vote, it would have abstained.[202]

As in the case of the UNESCO text bearing on the NWICO discussed earlier, the above UN text was a resolution, and as such endowed with but slight normative rank. By the early 1980s, the concept of a NWICO had not in fact been endorsed or precisely defined in any legally-binding instrument in either Organisation.

5. UN PUBLIC INFORMATION ACTIVITIES AND THE NWICO

During the 1970s Non-Aligned States began to seek closer General Assembly control over UN public information activities with a view to enhancing awareness (especially among Western publics) of such major UN policies as the NIEO and NWICO, as well as of the causes of groups such as the Palestinians and the blacks of Southern Africa which lacked the means to reach Western publics direct on any scale. Although not normative in a strict sense, reform in this area is treated by the Non-Aligned countries as a necessary aspect of a NWICO.[203]

At Tunisian initiative on behalf of the Group of 77,[204] the General Assembly decided at its 33rd session in 1978 to set up a 41-member Committee to Review United Nations Public Information Policies and Programmes (later renamed Committee on Information), on which the West held 10 seats, the Non-Aligned 27 and the Soviet bloc 4.[205] (The last such review dated back nearly thirty years to the time of the Korean War, when a more effective UN public information role was sought by the USA.) Competition for the seats was described by the Committee's Tunisian Chairman as unusually keen,[206] and it was decided the following year to increase the membership to 66.[207]

In 1979, following discussion in the Committee on Information on the basis of an Indian draft,[208] a resolution on UN public information activities[209] was adopted by consensus by the Special Political Committee and by the plenary of the General Assembly.[210] The resolution called on the Secretary-General, among other things,

* to ensure 'equitable participation of personnel from the developing countries in the staff of the Department of Public Information particularly in posts at the higher and decision-making levels';[211]
* to reconsider the priorities and programmes of the Department of Public Information in the context of the need to establish a NWICO;[212]
* to study the 'intensification of UN shortwave broadcasts';[213]
* to report on the feasibility, legal implications and cost of undertaking UN frequency modulation broadcasts in the Headquarters area;[214] and
* to invite Member States 'to grant to the United Nations Radio a share in their scheduled broadcast timetable'.[215]

Western States, however, did not associate themselves fully with the consensus. The USA and West Germany aired reservations as to the role of the Department of Public Information (DPI) and other UN organs in 'promoting the establishment of new orders that require significant changes in international and national structures' as was the case with the NIEO and NWICO, and stressed the need for 'objectivity' in United Nations publications and media services.[216] The UK, meanwhile, considered the widespread image of the UN to be a fair reflection of reality.[217]

But it was the issue of UN broadcasting, and especially the relationship with domestic broadcasting channels, which attracted the strongest Western criticism. As the USA was to remark, these portions of the resolution had in fact been discussed neither by the Committee on Information nor by the reduced-membership *ad hoc* Working Group set up by the Committee in 1979.[218] The reports of the Working Group had been welcomed by all the leading Western delegates, whose margin of influence on both the latter bodies was greater than in the full-membership Special Political Committee, as 'pragmatic' and 'constructive'.[219] The UK, Ireland for the EEC, Finland for the Nordic countries, the USA, Canada and Australia declared in explanations of vote that they could not give effect to these parts of the text as they did not control broadcasting stations directly.[220] The UK added that the UN should not adopt what it termed 'hasty and ill-prepared' proposals.[221]

The question of improving the UN's own broadcasting facilities was also to prove sensitive, and in fact bore upon the Middle East conflict. The Committee on Information had suggested that the UN resume use of the frequency assigned to it in New York (but loaned since 1966 to New York University) for its own broadcasting 'in order to counter the trend towards partial coverage of UN activities which had recently become evident in the Headquarters area'.[222] (In the circumstances, it would seem reasonable to interpret this formula as meaning pro-Israeli coverage.)

As it happened, the most sustained criticism of trends in UN public information policy came from Israeli spokesmen, who objected to what they considered to be a series of partisan UN publications on the question of Palestine. Israel particularly doubted that information disseminated by the Assembly's Committee on Exercise of the Inalienable Rights of Palestinian People, or by the Special Unit on Palestinian Rights created within the Secretariat by Assembly decision, could be anything but biased.[223]

Israel further considered that, given the absence of unanimity on the Middle East conflict in the General Assembly, neither the UN Department of Public Information nor the Secretariat more generally could serve as producers of information on that subject. Suggesting that the Secretariat was morally free to adopt a stance other than that of the majority in the Assembly, the Israeli delegate called upon the Secretary-General to declare his position on certain publications prepared within the Secretariat, and intimated that unpleasant consequences might ensue for the UN if the Secretariat continued, as he put it, 'to promote the efforts of certain countries to bring about the destruction of Israel'.[224]

The USA expressed 'strong reservations' on the subject of United Nations broadcasting and, backed by the UK and Japan, endorsed the Secretary-General's proposal for prior studies and patience.[225]

Western and Israeli preferences were reflected in the resolution quoted above which had the effect of postponing decisions by requesting a study of the legal and financial aspects of the proposal. That this move might have been seen as a delaying tactic by the majority is suggested by the General Assembly call the following year for 'urgent measures with the host country' to resolve the problems at issue.[226]

It is, of course, too soon to judge the outcome of this particular aspect of the NWICO debate, although some estimate of its probable evolution may be hazarded. It may be assumed that, failing substantial improvement of indigenous capacity to reach Western publics direct, Third World countries will maintain pressure for reform of UN public information activities. There are also reasonable grounds for assuming that the developing countries might achieve some satisfaction as regards internal management of such activities, notably at the level of staffing. On the other hand, however, there is no particular reason to suppose that efforts to secure greater publicity for UN-produced information through established external media will be significantly more successful than other Third World initiatives in the communications field.

The debate continues and none of the outcomes reviewed above may be considered final.

At Soviet bloc initiative,[227] for instance, the General Conference of UNESCO decided at its 21st session in 1980 to convene a meeting in 1983 to examine application of the 1978 Media Declaration, despite Western warnings against reopening discussions on that subject.[228]

Similarly, Third World attempts to set standards for the reordering of global information relationships seem likely to be pursued. Moreover, the debate continues to ramify both into other UN Agencies (notably ITU and FAO) and into areas other than formal standard-setting (e.g. informatics policy[229]).

At the same time, a number of Third World and East European spokesmen (notably those of Colombia, Cuba, East Germany, Egypt, Guyana, Iraq, Libya, Tunisia, Upper Volta, the USSR and Yugoslavia) have begun to question the growing tendency to refer policy issues to non-majoritarian arenas, a practice which they see as undermining the 'sovereign authority' of the General Conference and as restricting the 'freedom of expression' of Member States in that body.[230] By the same token, as mentioned in Chapter 1, they have criticised the concept of 'consensus' where this is seen as an instrument designed to secure outcomes corresponding too closely to the preferences of the Western minority.[231]

Conversely, however, there is no particular reason to suppose that the vigilance of Western States and mass media with respect to UNESCO activities in this field will slacken. Indeed, press reports announcing concerted Western confrontation with M'Bow over communications issues, canvassing budgetary reprisals, and recording efforts by influential media organisations – not at least at congressional hearings – to encourage the USA to withdraw from UNESCO had begun to multiply by the early 1980s.[232] Debates had also been held in response to Western criticism on ways in which the Agency's standard-setting activities might be reformed.[233] On 29 December 1983, as mentioned earlier, the Reagan Administration made public its intention of withdrawing the USA from membership of UNESCO at the end of the following year, citing among the principal grounds for the decision the fact that the Agency had 'exhibited hostility towards the basic institutions of a free society, especially . . . the free press' and its efforts to introduce a 'new world information order'.[234] In so doing, the Secretary of State nonetheless referred to the efforts the Director-General had made to secure results acceptable to the West. On 1 January 1985 US withdrawal took effect, and on 11 February 1985 the Secretary of State announced that he had appointed a Committee of Ten to evaluate reforms undertaken by UNESCO.[235]

The Thatcher Government in turn let it be known on 22 November 1984 that the United Kingdom would withdraw from the Agency by the end of 1985 unless reforms were effected by that time.[236] It did so in much the same terms as the US Government and reportedly in response to high-level American promptings.[237] The UK government confirmed its decision on 5 December 1985[238] and duly pulled Britain out of UNESCO with effect from 1 January 1986. Certain other Western Governments, notably those of Japan, West Germany and the Netherlands, have also hinted that they might follow suit;[239] and on

20 March 1985 a meeting of the Geneva Group, which comprises the twelve largest Western contributors accounting for some 70 per cent of the UNESCO budget, decided that the shortfall created by US withdrawal should not be made good but that instead selective cuts should be made in the programme approved in 1983 to match the reduced funding available.[240]

But it should be noted that the withdrawal decisions did not go unopposed either in the USA or in the UK. The State Department was split on the decision[241] and, perhaps more significantly, the move was strongly criticised by the US National Commission for UNESCO which groups American non-governmental bodies active in UNESCO's fields of competence. In the event the Commission's three Vice-Chairmen, of whom Leonard Sussman of the Inter-American Press Association was one, drew up a document designed to provide a more balanced picture of American positions on the UNESCO issue. In this document the Commission held, among other things, that: the State Department had consistently ignored its opinions and advice; that the timing of the American announcement was hard to justify in view of statements by leading US delegates to the effect that the 1983 General Conference had been among the least politicised and most constructive from the US point of view for some time; that the decision was supported by none of the 83 American Embassies and consulates consulted and by none of the 13 federal Agencies asked for their views; and that the intellectual level of US participation in UNESCO in preceding years had not been up to standard, too many members of US delegations having been appointed for internal political reasons rather than for their competence.[242]

Similarly, shortly before the UK decision, the Executive Board of UNESCO at its autumn 1984 session had adopted a range of proposals for reform, many originating from the United Kingdom. No UK proposals were rejected and British members publicly expressed their satisfaction.[243] Equally by the time the British pull-out was confirmed in December 1985, the view had become fairly widespread in Western circles that UNESCO was on the whole mending its ways.[244]

In the circumstances the decisions of the Reagan and Thatcher governments seemed to some to have been prompted by considerations of an essentially political nature rather than by the strict merits of the case.[245] Soon after the UK decision, a group of British academics, scientists and artists was reported to have joined ranks with like-minded politicians of all parties in a campaign to keep Britain in UNESCO.[246]

As far as the response of mass media is concerned, meanwhile, debates on communications policy continued to attract considerable numbers of Western journalists.[247] Moreover, news organisations from over twenty countries meeting in France in May 1981 served what the editor of *The Times* described as a 'resolute counterblast' to recent developments by adopting a declaration insisting on basic freedoms and urging technical rather than normative approaches to communications problems.[248] Press coverage of UNESCO has in the meantime increasingly tended to take the form of personal attacks on the management and life-style of the Director-General and has in some instances led senior Western staff members to publish replies.[249]

The Director-General, for his part, no doubt anticipating further confrontation and seeking to minimise unfavourable publicity, commissioned a study for 1983 from Charles Hargrove, former Paris correspondent of *The Times*, on UNESCO's image in the American and British press and ways in which it might be improved.[250] Working parties were also set up by the Director-General in July 1984 to look into different aspects of the running of the Organisation in response to criticism.

SUMMARY AND CONCLUSIONS

The scope and volume of debates on information policy continue to multiply, as does the number of arenas concerned with the subject in the UN system. In consequence, it has not been possible here to attempt an exhaustive review of developments in this field.

In our selection process, and especially in the space devoted to the UNESCO Media Declaration, we have consciously adopted the same criteria of significance as Western mass media. The purpose in so doing was to consider how and with what degree of success Western mass media and Member States reacted to those challenges in the information field to which they attached greatest importance.

We have shown that where the opposition of Western Member States and mass media was less than full scale, outcomes were more prescriptive and in many respects distasteful from the Western point of view. Such was the case, for instance, with the precursor resolutions to and early drafts of the Media Declaration, before mass media had been alerted to UNESCO communications debates. Such was also the case with the San José Conference, where Western States as observers had no formal power to influence proceedings, and where media concern was still confined to the print and broadcast media of North and Latin America.

On the other hand, where opposition was more thorough-going, outcomes were generally more favourable to the West. Full-scale trials of strength occurred in the full-membership arenas of the UNESCO General Conference and UN General Assembly, and once Western media were more broadly mobilised, with respect to the Media Declaration and to calls for a NWICO.

In these encounters the responses of Western States ranged from simple delaying measures to more or less explicit warnings of a budgetary nature and finally of course to the withdrawal of two leading states from membership. The principal tactics consisted in resort to minority-based procedures and in efforts to bypass if not delegitimise majoritarian principles.

This approach was reflected in referral of the subjects at issue to increasingly exclusive and unofficial arenas, mostly created for the purpose: for example, within UNESCO, the Drafting and Negotiation Group and its sub-group; the 'informal reflexion group'; the MacBride Commission; and the Intergovernmental Council of the IPDC; and within the UN, the Committee on Information and its Working Group.

The same approach was visible in Western appeals to 'consensus' where that concept, implicitly at least, was used to denote something other than a majority (even a majority comprising four-fifths of the membership). It was discernible, too, in persistent Western questioning of UNESCO's standard-setting activities more generally, and in a shift away from the normative approaches to global communications problems preferred in the postwar era towards more 'technical' solutions.

These responses on the part of Western States were reinforced by intensive media coverage seen by many (including some in the West) as a campaign to discredit the new majority and senior Secretariat staff, at times when both were especially vulnerable to pressure.

The outcome has been a number of texts and decisions broadly compatible with Western positions. The Soviet-sponsored Media Declaration, on which Western media focussed the most concentrated coverage, and which thus constitutes the most telling example, was effectively shorn of normative content.

In the case of the Third World call for a NWICO, too, normative approaches to communications problems on the part of the new majority have been largely stalemated. By the early 1980s, no legally binding text endorsing either the principle or a firm definition of a 'new order' had been adopted by either UNESCO or the UN. Nor did moves to reform UN public information activities as a partial means of compensating Third World communications-poverty seem destined to any appreciable measure of success.

The principal outcome of debate to date has been the creation of the IPDC, embodying the essentially technical approach and restricted membership preferred by the West. Even so, however, the institutional arrangements of this body are less than wholly satisfactory to Western powers (notably the USA and UK) which have in the event allowed the IPDC to remain financially under-endowed.

Meanwhile, the extent to which the UNESCO Secretariat has been placed on the defensive is evidenced by the cautious behaviour of the Director-General at various stages of the different debates and his attempts to limit confrontation by anticipating Western positions.

In sum, by resort to a variety of instruments, Western interests have so far succeeded in containing the new majority (and the Secretariat(s) as servants of that majority), and thus in preserving a determining say for the minority in the sphere of information policy.

At the same time, the interests challenged by the new majority in this particular field are endowed with what may be regarded as an unparalleled source of power, namely the capacity to publicise their side of an argument. Indeed, as we mentioned earlier, it has rather tended to escape notice, or at any rate comment, that in relation to debates on media policy mass media act to all intents and purposes as judges in their own cause.

The following chapters will consider developments in areas where the interests involved command fewer resources than the mass media, namely education, science, culture and race, to see how outcomes compare.

6 The Postwar UNESCO Debate on Regulation of Education

INTRODUCTION

As was shown in Chapter 3, promotion of international understanding as a means to peace, and the improvement of education to that end, were regarded by UNESCO's founders as central to the new Agency's tasks; and 'education for international understanding' was in fact to serve as the guiding framework for a number of UNESCO-wide projects.

Nevertheless, a certain amount of ambiguity prevailed with respect to the means by which such education was to be achieved. Indeed, while some Member States assumed UNESCO's constitutional commitment to education for peace to be largely attainable through liberal policies, others interpreted it as requiring explicit regulation of school systems.

This chapter will examine postwar UNESCO debates on international regulation and scrutiny of educational content in the interests of peace. It will concentrate on proposals for worldwide revision of textbooks under UNESCO auspices and for a Convention on the Direction of Educational Programmes towards International Peace and Security, but will also touch upon the debate on UNESCO involvement in Allied 're-education' of the German people.

First, it will briefly consider the postwar structure of UNESCO's policy-making bodies.

1. THE POSTWAR STRUCTURE OF UNESCO

Between 1945 and the early 1950s, the period which concerns us here, the West (that is, the USA, Latin American countries still for the most part adhering to US positions, Western Europe and the White Dominions) constituted a comfortable majority on UNESCO policy-making bodies, being regularly represented at the General Conference by between 30 and 40 Member States.[1] By contrast, representation for the Third World as a whole (Asia, Arab States and black Africa) ranged from a low of 7 countries at the 2nd session in 1947 to a high of 18 in 1949 and 1950. Black Africa in particular was consistently represented by either one State (Liberia) or none. Meanwhile, participation of the Soviet bloc in the Stalin era was irregular and, on a number of occasions, purely token in scale – notably at the 3rd session in 1948 and 5th session in 1950. The USSR itself took up active membership in 1954 and, until the Titoist breakaway, Yugoslavia was regarded by several Western observers as the unofficial mouthpiece for the Soviet Union.[2]

A similar situation prevailed in the Executive Board, which consisted of 18 members sitting in individual capacity although nominated (and in practice to varying degrees instructed) by States. During the first term of the Board, for instance, Western Europe accounted for 8 members and the Americas for 5, while the Third World and East Europe accounted for 3 and 2 members respectively.[3]

Having thus summarised the pattern of representation in UNESCO's main policy-making organs in the late 1940s and early 1950s, we may now turn to the debates of the time on regulation of educational content.

2. DEBATES ON UNESCO-SPONSORED REVISION OF TEXTBOOKS

In the immediate postwar era, a number of the then independent developing countries, notably Egypt, India, Lebanon and the Philippines, as well as a small number of Latin American and East European States (especially Mexico, Ecuador, Yugoslavia and Poland) expressed the view that 're-education' of the sort envisaged by the Allies for 'ex-enemy' countries should be extended to all nations, including the victorious peoples of the West. India and Mexico considered that not only the vanquished but also the victors required to be re-educated;[4] Ecuador, referring in particular to history textbooks, held that

> . . . it would be a good thing *not only for the Germans but for all the nations of the world* to revise their educational problems and the systems intended to solve such problems;[5] (emphasis added)

and the Yugoslav spokesman declared that

After this war the re-education of man – *and superman too* – is an imperative need of peace . . .[6] (emphases added)

Egypt proposed the issuing under UNESCO guidance of 'universal books', while the Mexican delegation tabled an amendment to proposals for UNESCO's Constitution, suggesting that an international commission of experts look into the problem of school texts, notably history books,

> in order to eliminate all statements tending to create a false feeling of racial superiority or national imperialism which may be contrary to the development of a spirit of human brotherhood and universal solidarity.[7]

The USA, too, at the conference for the establishment of UNESCO, appeared to favour action along these lines, as can be seen from a statement which we reproduce here at some length:

> . . . we suggest . . . that UNESCO should encourage all Member States to *direct* their respective educational systems to the *inculcation* of knowledge, attitudes and skills which contribute to international peace and security and to the support of the Charter of the United Nations. Therefore *a commission of representative educators* should be appointed *to survey the content and methods of national systems of education*, and to formulate recommendations for the adaptation of educational programmes to this end. In the US, considerable discussion and very serious consideration are being given to the proposal that at the November Conference there be a resolution of the General Conference of UNESCO which would *remind the governments of the UN that they have undertaken certain obligations* under the Charter which relate to the maintenance of peace and security and that therefore *it is to be expected that they will apply a sense of these obligations to the content and method of their education.*[8] (Emphases added.)

The original draft Constitution of UNESCO as drawn up by the Conference of Allied Ministers of Education (CAME) did not provide for international scrutiny of teaching materials, let alone mandatory regulation. Under Article II, the Organisation was simply to

> foster the growth . . . of educational and cultural programmes which give support to international peace and security,

and to 'develop and make available' educational and cultural plans and materials 'for such consideration and use as each country may deem proper'.[9] Under alternative French proposals, meanwhile, the Agency's work on educational content would be approached indirectly from the perspective of recognition of degrees and international mobility of students and teachers, rather than through direct attempts to promote international understanding as such.[10]

The Mexican amendment mentioned above was referred, along with the constitutional proposals prepared by CAME and by France, to a Drafting Committee composed of representatives of France, India, Mexico, Poland, the UK and the USA.[11] But the Mexican amendment was not reflected in the text drawn up by the committee and broadly endorsed by the relevant commission of the founding conference: the latter text stated that UNESCO would collaborate with Member States 'at their request' in studying such matters as teaching methods and curricula, and would define the goals of educational practice.[12] But no reference was made, either in this draft or in the final text of the Constitution, to an international textbook commission as such. On the other hand, rather stronger provision was made for respect of domestic jurisdiction of States than had been contained in either of the original draft constitutional texts.[13]

The question of generalised textbook revision was discussed again at the first session of the General Conference in late 1946 by the Education Sub-Commission. Poland held that some form of international control should be exercised on general and national history textbooks so as 'to prevent the distortion of events for war-like purposes', particularly in countries 'where harmful doctrines had taken root and where the desire for power dominated', but did not specify the form of control envisaged.[14] The Turkish delegate proposed the establishment of a 'revision committee for school textbooks, possessing effective censorship powers', while India favoured regional conferences to verify history textbooks.[15] The observer for Nicaragua and Costa Rica considered that revision should also apply to books on religious history, while France underlined the necessity of revising school-books for all subjects without exception.[16] Similar views were also to be aired by India, Lebanon, Mexico and the Philippines at the 2nd, 3rd and 4th sessions of the General Conference.[17]

The position of the USA, however, appeared more reserved in 1946 than the previous year. The USA responded to proposals for UNESCO-sponsored textbook revision by observing that

> there were no government educational textbooks in America and there was absolute freedom in the publication of schoolbooks. *UNESCO must not take on the role of censor, and alter or revise*

books which appeared in America, but should confine itself to the drafting of reports and recommendations, which would be submitted to American educational institutions.[18] (Emphases added)

The guardedness of the American position may have been due in part to vocal West Coast protest at what were seen as interventionist UNESCO plans liable to undermine the patriotic convictions of young Americans.[19] The above statement, and especially the exclusionary reference to American teaching materials, would in any event seem to suggest that the USA had envisaged that any international revision exercise would focus primarily on the materials of other countries or, at the least, that any panel selected under UNESCO auspices would be likely to view US materials favourably. So, too, would the view expressed by a senior US delegate (but not encouraged by the then Director-General, also an American) to the effect that UNESCO could hardly find a more suitable project than revision of the textbooks of the USSR and other countries.[20]

Following the above discussion New Zealand, seconded by Australia, moved that each Member State send the Secretariat representative collections of the textbooks used in educational institutions in their country, this motion being adopted by 11:2.[21] But a rider to the New Zealand amendment, seconded by the UK and adopted by 9:3, called on the Secretariat to report to the General Conference on its scrutiny of the books.[22]

The potential for diplomatic embarrassment inherent in such a procedure was clear and may well have been designed to deter the advocates of generalised textbook revision. Be that as it may, India seconded by Norway requested the Secretariat to report to the country concerned instead of to the General Conference, and this amendment was adopted by 9:0.[23]

Meanwhile, an amendment tabled by the Philippines and seconded by Egypt, and calling upon UNESCO to

prepare a *Charter* in the light of which the various countries *will* revise and modify their school textbooks . . . (Emphases added)

was adopted by the Education Sub-Commission by 12:3.[24]

In the programme resolution adopted by the Education Sub-Commission, and later endorsed by the full Programme Commission and plenary, these proposals were incorporated in diluted form.[25] The Philippines' call for a mandatory charter for textbook revision was replaced by a more permissive resolution calling on the Secretariat to draw up a 'set of principles' or 'code of ethics' which Member States would be free to follow or not.

The idea of creating a clearing-house of national textbooks as a basis for textbook revision was also retained, along with the principle – this time expressed in strengthened form – of reporting to the General Conference rather than to the country concerned.[26] The importance of such a public reporting system was argued in the introduction to the report of the Programme Commission drafted by the American rapporteur:

> Necessarily involved in [the proposal for a comprehensive revision of textbooks] is the assumption by UNESCO of a responsibility to report to the General Conference and to the United Nations and the world at large any instances of misuse of text-books which might be considered to constitute a danger to the peace. No question of censorship is involved here or elsewhere in UNESCO's programme. UNESCO is not the policeman of the mind nor the censor of the imagination. UNESCO is, however, charged, under its Constitution, with a duty to preserve peace . . . through the instruments of education, of science and of culture. It has, therefore, a clear responsibility, finally and in the last analysis, to call to the attention of the member nations of UNESCO and of the United Nations any misuse of the facilities of teaching which it considers dangerous to the peace.[27]

But the labouring of this point may, as suggested above, have been intended to discourage the sponsors of generalised textbook revision. Although study of the books would have been entrusted to the Secretariat in collaboration with National Commissions for UNESCO and other national bodies, the Secretariat would have had the coordinating role; and misgivings could be anticipated on the part of certain States as to the likely findings of studies conducted under the auspices of an essentially Western-run Secretariat. In this connection, delegates of a number of Third World and East European countries (notably India, China, Uruguay, Egypt and Czechoslovakia) remarked at the second session of the General Conference and subsequently that the staffing was far from reflecting the full range of cultures and beliefs represented in the Agency's membership.[28]

The interventionism of the initial proposals was watered down still further in the work programme approved by the Executive Board four months later. The Secretariat was instructed, among other things, to draft a 'model method of textbook analysis', including the development of principles by which each Member State 'might, as it sees fit, analyze its own textbooks and teaching materials'; and to initiate a study of the treatment of international cooperation in these textbooks. The word 'improvement' was also substituted for 'revision' in this and most later texts, and explicit mention of reporting to the General Conference on the findings of textbook scrutiny was dropped.[29]

Western Member States were to continue to treat the question of UNESCO-sponsored programmes of textbook revision with caution, the UK in particular regularly entering reservations with respect to any proposals which might imply either undue uniformity of educational content or improvement of textbooks 'by the direct action of governments'.[30]

Gradually, the idea of worldwide textbook revision under UNESCO auspices disappeared from the agenda. Each year, the Organisation distanced itself further from suggestions of direct involvement in the revision of teaching materials, confining itself to an exhortatory, stimulative and advisory role. Thus in 1948 and 1949, the General Conference instructed the Director-General 'to further the improvement of textbooks and teaching materials';[31] in 1951, 'to stimulate Member States . . . to proceed with the revision of their history and geography textbooks';[32] and in 1952 simply 'to assist Member States in improving curricula, methods, textbooks and teaching materials'.[33]

Similarly, instead of the code of ethics canvassed earlier, UNESCO published a Handbook in 1949 containing a 'model plan' for the analysis and improvement of textbooks and teaching materials which was sent to Member States for comment.[34] In his report for that year, the Director-General effectively disclaimed further responsibility for the subject on the part of the Secretariat, stating that

> The programme for improvement of textbooks has now reached the stage where much of the initiative must pass to Member States

and adding that

> for the present, bilateral agreements may prove more practicable than multilateral ones.[35]

Member States, meanwhile, were simply 'invited' by the General Conference in 1950 'to initiate or pursue examination of their textbooks' and in 1951 'to undertake or continue examination of their textbooks'.[36]

Thereafter, UNESCO activity in the field of textbook improvement was to take the form chiefly of sponsorship of seminars for members of the teaching profession and others involved in textbook production, and publication of a number of guides to the teaching of specified subjects.[37]

3. THE PROPOSED UNESCO CONVENTION/ RECOMMENDATION ON THE DIRECTION OF EDUCATIONAL PROGRAMMES TOWARDS INTERNATIONAL PEACE AND SECURITY

Proposals for the drafting of a legally-binding text on the question of school programmes were also put forward in the postwar years but, like those for generalised textbook improvement under UNESCO aegis, were ultimately abandoned.

In 1947, at the 2nd session of the General Conference to which it was host, Mexico tabled proposals for a Convention on the Direction of School Programmes towards International Peace and Security, which would bind States legally to revise their educational systems, methods and materials in the manner and to the extent necessary to secure peace and international understanding.[38] The original proposals envisaged among other things that a commission of experts would

> edit a text in which shall be expressed a body of pedagogic principles, systems of education, plans of study, etc., for the international understanding which the Member States should bind themselves to implant within their respective jurisdictions.[39]

Mexico held the likeliest source of future war, and hence the area where reform was most pressing, to be the 'well-educated and industrialised nations' (although it may be noted that they urged recourse to educators in the USA and Switzerland in carrying through such reforms).[40]

A second and briefer motion tabled by Mexico to give effect to its proposals was worded in terms closer (through its inclusion of reference to domestic constitutional provisions) to those traditionally used by the USA and its supporters.[41] Endorsed by Cuba and Egypt, supported 'whole-heartedly' by the USA, and adopted after minor amendment by the General Conference, the motion instructed the Director-General

> to prepare for the consideration of the 1948 General Conference a draft convention under the terms of which the Member States *may*

agree *within the limitations and powers of their respective constitutional and legal provisions* regarding the control and administration
of education, to *direct* the programmes of their respective educational systems at all levels to the needs of international peace and
security . . .[42] (Emphases added.)

But little was in fact to come of this undertaking. Briefed by the
Secretariat, the Chairman of the Executive Board announced in May
1948 that no action could be taken on the subject that year or next for
lack of staff and funds.[43] (These grounds seemed unconvincing to the
French and Australian members of the Board, in whose view the
project followed directly from the Constitution and required a
minimum of financing and personnel.[44]) The General Conference that
year again instructed the Director-General to prepare a draft of a
convention, but on this occasion specified no time-limit.[45]

The Secretariat for its part displayed little enthusiasm for the
project. In a memorandum to the Director-General in May 1949, the
head of the education sector, a former delegate of New Zealand,
advised deferment of the drafting of a convention on grounds of
technical difficulty (e.g. in defining what was meant by 'an educational
programme directed towards peace and security'; in identifying the
appropriate authorities in each country and the scope of their powers;
in deciding who should monitor implementation; etc.).[46]

The fourth session of the General Conference, on the basis of a
Secretariat document, instructed the Director-General simply to 'take
steps towards' the drafting of a convention.[47] The Secretariat then
decided to convene a meeting of experts to consider the advisability of
drafting one or more conventions, or a recommendation on the
subject. Held in November 1949, the meeting brought together nine
experts of whom 5 from the West (France, Italy, Norway, UK and
USA), 4 from the Third World (Egypt, India (2 experts) and Mexico),
an additional 'special consultant' from the UK and no experts from
East Europe.[48]

The UNESCO Legal Adviser, a French national, set the tone of the
debate by counselling that a legally-binding convention would not be
easy to draft, given the differences in school systems and the
unpropitious climate.[49] The experts concurred in the view that a
recommendation (i.e. a non-binding instrument) would be more
appropriate at that stage, although referring to the Director-General
the question of whether to mention in the recommendation the possibility that it might lead on to a convention or series of conventions,[50]

The recommendation as drafted and unanimously approved by the experts[51] specified, among other things, that school programmes should: stress the conception of the equality of all human beings set forth in the Universal Declaration of Human Rights, including the equal right of every nation to direct its life; present the work of the UN and the Specialised Agencies as a most significant move towards promoting the peace and well-being of all peoples; and promote the study and practice of active responsibility and loyalty to the local and national community as the basis for the 'wider loyalty to the world society to which all other obligations should be subordinate'. The measures of implementation, meanwhile, were all expressed in liberal form.

The American Acting Director-General, in advising the Executive Board to submit the draft recommendation to the 5th session of the General Conference, judged it preferable not to include a reference to possible future conventions.[52] The Board, after substituting the word 'improvement' for the term 'revision' of textbooks,[53] decided to begin by circulating the draft to member States for comment.[54]

The response of Western States to this consultation gave little indication of eagerness to pursue the project. None of the Member States which replied to the call for comments expressed contrary opinions, but substantive replies were in fact received from only 11 countries.[55] Of these, Australia, Canada, the Netherlands and the UK entered reservations of a constitutional and legal character relating to States' rights in federal countries and to the principle of freedom of education which, they explained, precluded government influence over the choice and drafting of textbooks in their countries.[56] The written comments of the British Government, for instance, declared that 'it is necessary for the United Kingdom to enter a caveat to this recommendation in so far as it assumes the ability of the State to impose curricula changes from above'.[57] The British Minister of Education went further, expressing doubts as to the need for action on this project.[58]

The USA, for its part, communicated no written comments on the draft. But although never explicitly going back on its earlier support, the USA appears to have made no further moves to advance adoption of an instrument. The sudden decline in US participation may have been due to the fact that, as mentioned in Chapter 4, the Brickerite movement to limit US adherence to international instruments which might invalidate federal or State laws (notably legislation permitting race discrimination), and which was to result in American withdrawal from the drafting of such texts, was already underway by 1950.[59] In any event the Executive Board, instancing the small number of replies received, instructed the Director-General to present a progress report to the 6th session of the General Conference in 1951, but without recommending further action.[60]

The item was duly placed on the agenda of the 6th session[61] where, in view of the UNESCO-wide nature of the issues addressed, it was agreed to include it among the resolutions of a general rather than of a purely educational character.[62] However, the subject was not in fact discussed again during that session and, thereafter, the question of a standard-setting instrument to promote 'education for peace' was to remain in abeyance for some twenty years.

The failure to conclude the discussion at the 6th session of the General Conference is explained neither in the conference records nor in subsequent internal correspondence.[63] This outcome may have been due to an accident in conference management. At the same time, it appears clear enough that leading Western States were not over-anxious to pursue the debate. In view of their repeated reference to domestic constitutional provisions, and in the absence of evidence to the contrary, it would seem reasonable to assume that these States might have felt some uncertainty as to whether liberal principles could in fact be assured of prevailing in debate and, in the circumstances, preferred to let the matter rest.

————————

However, as can be seen from debates briefly discussed below on participation by UNESCO in the 're-education' of 'ex-enemy' peoples, leading Western powers in the postwar years did not invariably rule out interventionist methods or UNESCO involvement therein.

4.　UNESCO AND THE 'RE-EDUCATION' OF 'EX-ENEMY' PEOPLES

The question of UNESCO involvement in Allied programmes for 're-education' of Axis peoples and especially of Germany was raised by the Netherlands in 1946.[64]

The principle of 're-education', i.e. control by the occupying powers temporarily constituting the State over the form and content of education dispensed to defeated populations, was in this instance challenged by no Member State. (Indeed, the paradox whereby vanquished peoples were 'forced to be free' by the victorious liberal democracies has frequently been remarked upon.[65])

But the issue of what specific content to impart to such education was to occasion heated debate in the Executive Board[66] and General Conference[67] for several years. Legalistic in form, the debate in fact overlapped in substance with cold-war politics. (The discussions to be described below did not arise in connection with Japan where there was only one occupying power.)

American and British delegates, with a view to enhancing the legitimacy in German eyes and thus the effectiveness of 're-education', strongly urged UNESCO involvement in Allied programmes, the USA seeking help in particular with the revision and preparation of textbooks.[68]

However East European spokesmen, notably those of Czechoslovakia and Poland, treated the matter differently. As a small minority, these delegates could not expect to have a determining say in the content of 're-education' under UNESCO auspices. Resorting to procedural tactics, they held that any UNESCO involvement would have to be approved by the Allied Control Council (ACC) on which the USSR – not at the time a Member of UNESCO – was represented.[69] UNESCO's approach to the ACC having been rebuffed, East European members claimed that the Agency had no right thereafter to enter into negotiations with individual Zone Commanders.[70] These delegates consistently and forcefully contended that 're-education' was a political matter for which UNESCO had no jurisdiction and that, by intervening in Western zones alone, the Agency was contributing to the division of Germany and laying itself open to charges of partisanship.[71]

It may be noted that despite heated discussion over several years, this minority view received relatively little Western coverage. In the standard works on UNESCO, either the debate is ignored or the East European objections are presented with little attempt at explaining the grounds for opposition. A work on UNESCO by two Americans, Walter Laves (Deputy Director-General of UNESCO at the time of the debate) and Charles Thomson, for instance, writes off the Soviet bloc position in five lines as obstructionist.[72]

In the event, the majority in the Executive Board and General Conference, along with the British Director-General, Julian Huxley, and his American Deputy, Walter Laves, were to endorse the American, British and French view that UNESCO was entitled to contact and work with those occupying powers interested in co-operation with the Agency, which in practice meant the three Western allies.[73]

But the Board and General Conference were also circumspect, and their decisions can be seen to have taken at least some account of East European objections. Thus while all UNESCO activities in Germany remained subject to approval by the 'appropriate allied authorities' (interpreted as the relevant zonal power), efforts were made to preserve the appearance of independence. In particular, following a protest from Poland on what it deemed the unauthorised and ceremonial opening of UNESCO offices in Stuttgart,[74] and discussions in the Executive Board stressing the importance of distancing the Agency from the military authorities, care was taken to establish UNESCO offices in premises separate from those of the latter.[75]

Moreover, the programmes adopted[76] were to be regarded by Western members as modest.[77] Confined at first largely to studies of education problems in Germany and of ways in which UNESCO might best contribute to their solution, they were to involve such activities as translation and distribution in Germany of UNESCO publications, and easing the exchange of selected Germans and of publications 'calculated to further the aims of UNESCO' between Germany and other countries.[78]

Similarly, rather than engaging in direct revision or production of textbooks, the Secretariat was authorised for example to make available for use in Germany the 'principles, criteria and model plan' devised by UNESCO for textbook improvement in general, as well as adequate source and monographic material; to compile and dispatch to Germany bibliographies on textbook improvement; and to be available for consultation on request by Allied authorities.[79]

But despite the minimalist nature of the activities and the concern to keep occupation authorities at arms length, it remains that the postwar majority could, in the selected case of Germany, be seen as having encouraged UNESCO along paths that were nonetheless interventionist, and as having supported such a course of action in spite of its implications in terms of prevailing Cold War politics.

SUMMARY AND CONCLUSIONS

By 1951, formal proposals both for worldwide textbook revision under UNESCO auspices and for international regulation with respect to school programmes more generally had been abandoned. As has been shown, these outcomes can to no little extent be attributed to lack of active support either from the then majority of Western States and their supporters, or from the largely Western-run Secretariat.

Indeed, it emerges from the debates reviewed in this chapter that leading Western States, although actively seeking UNESCO participation in Allied re-education programmes in Germany, did not interpret UNESCO's constitutional commitment to 'education for peace' as binding them to monitor the content of education systems on a universal basis for conformity with the ideals of peace and international understanding. In this sense, 'education for peace' could be said to have been treated by the postwar majority within UNESCO as synonymous for practical purposes with education by and for liberal democracy.

7 The Contemporary UNESCO Debate on Regulation of Education

INTRODUCTION

This chapter will consider UNESCO standard-setting activities in the field of education in the mid-1970s to see how the results compare both with those in the education field in the postwar era and with contemporary developments in the communications sphere.

Educators were from the start well represented in UNESCO circles. Education was conceived by many of UNESCO's founders as the key activity of the new Agency: Ministries of Education had after all provided the wartime impetus for its creation; in many countries, they were to remain the coordinating bodies for national policy on UNESCO matters; and for some time education was the leading programme sector in the Organisation. But, in most countries and for the most part, teachers are also on the public payroll. Consequently they may be considered as commanding fewer material resources and as being less independent of the State than, for instance, media interests.

The purpose of this chapter is thus to consider how far the relatively weaker position of teachers as compared with mass media may have affected the outcome of standard-setting activities in the sphere of education. It will do so by examining the debates on three Recommendations adopted between 1974 and 1976.

1. THE RECOMMENDATION CONCERNING EDUCATION FOR INTERNATIONAL UNDERSTANDING, COOPERATION AND PEACE AND EDUCATION RELATING TO HUMAN RIGHTS AND FUNDAMENTAL FREEDOMS (UNESCO, 1974)

The above Recommendation,[1] adopted by the General Conference of UNESCO in 1974, contains a number of prescriptions concerning the goals and content of education.

128

Originating from a Polish motion[2] and following on from a number of East European initiatives of the mid-to-late 1960s,[3] the proposal for a Recommendation met with some initial reluctance of principle on the part of Western States and notably of the USA.[4] But the latter soon succeeded in extending the scope of the proposed instrument to include education relating to human rights and fundamental freedoms.[5] Thereafter, as can be seen in the pronouncements of the Nordic and EEC States, Australia, New Zealand, Switzerland and the USA,[6] Western States adopted a generally supportive stance and focussed their comments on the specifics of Secretariat drafts.

The drawing up of a preliminary report and draft recommendation[7] was entrusted to Jean Guiton (a retired French staff member who had been involved in the inconclusive attempts to draft a recommendation on the subject in the 1940s) under the supervision of Donald Irvine, an American official. In the light of written comments from Member States,[8] the Secretariat proceeded to draw up a revised draft Recommendation.[9]

At the Special Committee of Government Experts held in April–May 1974 to finalise a draft for submission to the General Conference, just over half of the amendments[10] (89 out of 167) were tabled by Western States,[11] and in particular by the USA (35 amendments).[12] Western powers sought, among other things, insertion of additional references to 'fundamental freedoms', to domestic constitutional provisions, and to 'free access to facts, opinions and ideas' as the basis for 'critical understanding'; dilution of certain recommendations to States (e.g. from 'should ensure' to 'should endeavour to ensure'); and deletion of a number of references to ethical and moral considerations, to 'direct action' to solve problems, and to the listing of certain phenomena as 'major problems' to whose understanding and solution education should contribute.

The Soviet bloc submitted 12 amendments[13] which, like their earlier written comments,[14] aimed mostly at strengthening the wording of certain passages and at inclusion of references to 'peaceful coexistence', to the 'social duties' of the individual, to development of a 'just' peace, to the 'problems' of zionism, nazism and neo-nazism, to the 'inadmissibility of using science and technology for warlike purposes', and to non-interference by States in each other's internal affairs.

Third World countries initially played only a limited part in the drafting process. The 40 developing countries represented at the intergovernmental meeting constituted a two-thirds majority.[15] But only 9 tabled amendments; nearly two-thirds of these (38 out of 60) were authored by Mexico[16] and aimed essentially at condensing what was by common consent a wordy text, while the remainder were mostly directed at minor aspects of the subject.[17]

The draft approved by the intergovernmental meeting[18] was subsequently to be described by Canada as generally 'progressive and liberal'.[19] It contained no reference to the 'responsibilities' of educators, none having in fact been proposed either in Secretariat drafts or in amendments tabled by Member States.

The goals of education were spelt out in the following statements, all introduced by the impersonal and thus liberal formula 'education should . . .':

> Education should be infused with the aims and purposes set forth in the Charter of the United Nations, the Constitution of UNESCO and the Universal Declaration of Human Rights . . .[20]
>
> . . . education . . . should develop a sense of social responsibility and of solidarity with less privileged groups . . .[21]
>
> Education should stress the inadmissibility of war, force and violence and should bring every person to understand and assume his or her responsibilities for the maintenance of peace. It should contribute to international understanding and strengthening of world peace and to the activities in the struggle against colonialism and neo-colonialism in all their forms and manifestations, and against all forms and varieties of racialism, fascism and *apartheid* as well as other ideologies which breed national and racial hatred and which are contrary to the purposes of this Recommendation.[22]
>
> Education should be directed both towards the eradication of conditions which perpetuate and aggravate major problems affecting human survival and well-being – inequality, injustice, international relations based on the use of force – and towards measures of international cooperation likely to help solve them. Education . . . should relate to such problems as:
>
> (a) equality of rights of peoples, and the rights of peoples to self-determination;
>
> (b) the maintenance of peace; different types of war and their causes and effects; disarmament; the inadmissibility of using science and technology for warlike purposes and their use for the purposes of peace and progress; . . .[23]

Similarly, in the following provisions relating to 'ethical and civic aspects' and to teacher preparation, the action envisaged by States is indirect:

Member States should take steps to ensure that the principles of the Universal Declaration of Human Rights and of the Convention on the Elimination of All Forms of Racial Discrimination become an integral part of the developing personality of each child, adolescent, young person or adult. . .[24]

Member States should urge educators . . . to use methods which appeal to the creative imagination of children . . .[25]

Member States . . . should . . . provide teachers with motivations for their subsequent work: commitment to the ethics of human rights and to the aim of changing society, so that human rights are applied in practice . . .[26]

The recommendations to Member States with respect to production and improvement of teaching materials were also liberal in form:

Member States should promote appropriate measures to ensure that educational aids, especially textbooks, are free from elements liable to give rise to misunderstanding, mistrust, racialist reactions, contempt or hatred with regard to other groups or peoples;[27]

Member States should encourage wider exchanges of textbooks . . . and should, where appropriate, take measures, by concluding, if possible, bilateral and multilateral agreements, for the reciprocal study and revision of textbooks . . . to ensure that they are accurate, balanced, up-to-date and unprejudiced and will enhance mutual knowledge and understanding between different peoples.[28]

So, again, was the provision inserted at Finnish initiative[29] to the effect that 'there should be a special component of mass media education in teaching to help pupils to select and analyse information conveyed by mass media'.[30]

Despite their liberal formulation, the above provisions bearing on the goals of education and on the role of the State are clearly more prescriptive than parallel provisions in the Media Declaration of 1978. Nevertheless they were endorsed by Western States, whose objections both in writing[31] and in the course of often heated debate[32] addressed not the principle of prescription but rather the specific nature of the educational goals and State roles to be prescribed. Thus the British delegation, although recording a formal reservation to any paragraph beginning 'Member States should' on account of the decentralised nature of the UK educational system,[33] was to declare that it favoured adoption of the instrument.[34]

But although the above draft was approved unanimously by the intergovernmental expert meeting, a Peruvian motion at the 18th session of the General Conference was to mobilise a majority behind changes which a number of Western States were to pronounce unacceptable.

The delegate from Peru, then under left-wing government, tabled an amendment in the Programme Commission proposing insertion of the following paragraphs:

Education should include critical analysis of the historical and contemporary factors of an *economic* and *political* nature underlying the *contradictions* and divisions between countries, together with ways of overcoming these contradictions, which are the real impediments to understanding, true international cooperation and the development of world peace.

Education should emphasise the *true interests* of peoples and their *incompatibility* with the *interests of monopolistic groups* holding economic and political power, which practise exploitation and foment war. (Emphases added.)[35]

This proposal was adopted in Commission by 32:8:32, and the text so amended as a whole by 72:1:6.[36]

A Nordic amendment[37] designed, according to its authors, to express the same ideas in milder form with a view to securing the desired consensus, was presented in plenary and backed by several Western States, notably Canada, France, Italy, the Netherlands, Switzerland and the USA.[38] But the representatives of a number of left-wing African governments (e.g. Algeria, the Congo, Guinea and Niger), as well as of Nigeria, Cuba and two East European States, spoke in favour of the Peruvian wording,[39] and the Nordic amendment was ultimately rejected by a narrow majority of 37:39:17.[40]

Meanwhile, in the course of debate on the above two paragraphs, the spokesman for Guinea had orally proposed an amendment to one of the paragraphs specifying the goals of education, in order to distinguish what were described as 'wars of aggression and domination' from 'wars of liberation'.[41] Five African and Arab delegates (Algeria, the Congo, Liberia, Niger and Nigeria) along with the People's Republic of China, Cuba and Ukraine voiced agreement[42] with this amendment, which was adopted by the far larger majority of 61:11:20.[43] The amended portion of the relevant paragraph reads:

Education should stress the inadmissibility of recourse to war *for purposes of expansion, aggression or domination*, or to the use of force or violence *for purposes of repression*, . . .[44] (Emphases added.)

It may be assumed that both the Peruvian and the Guinean amendments were largely unanticipated. Peru had, after all, presented no such proposals at the earlier intergovernmental meeting and had joined in the latter's unanimous adoption of a revised draft, while the Guinean amendment was presented in oral form at the last minute. As such, the two proposals provided potential opponents with little opportunity to rally effectively. It may in particular be noted in this respect that the Secretariat was aware of little press attention to the proceedings,[45] media interest at the 1974 General Conference being concentrated (as mentioned elsewhere) on the 'Israel resolutions' and election of a new Director-General.

A French motion for adjournment of the vote in General Conference plenary having been rejected, the Recommendation containing the above alterations was approved by 76:5:15,[46] over the opposition of Australia, Canada, France, West Germany and the USA.[47]

However, the delegates of the UK and Portugal, explaining their votes, declared that they had voted for the text as a whole.[48] Similarly, the delegate of post-Allende Chile held that the text contained no unacceptable concept,[49] as in fact did two lawyers who had served on US delegations to relevant meetings.[50] Moreover the USA, despite its negative vote, took measures to implement the Recommendation, with the general spirit of which it pronounced itself in sympathy.[51]

In fact, apart from the rather dramatic climate surrounding the last stages of the drafting process, the Recommendation gave rise to relatively little opposition in any quarter. Western States did not object to the principle of prescribing certain goals for education, so long as the prescriptions remained liberal in form. Soviet bloc States, for their part, had an interest as initiators of the instrument in not jeopardising its adoption by overplaying their hand: while prepared to take the floor in plenary in support of the Third World amendments, they neither pressed for more prohibitive or interventionist forms, nor sought reference to practitioner responsibilities.

2. THE REVISED RECOMMENDATION CONCERNING TECHNICAL AND VOCATIONAL EDUCATION (UNESCO, 1974)

The aim of the above Recommendation[52] was to update an earlier (1962) UNESCO instrument on the same subject, essentially to take account of the pace of technological change and its impact on employment.

An early proposal for revision of the 1962 Recommendation was made by the USA in 1968 and was echoed by several Member States in 1971.[53] A preliminary report and draft text[54] were drawn up in September 1973 by an American staff-member, Mr H. Foecke.

By the time Member States were invited to comment on the draft in 1974, the changes which had been seen to warrant revision were accelerating. The oil crisis of 1973 was aggravating underlying trends to technological unemployment and surplus capacity, and the development plans of non-oil-exporting Third World countries were especially affected. States of East, West and South, faced in varying degrees with problems of energy shortage, external debt and unemployment (including 'educated unemployment'), thus shared an interest in maximising domestic technical know-how and problem-solving capabilities.

Written comments by Member States[55] on the Secretariat's preliminary draft in the event revealed consensus across the political spectrum both on the timeliness of revision of the earlier instrument and on the general considerations underlying the Secretariat text.

Third World countries (in particular Cameroon, Colombia, Kuwait, Laos, Liberia, Peru and Tunisia) saw technical and vocational education as a crucial factor in overall development.[56] Lacking many of the necessary resources, they pressed vigorously for greater assistance – both through UNESCO and bilaterally – in constructing and carrying out programmes appropriate to local conditions.

General agreement was evident, too, concerning a need both to enhance the status of technical and vocational education relative to more traditional or 'academic' curricula, and to incorporate more elements of a technical nature in general education from an early stage.[57] The principle of stressing breadth and flexibility in the substance and organisation of technical/vocational education in order to maximise adaptability and transferability during working lives was also widely endorsed, as was that of planning it in such a way as to achieve a satisfactory match with national manpower requirements (whether through central planning or 'realistic guidance' as to likely job outlets).[58]

A further area of agreement concerned the need for practical components in technical and vocational education, notably through periods spent in the relevant occupational sector and through association of employers in the design and evaluation of courses. Contention in this connection was confined to the extent to which the private sector should influence the form and content of education, the USSR,

East Germany and Finland favouring less[59] and Switzerland and the USA greater involvement.[60] Positions were reconciled by avoidance of such terms as 'business' and 'management', and resort to more neutral turns of phrase ('employers', 'industry', 'enterprises'. . .).[61]

Revision of the earlier text to place technical and vocational education in the context of the newly-evolved concept of 'life-long learning' and to stress its contribution to enhancing the quality of life and productiveness of leisure were also broadly supported.

A meeting of government experts, at which Third World countries accounted for three-fifths of the 49 States represented,[62] was held in May 1974 to finalise a draft for the General Conference.

The objectives of technical and vocational education were redefined in the Revised Recommendation to specify that this type of education should

(a) contribute to achievement of society's goals of greater demo-
cratisation and social, economic and cultural development, while at the same time developing the potential of individuals for active participation in the establishment and implementation of these goals;

(b) lead to an understanding of the scientific and technological aspects of contemporary civilization in such a way that men comprehend their environment and are capable of acting upon it while taking a critical view of the social, political and environmental implications of scientific and technological change.[63]

This wording was based on Secretariat proposals,[64] modified at French initiative[65] to add the notion of active influence on the social environment to that of mere understanding. Although its key terms are not defined, it can be seen that the above passage is more normative than corresponding portions of the 1978 Media Declaration.

The Revised Recommendation also contains a few references to 'responsibilities' and prescriptions relating to teachers and administrators. These too reflect the wording of the Secretariat's original draft,[66] amended in one case at French instigation:[67]

All programmes of technical and vocational education . . . should . . . stress a sense of professional values and responsibilities from the standpoint of human needs . . .[68]
Programmes . . . should be developed with particular attention to
(a) the inclusion of components directed to developing attitudes

whereby those with particular responsibilities in technological fields constantly relate their professional tasks to larger human goals . . .[69]
Teachers . . . should . . . develop the ability to relate [a broad range of specialities] to the larger social, economic and historical and cultural context . . .[70]
Administrators should keep up to date . . .[71]

But the treatment of responsibilities in the above few provisions may be regarded as relatively abstract, and in the event occasioned no objections on the part of Western States.

Meanwhile the Democratic Republic of Germany secured insertion in the preamble of the following reference to peace:

Recognising that technical and vocational education have to contribute to the maintenance of peace and friendly relations between the various nations, . . .[72]

However, a further East German draft amendment[73] to specify in an operative paragraph that 'the general part' of technical and vocational education should 'serve the requirements of peace and relations of friendship between countries with different political and social systems' was rejected. So, too, was yet another East German proposal that the preparation of guidance staff should include politics.[74]

But these were in fact the sole Soviet bloc attempts to relate technical and vocational education to 'education for peace and international understanding', and no suggestions were presented by these States for revision of the liberal formulation of the Secretariat's drafts along more interventionist or 'negative' lines.

Moreover, only three East European countries (East Germany, Hungary and Poland) sent delegations to the intergovernmental meeting convened in Paris in May 1974 to finalise the draft Revised Recommendation, as compared with eight in the case of the meeting – also held in Paris in May 1974 – to consider the draft Recommendation on education for international understanding discussed earlier.[75] The text as revised by the meeting of governmental experts[76] was adopted unanimously by the meeting itself[77] and, after one minor amendment in the Programme Commission,[78] by the General Conference plenary.[79]

The Soviet bloc would in fact seem to have concentrated its efforts to regulate educational content in 1974 on the Recommendation on education for international understanding which, adopted at the same session of the General Conference, was not only a Soviet bloc project but dealt more centrally with content. Indeed, the stress in the Revised Recommendation on Technical and Vocational Education on preparation for flexibility implied constantly evolving content and thus virtually precluded specification of subject matter. The focus instead was on structures, funding, integration with other forms of education, and linkages with the broader economy. In this intrinsic sense, the Revised Recommendation offered fewer openings for advocacy on behalf of 'education for peace'.

The importance explicitly attached to the Revised Recommendation by Third World delegates would no doubt also have served to limit the vigour with which the Soviet bloc (and developing countries themselves) might otherwise have pressed positions unacceptable to the West. But in any case, in the circumstances of the time, States across the board proved broadly to share an approach which could be seen not only to place a premium on raising technical skill levels as against acquisition of more academic types of knowledge in technical and vocational education itself, but also to involve some degree of 'technicisation' of curricula in general education.

3. THE RECOMMENDATION ON THE DEVELOPMENT OF ADULT EDUCATION (UNESCO, 1976)

The central purpose of the above Recommendation,[80] which arose out of a UNESCO world conference on adult education in 1972, was described by the American Deputy Director-General, John Fobes, as being to 'mobilise political support' for the development of adult education in the perspective of life-long learning.[81]

The preliminary report and draft were prepared under contract by a French national, Mr Bellogé, supervised by a Danish staff member, Mr Paul Bertelsen.[82] On the basis of comments received from Member States,[83] a revised draft was prepared in April 1976.[84]

By this time, global economic recession was intensifying and with it the scale of actual or potential social unrest. In the circumstances, States of North and South alike had a continuing interest in attempting to sharpen their relative competitive positions by raising the general level of skills within their borders. But they could also be seen as having an interest, at the very least, in defusing possible support for radical protest or reform by promoting enhanced individual fulfilment at the social and cultural levels among those worst hit by recession.

Preoccupations of this order were discernible in the approaches of States to the draft Recommendation on adult education. As in the case of the Revised Recommendation on Technical and Vocational Education, albeit to a slightly lesser extent, the positions of States of the West, Soviet bloc and Third World were to display a large measure of harmony both with respect to the need for an international instrument and with respect to many basic aspects of the Secretariat's draft.

The themes recurring most frequently in Secretariat drafts,[85] in Member States' comments[86] and in draft amendments[87] were those of rapid social change and the need to develop the ability to cope with, adjust to and/or influence the direction of change.

Meanwhile, several countries in each of the three conventional groupings considered that the preliminary draft insufficiently reflected such concepts as 'life-long education', 'the learning society' and 'self-directed instruction'; that it needed to relate adult education more closely to national development plans and/or to community development; that it took too little practical account of the problems of the least privileged and of women; and that it should strengthen the provisions on financing.[88] A number of Western and Third World States also shared the view that the draft wrongly conceived of adult education as being 'particularly' concerned with those in or seeking employment.[89]

Other themes stressed across the board were the relevance of adult education to creation of 'critical' awareness and/or understanding of socio-economic conditions; to promoting active and 'responsible' participation in all social spheres; to improving the quality of life and leisure; and to stimulating a spirit of mutual assistance and solidarity among adult learners as against that of competition.[90]

By the same token, such differences of opinion as arose were divided as much within as between the three sets of countries (although a more pronounced tendency was observable among Third World countries to view adult education in the context of literacy work,[91] and among Soviet bloc States – which hesitate to admit to the existence of unemployment in their societies – to stress the upgrading of skills and general knowledge only among workers.[92])

Thus, for instance, Canada, Spain and the USA shared with East Germany and Poland the view that the accent in adult education should be placed less exclusively on vocational/economic aspects and more on enhancing the social/cultural/political development of the individual and/or of the community.[93]

The extent of agreement was evidenced by the tabling at the intergovernmental meeting responsible for finalising a text for the General Conference of over twenty joint amendments sponsored by various combinations of, on the one hand, Belgium, France, West Germany, post-Salazar Portugal, Finland, Norway and occasionally the UK and USA; and on the other hand Yugoslavia, Iran and a number of African States of diverse political persuasion.[94] (Not the least telling of these, in times of generalised bureaucratic cutbacks, was a numerically well-backed proposal[95] further supported by Canada and Sweden,[96] for increased staffing and funding of the UNESCO adult education unit.) Conversely, the large number of amendments presented in all[97] (275, over half sponsored by Western delegations) was misleading insofar as many aimed chiefly at compression and stylistic improvement of the text.

Joint proposals of the sort just described led to revision of the principles on which it was recommended that adult education should be based. For example, at the suggestion of Portugal, Yugoslavia, the Central African Republic and the Congo,[98] education should be planned

> with a view to transformation of the working environment and of the life of adults . . .[99]

(although the direction of such transformation was not specified); while at the instigation of West Germany, Portugal, Yugoslavia, the Central African Republic, the Congo and Senegal,[100]

> it should contribute to the economic and social development of the entire community.[101]

Nevertheless, some disagreement was to emerge along broadly traditional lines in relation to the goals of adult education. Thus, at the initiative of Finland, Czechoslovakia and Hungary,[102] 'promoting work for peace, international understanding and cooperation' was added to and listed first among the aims to which adult education should contribute;[103] while at the suggestion of the same three States together with Ethiopia and Norway,[104] a similar reference was also included in the preamble.[105] American attempts either to delete these references or to reorder the priorities[106] were unsuccessful.

Some contention also arose in connection with references to mass media. For instance, Western delegations (notably those of Canada,

Denmark, Netherlands, the UK and the USA) sought deletion[107] of one of the aims to which the Secretariat had proposed that adult education should contribute, namely

> developing the necessary discernment in using mass communication media, in particular radio, television, cinema and the press, and interpreting the various messages addressed to modern man by society.[108]

In the event, apart from replacing the word 'man' by the words 'men and women', the intergovernmental meeting retained the original Secretariat wording.[109] However, the revised draft not only referred to guaranteeing the freedom of expression of mass media,[110] but contained no prescriptions regarding media content, and as it happened Western States did not reopen debate on this point at the General Conference.

One of the very few provisions to be the subject of a draft amendment at the General Conference also bore – implicitly at least – on media content and regulation, notably with respect to sex-typing of social roles. The USA unsuccessfully moved[111] deletion of a provision in the section on contents,[112] representing a modified version of an earlier Portuguese and Yugoslav proposal,[113] to the effect that adult education should aim at

> the emancipation of men and women from preconceived models imposed on them by society . . .[114]

A number of Soviet bloc suggestions were also overruled or diluted, including proposals for reference to 'the obligation of the State to promote the desire of adults for education' and to 'moral preparation for active social participation'.[115] Meanwhile a Czechoslovak proposal that the content of adult education include

> education for peace and measures to counteract war propaganda and incitement to hatred on grounds of race, politics or nationality,[116]

although reflected in the revised Secretariat draft,[117] was later dropped[118] following adoption of a synthesised version of the relevant paragraph proposed by Denmark.[119] However, neither the Soviet bloc nor the Third World engaged in any noticeable effort to prescribe 'duties' for educators of adults or to replace the impersonally-worded sections on the aims, principles and content by more interventionist or 'prohibitive' phraseology.

While prescribing certain goals for adult education, including promotion of peace, the Recommendation thus remained liberal in form. The revised draft[120] was adopted unanimously by the inter-governmental expert meeting of June 1976[121] and, after minor amendment and minimal debate in the Programme Commission, by the General Conference at its 19th session.[122]

The debate on the Recommendation on Adult Education may thus be said to have revealed a fair degree of harmony between the major groupings of States. True, being related less exclusively to employment and more to personal development than the Revised Recommendation on Technical and Vocational Education, the adult education text afforded somewhat greater scope than the former for controversy over goals and content.

But like the former instrument, it was not primarily concerned either with content or with a Soviet bloc project. Moreover the session of the General Conference to which it was presented for adoption in 1976 was also, as shown in Chapter 5, the session where confrontation over the Media Declaration (which, by contrast, was a Soviet bloc initiative) intensified seriously. In addition to these factors, Western, Eastern European and Third World States, all in the grip of global recession, largely shared a conception of adult education as a means not only to skill enhancement, but also to 'responsible participation'.

SUMMARY AND CONCLUSIONS

Some twenty-five years after the failure of the first attempts at drafting a standard-setting text on education for peace and international understanding, the new majority within UNESCO, led by the Soviet bloc, secured adoption of a Recommendation on the subject expanded at Western initiative to include education relating to human rights and fundamental freedoms.

The three standard-setting instruments considered in this chapter all remained liberal in form, calling for only indirect action on the part of States and laying down no duties on the part of practitioners to dispense any specific educational content.

At the same time, the three Recommendations were also all more prescriptive with respect to the goals of knowledge than the 1978 Media Declaration. The contrast was most marked in the case of the Recommendation on education for international understanding, the only text of the three to be primarily concerned with content. But as we have seen, in none of the instruments (with the possible exception of a few aspects of the latter text amended at Third World initiative) did the level or content of prescription exceed the bounds of acceptability to leading Western States.

In the event, however, achievement of these outcomes did not require the mobilisation of teachers' organisations or mass media, nor could they even be attributed to the fact that the officials involved were all Western. Rather, they may be chiefly explained by the fact that the new majority did not press for any greater degree of regulation. This restraint, in turn, was shown to be attributable in the case of the Recommendation on education for international understanding to the interest of Soviet bloc States in not jeopardising a standard-setting project they had initiated by pressing their policy preferences to extremes.

The Recommendations on Technical and Vocational Education and on Adult Education, meanwhile, were neither Soviet bloc initiatives nor centrally concerned with content. In addition, the fact that Third World States attached especial importance to the former and to securing Northern assistance in implementing it favoured restraint on the part of both developing and East European States in that instance. Moreover the three major groupings of States broadly concurred in their approaches to these two Recommendations as means of coping with change and potential public disaffection in the mid-1970s, technical/vocational education and adult education being conceived in practice on all sides as conducive not only to raised skill levels but also to 'responsible participation'.

8 Scrutiny of Textbooks used in UNRWA/ UNESCO Schools: A Precedent for 'Politicisation'?

INTRODUCTION

This chapter will examine a set of developments within UNESCO which may plausibly be regarded as a precedent for 'politicisation', as that term is conventionally understood in the West, but which has not – either at the time or since – been presented as such. The events in question concern the UNESCO-sponsored screening, following the June 1967 Middle East war, of textbooks used in the education of Palestinian refugees in UNRWA/UNESCO schools.

The subject was debated at length in the Executive Board of UNESCO between 1967 and 1971,[1] but the records remain largely unresearched and the episode itself passed virtually unnoticed in Western circles. The very unfamiliarity of the incident is central to our argument on 'politicisation'.

It may be recalled that, in Chapter 1, the concept of 'politicisation' as used by Western policy-makers and commentators was found to comprise the following components: (a) the intrusion of 'extraneous politics' arising from altered power relations in the wider environment; (b) challenges to established Agency policy (and, in the specific case of UNESCO, to the principle of freedom of information); (c) the operation of a double standard in the upholding of national sovereignty; and (d) the exercise of 'selective morality'.

The purpose of this chapter will be to analyse the Executive Board decision to screen the textbooks to see how far it may be held to correspond to 'politicisation' so defined. First, we shall briefly review the origins and outcome of the debate as well as the representation of the contending interests on the Board at the time of the relevant decisions.

1.   THE ORIGINS AND OUTCOME OF THE DEBATE

Since 1950, the United Nations Relief and Works Agency for Palestine Refugees in the Near East (UNRWA) and UNESCO have jointly administered a programme of education for Palestinian refugees.[2] UNRWA, based in Beirut, held its mandate from the UN General Assembly and was assigned administrative responsibility for the programme; UNESCO, based in Paris, was allotted substantive (educational) responsibility.[3] UNRWA and UNESCO established and administered schools for Palestinian refugees in territory under the formal sovereignty, the informal sovereignty, or the administrative control of the four Arab States bordering on Israel (Egypt, Jordan, Lebanon and Syria). The programme was governed by the terms of an agreement between UNRWA and UNESCO,[4] which required the two Agencies to act in consultation 'with the governments concerned'.[5]

As a consequence of the 1967 war, UNRWA/UNESCO schools attended by some 55000 refugee children in the Gaza Strip, the West Bank, the Golan Heights and East Jerusalem came under *de facto* Israeli control.[6] In the non-refugee (i.e. national) schools in the Golan Heights and East Jerusalem, the Israeli authorities replaced existing textbooks with those prescribed for use in Arab schools in Israel. Meanwhile, in national schools in the West Bank and the Gaza Strip, Israel introduced Israeli-edited versions of Jordanian and Egyptian textbooks.[7]

In the case of the UNRWA/UNESCO schools in the occupied territories, the Israeli authorities began to impound textbooks from June 1967 onward, proceeding either to discard or to revise them. They notified UNRWA accordingly, adding that they were compiling a file which, they claimed, would prove that the schools were imparting distorted history and that they were 'systematically indoctrinating the children [in them] with hatred against Israel'.[8] However, the Israeli authorities did not notify UNESCO, the Agency with substantive responsibility for the programme, that they had embarked on this course of action.[9]

The Commissioner-General for UNRWA, when approached by the Israeli authorities, agreed to defer to their wishes regarding the content of education dispensed in UNRWA/UNESCO schools although, rather than retaining for use in the schools books physically edited by Israel, the UNRWA Secretariat issued 'teaching notes' reproducing the Israeli-approved texts.[10] Thus, for practical purposes, the Commissioner-General for UNRWA treated Israel as one of 'the governments concerned' under the UNRWA/UNESCO agreement mentioned above. An important reason advanced for so doing was adverse media coverage, notably in the Israeli press and on French television.[11]

UNESCO, meanwhile, became aware of the above developments through unfavourable Western publicity regarding the textbooks,[12] and the question arose of whether or not it should pursue the same course as UNRWA. The Director-General of UNESCO considered that the Secretariat could not settle the question – and specifically could not include Israel among 'the governments concerned' under the UNRWA/UNESCO agreement – on its own authority, but would require a policy decision on the part of the Agency's governing bodies.[13]

The Director-General therefore referred the matter to the Executive Board, requesting that body to decide whether or not UNESCO should continue to administer the programme with UNRWA and, if so, whether it should emulate the UNRWA policy of accommodating Israeli preferences with regard to educational content.[14]

On 3 November 1967, the Executive Board authorised continued cooperation with UNRWA for the education of Palestine refugees in both Arab- and Israeli-administered territory.[15] But at the same time, it decided that the education so dispensed should conform to certain standards,[16] the standards in question representing an unweighted amalgam of the criteria proposed respectively by the Arab States[17] and by Israel.[18] (For the text of the decision, see Appendix III.)

The implication of this decision, as the Director-General saw it, was that the textbooks would have to be examined.[19] At subsequent meetings, the Executive Board made this implication explicit and agreed (at the Director-General's suggestion)[20] that the task be entrusted to a Commission of 'outside experts', to be set up for the purpose, rather than to the Secretariat.[21] A Commission consisting of three Western 'Arabists' (one each from the USA, France and Turkey)[22] was duly appointed, and reported on its scrutiny of the textbooks in February 1969.[23]

2. REPRESENTATION ON THE EXECUTIVE BOARD IN 1967–8

The policy decisions to screen the textbooks and to set up an expert commission were taken during 1967 and 1968 by the Executive Board, a restricted-membership body sitting between sessions of the General Conference and consisting at the time of thirty members.*

Of the main protagonists, Israel happened to be a member of the Board for all of the sessions at which the subject was discussed except for the last two meetings on the subject in 1971. Two of the Arab host States, namely Egypt† and the Lebanon, were also represented. Meanwhile those Arab countries directly concerned but not members of the Board were entitled, as Member States, to be heard by the latter although not to vote.

The Palestinians, as the third party centrally affected, enjoyed no direct representation, the debate having taken place several years before the PLO was granted observer status within the UN system. (The Arab States, of course, often spoke in the vocabulary of Palestinian welfare, but an identity of interests should not be too readily assumed. The fact that certificates issued by Israel following examinations held under its supervision in the occupied territories in 1968 were not recognised by Arab governments when presented in support of applications for admission to higher levels of education in the Arab countries provides an example of the limits to shared Arab State and Palestinian interests.[24] The refusal of the Arab States to allow continued use of the provisional teaching notes mentioned earlier after the Commission of Outside Experts had cleared for use those textbooks they replaced, but before Israel had authorised import of the books into the relevant territories, illustrates the point further: in many cases UNRWA/UNESCO schools were left for up to a year with no teaching materials at all.[25])

Meanwhile, the Soviet bloc was represented on the Board by three members (from Hungary, Rumania and the USSR). These members on the whole endorsed the Arab position, although the Rumanian stance tended to be more ambivalent.[26] The Arab side could therefore generally count on mustering 5 votes.

Seven African and 3 Asian countries (of which Iran and Japan) were also represented on the Board, but took relatively little part in negotiations and adopted no clear position on the policy issues. Of the former, meanwhile, the Nigerian and Ivory Coast members were to declare that they were in receipt of aid from and were on good terms with Israel.[27] Latin America accounted for 6 members, who were to

---

*For the list of members, see Appendix IV.
† During the period under review, Egypt's name changed twice. For simplicity, we shall refer throughout to 'Egypt'.

prove active in seeking a compromise between Israeli and Arab positions. Finally the West, including the USA, held a balance of 8 votes.

Let us now consider how far the Board's decisions of 1967 and 1968 match the definition of 'politicisation' set out earlier.

3. AN INTRUSION OF 'EXTRANEOUS' POLITICS?

First, to what extent should the sequence of events described above be seen as an intrusion of 'extraneous' politics? Clearly, the situation was a direct product of political and military developments external to UNESCO; specifically, it was the result of Israel's victory in the June 1967 war and of altered power relations in the area. It would therefore seem to correspond to 'politicisation' at this first level. Nevertheless, it could be argued that since Israel did not seize UNESCO of the matter officially, it was not responsible for 'politicising' the Agency's proceedings. Indeed, as we have seen, the proximate initiator of debate on the textbooks was the Director-General.

However, this would seem to be an unduly restrictive reading of the situation. It seems fair to conclude that, by entering schools which (as we shall see) Israel itself defined as 'international', and by altering the content of their teaching materials without the authority of the international Agency substantively responsible, Israel constructively 'politicised' the issue. The words of the Israeli member of the Board would seem to support this view of the matter:

> [Israel] had not thought it appropriate to raise a political issue before the Board, but had sought – as on other occasions – to make [sic] a constructive approach to the problem.[28]

The alternative to formal discussion of the changed political circumstances (Israeli occupation) and their direct educational consequences (censorship) would have been to acquiesce silently, and in that sense to legitimise the accomplished fact. It was precisely for his failure to challenge the legitimacy of Israeli actions on the ground, and indeed for what was seen as his readiness to legitimise them by treating Israel as one of 'the governments concerned' under the UNRWA/ UNESCO agreement, that the Arab States had criticised the Commissioner-General for UNRWA.[29] It therefore seems reasonable to assume that considerations of this order underlay the decision of the Director-General of UNESCO to consult the Executive Board before following suit.

4.   A CHALLENGE TO ESTABLISHED POLICY?

It will be argued below that the decision to screen the textbooks used in the education of Palestinian refugees constituted a departure from established policy at two levels. First, it reversed the specific UNRWA/UNESCO policy of non-intervention in educational content; secondly, it reversed the consensus on non-intervention more generally.

A.   Reversal of UNRWA/UNESCO policy of 'integration' and non-intervention

Prior to June 1967, UNRWA and UNESCO had provided no separate education system for the refugees but had, instead, based their policy on the principle of 'integration' with the systems of the Arab host States. By this was meant that no special textbooks would be prepared for UNRWA/UNESCO establishments; instead these establishments would use, unscreened and unaltered, the curricula and teaching materials prescribed for use in the schools of the host States.

Historically, there were a number of grounds for adopting this approach.[30] One reason was that, as a result of its perennial financial precariousness,*[31] UNRWA was unable to fund a fully comprehensive education system and, in particular, operated no secondary schools. Consequently, the children tended to pursue their secondary and higher education in institutions in the host countries. The refugee children's overall prospects were in fact seen as dependent largely upon their passing State examinations in the Arab host countries and upon receiving Government certificates from those States. Moreover, the possibility that it might at any time have to cease operations for financial reasons had obliged UNRWA to think in terms of potential successors and, until 1967 at least, the most likely candidates for the role seemed to be the Arab host States.

But the most crucial reason for the policy of 'integration' and non-intervention, for the purposes of the present argument, was that it had been felt that any attempt to create a separate, 'internationally-orientated' and 'politically innocuous' system would have involved the

---

* Unlike UNESCO, UNRWA has no regular budget but is funded wholly by voluntary contributions, supplied mostly by the West. The Arab States, holding the West responsible for the refugee status of the Palestinians, have not contributed on a large scale to UNRWA as such, but have matched or exceeded the latter's payments in 'counterpart expenditure'.

two Agencies in highly sensitive issues of political judgement.[32] In the words of the Commissioner-General for UNRWA,

> Such an attempt would have led the Agency into a direct collision with the host countries in matters of a highly political and controversial nature where not merely the interpretation of facts and events but even the very facts and events themselves are widely disputed. As a purely humanitarian Organisation, UNRWA has no competence in political matters and would have been treading on very dangerous ground if its officials had attempted to censor the textbooks prescribed by the host governments. This would have involved exercising a necessarily subjective judgement of their truth and objectivity.[33]

It would thus have compelled UNRWA and UNESCO to engage in explicit politics, and thereby to exceed what were normally treated as technical and humanitarian mandates.

(Although we do not intend to enter into the substantive debate on the content of the textbooks,[34] an example of the problems involved in the preparation of 'neutral' textbooks may be helpful. The drawing and labelling of maps probably serves the purpose as well as any: for Israelis, as for most Western States, the territory lying between Egypt, Jordan, the Lebanon and Syria is 'Israel'; for many Palestinian and Arab observers, however, it is more accurately described as 'the usurped portion of Palestine'.)

It is, of course, possible to take issue with the above rationalisations for the UNRWA/UNESCO policy of non-intervention, as Israel pointed out that it had attempted to do on more than one occasion before 1967.[35] It remains, however, that the decision to screen the textbooks represented a reversal of established practice, prompted by Israeli military victory.

B. Reversal of liberal principles

Besides reversing the specific policy of the UNWRA/UNESCO education programme, the decision in favour of intergovernmental control of the textbooks represented a departure from UNESCO's policy of non-intervention more generally.

To understand how these reversals came to be sanctioned, it is necessary to examine the positions advanced by the contending parties in the Executive Board.

(a) Israel's position: control of 'international' (UNRWA/
UNESCO) education in the interests of peace

As we have seen, Israel favoured revision of the textbooks, either
under its own auspices or, failing this, under UNESCO aegis. Israel
was to define the principles at stake as less political than humanitarian
and ethical.[36]

The humanitarian consideration, the Israeli Board member contended, was to ensure that the Palestinian children continued to
receive education. The ethical concern, meanwhile, was to guarantee
that the content of education in UNRWA/UNESCO schools con-
formed to the ideals laid down in the UN Charter, in UNESCO's
Constitution, and in Article 26(2) of the Universal Declaration of
Human Rights.* Indeed, a central if not the major aspect of the Israeli
case was its insistence on the 'international' character of the UNRWA/
UNESCO schools.[37] In Israel's view, the fact that these schools were
'international' or 'internationally sponsored' rendered the need to
guarantee ethical content especially pressing. The Israeli member
claimed that 'hatred had been taught for years under the UN flag', and
that such a situation was intolerable.[38]

Israel went further, extending the argument beyond the schools as
such to encompass any student sponsored by UNRWA. It sought to
maximise the scope of any scrutiny exercise, urging that it apply to
teaching materials used in UNRWA/UNESCO establishments not
only in the occupied territories but also in Arab-administered territory
and, indeed, in any school attended by pupils 'receiving grants,
allowances or subsidies from UNRWA'.[39] (Potentially, as the Lebanese and Syrian spokesmen remarked, this opened the door to scrutiny
of teaching materials employed in every school in the Arab world,
including foreign schools where curricula might match those in use in
the parent countries.[40]) Similarly, at the same time as describing its
own involvement in the running of the schools as minimal, Israel was
regularly to stress the 'international' – and thus implicitly more neutral
and legitimate – character of the scrutiny exercise itself.[41]

In the name of peace, Israel thus sought so far as possible to
'depoliticise' the education of Palestinian refugees. In this spirit, Israel
urged that the official insignia of issuing countries be removed from
Arab textbooks so as to 'avoid political implications' in UNRWA/

---

* The text of this Article is reproduced in the Executive Board decision of 3 November
1967 (see Appendix III).

UNESCO establishments, and suggested that they be replaced by UN or UNESCO emblems.[42] At a later stage, Israel also endorsed a proposal by the Commission of Outside Experts that UNESCO prepare model textbooks for the UNRWA/UNESCO schools.[43]

For Israel, to summarise, the issue at stake was ethical content of education identified as 'international'.

(b) The Arab States' position: freedom of education

The Arab States defined the matter rather differently.[44] In the Arab view the matter was at heart political, rather than humanitarian or ethical, since it stemmed from Israel's occupation of Arab territories and from its censorship activities on the spot.[45]

The Arab members maintained that UNESCO-sponsored screening of the textbooks would be tantamount to legitimising Israeli occupation and expansionism.[46] In their view, moreover, it would encourage Israeli tactics of cultural and political assimilation by denationalising the textbook, the pupil, and ultimately the nation.[47] The exercise, they argued, would amount to pacification through control of culture and would work to the advantage of objective Israeli interests.

Spokesmen for the Arab and Muslim view (most notably Algeria, Egypt, Jordan, Pakistan and Syria) claimed that if there was hatred among the children, it was hatred of aggression; and that such hatred should be attributed not so much to indoctrination as to the historical and material facts of Zionist/Israeli treatment of the Palestinian people.[48] The circumstances of the Palestinians, Arab members contended, were themselves political; hence to 'depoliticise' their education while leaving their situation unaltered would be political in the extreme.

In other words, the Arab side considered what it saw as the rewriting of Palestinian history to be profoundly political. In opposition to Israel's call for the control of Palestinian education in the interests of 'peace', they stressed the principle of freedom of Palestinian culture and the refugees' right to a history of their own.

In support of their position, the Arab members invoked Article 26(3) of the Universal Declaration of Human Rights, endorsing parents' prior right to choose the education dispensed to their children. Similarly, they invoked a 1956 UNESCO resolution on the 'free functioning of education', which advocates compatibility of education with the traditions of those educated:

. . . everywhere education shall respect the cultural, religious, national and linguistic traditions of the inhabitants and its nature shall not be altered for political reasons.[49]

(This text had been adopted by UNESCO at the time of the Suez crisis, when a situation analogous to that prevailing after the June 1967 war had been anticipated.) Finally, Lebanese spokesmen explicitly called attention to the freedom of educational establishments in the Lebanon to select their own textbooks.[50]

Ultimately, however, the Arab members consented to the revised terms of UNESCO cooperation with UNRWA. In so doing, they were no doubt motivated not only by recognition of their own minority position on the Executive Board, but by the likelihood that a refusal would put an end to the UNRWA/UNESCO education programme and in the process earn them considerable opprobrium. Syria alone consistently refused, on principle, to condone or take part in the screening exercise.[51]

(c)   The position of the Director-General

The position of the Director-General, René Maheu of France, was important for both institutional and personal reasons. Institutionally, the Director-General was responsible for introducing and setting the terms of the debate; personally, he was a 'strong' executive head of acknowledged intellectual calibre.

For the Director-General, the prime consideration would seem to have been to safeguard what he termed UNESCO's 'moral authority'.[52] Maheu's words and actions reveal a consistent concern to distance the Secretariat from any scrutiny exercise and to strike a balance which would be regarded as fair by all concerned.[53]

In several respects, the Director-General's policy was unfavourable to Israel. As we have seen, he refused to allow either Israel's policy or UNRWA's subsequent compliance to become UNESCO policy by default. He also adhered throughout to the official UN stance on Israeli occupation, and to the view that occupation conferred on the occupier no legal right to be consulted regarding educational content.[54]

However, on the central question of the legitimacy of intergovernmental controls, the Director-General was to espouse the Israeli rather than the Arab definition of the matter. Characterising the problem before UNESCO as ethical rather than political, the Director-General asserted UNESCO's general jurisdiction with respect to questions relating to the content of education for which, he stated,

> UNESCO is competent not only within the framework of the UNRWA/UNESCO agreement, but also according to its very Constitution . . .[55]

It is highly significant, however, that not long afterwards the Director-General should have pointed out that the exercise was the first of its kind in UNESCO history.[56]

(d)   The Western position

Finally, the position of Western States and their supporters. The role of these States was crucial not only in view of their traditional advocacy of liberal principles but because, as shown above, they held a balance on the Executive Board at the time of the initial policy decisions.

The stance of leading Western members of the Board proved, in the event, to be noticeably muted. The USA and UK, in particular, seldom took the floor; and when they did, they confined themselves for the most part to abstract commendations of the principle of objectivity. The American member of the Board, for instance, in a brief endorsement of the decision to monitor the content of the education provided in UNRWA/UNESCO schools, declared himself in favour of

> any solution which would enable UNESCO and UNRWA to ensure that the textbooks used were of an objective nature and that the education provided would prepare students to live constructive lives in their own societies.*[57]

French members of the Board, on the other hand, proved slightly more forthcoming on the subject of UNESCO's peace-making role (*action pacificatrice*).[58] Meanwhile members from Italy, the Netherlands and Switzerland spoke positively in support both of screening the textbooks and of creating an expert Commission,[59] and on occasion sponsored jointly with Latin American members what were presented as 'compromise' resolutions.[60]

It should be noted, however, that the 'compromise' in such motions related to the particular guidelines for examination of the textbooks, not to the principle of monitoring as such. Between monitoring the

* The meaning of the term 'own societies' in relation to the refugees is not entirely clear.

textbooks and not monitoring them, clearly no compromise was possible; and the eight Western members, along with the six Latin Americans and Israel acquiesced in the principle of intergovernmental control.

But at no point did Western spokesmen allude to the principles of freedom of information or professional pluralism, even as considerations of a secondary order. The position adopted by Israel, the Western members and the Director-General amounted to a statement of UNESCO's duty, by virtue of its ethical and constitutional commitments, to regulate the content of education dispensed to Palestinian refugees in the interests of peace.[61]

This position cannot be faulted in a strict constitutional sense. But it obscures the fact that, as shown in earlier chapters, UNESCO's ethical commitment had not previously, and to date still has not been taken by Western Members to justify intergovernmental control over information and textbook content. Even in the case of German 're-education', as shown in Chapter 6, UNESCO involvement did not take the form of direct scrutiny of teaching materials.

5.   A DOUBLE STANDARD ON NATIONAL SOVEREIGNTY?

Let us now consider whether the scrutiny exercise involved a double standard in the upholding of national sovereignty.

Much of the debate centred on whether or not the national sovereignty of Arab States was in fact involved at all. As we have seen, a central element of the Israeli case was its emphasis on the international identity of the UNRWA/UNESCO programme, and the special need to ensure the ethical content of internationally-sponsored education.

Once again, however, the Arab States defined the matter differently. The Arab view, expressed most forcefully by Syria, held that to characterise the scrutiny exercise as concerning only internationally-sponsored education was misleading. The teaching materials at issue were prescribed first and foremost for use in national education systems, and only coincidentally for use in 'international' schools.[62]

Since the texts used in UNRWA/UNESCO schools and those used in host State education establishments were identical, it would be impossible to distinguish between the two for purposes of scrutiny. Examination of textbooks used 'internationally' would necessarily involve screening of national education systems and, hence, in the view of the Arab States, violation of their sovereignty in this field.[63] For the Arab States, therefore, the relevant criterion was not the source of sponsorship (international), but rather the source and primary use of the textbooks (national).

At the time of the initial decision of principle, the Director-General, Israel and the Western States glossed over the fact that the texts were used in the host countries' own schools, or else defined it as secondary. In introducing the debate, for example, the Director-General express-ed the view that the textbook issue 'did not concern national schools' and thus 'did not involve interference in the internal affairs of States',[64] thereby endorsing the Israeli rather than the Arab view of the matter. Western members, for their part, did not broach the question of sovereignty at all.

However, at later stages of the exercise, the Director-General explicitly recognised that, despite the international character of the schools, 'they are nevertheless integrated into national structures', and that the Arab States' concession had been noteworthy.[65] The Director-General also stated that to acknowledge rights of educational over-sight for the occupying power in this particular instance would be 'especially abnormal, given that the textbooks in question are used in non-occupied parts of the countries concerned'.[66] Israel too, although making a different point, was later to remark that the books were used throughout the host States' school systems.[67]

These statements must surely be regarded as highly revealing. Indeed, it might well have appeared to pro-Arab opinion that the prevailing definition of the exercise as purely 'international' in incidence was a sleight of hand, concealing a double standard with regard to national sovereignty. For the majority definition of the problem as one unrelated to national sovereignty had important moral implications, to which we now turn.

6. AN EXERCISE IN SELECTIVE MORALITY?

It remains in this section to consider whether the decision to screen the Arab textbooks constitutes evidence of selective morality on the part of supporters of the decision; and this question relates directly to the discussion on national sovereignty.

If the exercise was defined as affecting only internationally-sponsored schools and students or, still more narrowly, only the

UNRWA/UNESCO education system, then it could be treated as unique. Israeli strategy was to stress uniqueness, and it was the argument from uniqueness which prevailed. Definition of the moral issue as ethical content of internationally-sponsored or UNRWA/ UNESCO education, rather than ethical content of education in general, enabled Israel to claim that the content of its own teaching materials was irrelevant.[68] Hence the scrutiny exercise was, in the event, to remain confined to Arab teaching materials. Textbooks used in Israel were never submitted to screening; nor, *a fortiori*, were those of other countries.

But if it were admitted that scrutiny of materials used in UNRWA/ UNESCO establishments inevitably – and primarily – affected national education systems, then the principle of screening would have to be viewed as general in application: intergovernmental control of national education systems in the interests of peace must be regarded as universally legitimate, or not legitimate at all. At a minimum, a finding that Arab national sovereignty was involved would have required reciprocal scrutiny of Israeli textbooks, for which the Arab States – in references to 'extending the competence of the Commission' – were repeatedly to call.[69] (Arab spokesmen, on occasion quoting studies by Israelis and/or former Zionists, claimed that Israeli textbooks glorified the country's military exploits and dealt pejoratively with Arabs.[70])

From the Arab perspective, moreover, the criterion of 'international sponsorship' might well have seemed to demonstrate Western bad faith, insofar as it overlooked the origins of the UNRWA/ UNESCO education system. That system, after all, was not a given, but could itself be seen as a direct outcome of the forcible and Western-aided establishment of the State of Israel against the wishes of the inhabitants of Palestine. To scrutinise the textbooks of the hosts to the UNRWA/UNESCO system could thus have been deemed to add insult to injury.

What the decision might therefore conceivably have suggested to sympathisers of the Arab view was a certain selectiveness in the commitment to 'freedom of information', specifically a commitment diminished in the case of Palestinian refugees and their Arab hosts.

In their defence, Western States may have concluded that they were acting in the best interests of the Palestinians. If the practical alternatives were either to permit direct Israeli censorship, or to abandon support for the education programme for Palestinian refugees altogether, then revision under UNESCO auspices might well have appeared the lesser evil. It could also reasonably be argued that, given Israel's material control over the territories, to adopt a confrontationist approach would have been futile.

Nevertheless, it is not clear that these considerations need have prevented Western States from advancing any defence whatsoever of the other principles involved, even if only in token obeisance. Equally, had Western States supported calls for reciprocal scrutiny of Israeli textbooks, then the cause of objectivity – at least within the narrow context of Arab–Israeli relations – might have been seen to have been more nearly served. The morality of a stance does not, after all, depend on the power of the moral agent.*

Be that as it may, the adoption by leading Western States (notably France, the USA, the UK, Switzerland and the Netherlands) of a more vocal moral stance once circumstances turned against Israel at later stages of the exercise,[72] as well as with regard to the 1974 UNESCO 'Israel resolutions' and the 1975 UN resolution on zionism, afford a contrast with their mildness on the occasion examined here.

7. WESTERN COVERAGE OF THE EPISODE

Western coverage of the events examined above was minimal, at least by comparison with the level of attention devoted to subsequent developments less favourable to Israel, so that Western publics have remained largely unaware of the precedent.

The subject has been touched upon in Anglo-Saxon academic circles, but mostly in works on UNRWA;[73] as such, it has not been related to the wider debate on 'politicisation' of UNESCO. In recent scholarship on UNESCO itself, meanwhile, the textbook episode is not discussed. In an otherwise informative study of UNESCO and world politics, for instance, James Sewell fails to refer to it at all.[74] Professor Hoggart, who devotes half a chapter in his widely-read 'insider' account of UNESCO to the 1974 'Israel resolutions', does not mention it once.[75] The leading English-language journals in the field of international relations appear scarcely to have covered the incident

---

* The point can be illustrated by an anecdote. In January 1980, the US Ambassador to the UN Security Council submitted a draft resolution calling for Soviet withdrawal from Afghanistan, in the certain knowledge that it would be vetoed by the USSR. He explained this apparently futile gesture in the following terms: 'Just because you know someone is going to be intransigent doesn't mean you shouldn't haul them before the bar of justice.'[77]

either; and official and semi-official accounts of UNESCO involvement predictably gloss over the political dimensions of the issue.[76]

On the contrary, where Western media did broach the subject, they would seem to have done so chiefly to condemn the Arab side: it may be recalled that the Commissioner-General for UNRWA cited adverse Western publicity as an important determinant of his policy towards the Israeli occupying authorities. Indeed, stressing what they identified as Arab anti-semitism, Western media publicised the most extreme – and on occasion fictitious – features of the Arab textbooks.[77]

UNESCO *Press Reviews* (compiled at the time on the basis of material supplied by press clippings agencies, National Commissions for UNESCO, UNESCO Field Offices, UN Information Centres and 'other sources covering 32 Member States'[78]) reveal no coverage of the debate in the Western press, nor do indexes to leading British and American newspapers.[79] *The Times Index*, for instance, contains no entry on the debate; by contrast, challenges to Israel were the subject of 10 out of 13 items on the UNESCO General Conference in 1974.[80] Similarly, the *New York Times Index* for 1967 contains one item on the Executive Board's 'compromise resolution' on the textbooks, while 40 out of 43 items on the 1974 session of the General Conference were devoted to the 'Israel resolutions' and reactions thereto.[81]

The gap in coverage concerning the Executive Board decisions on the Arab textbooks, when combined with the scale of publicity focussed on later challenges to Israel and to zionism, may be seen to have the effect of implying an Arab monopoly on unreasonableness and, in this way, of reinforcing the prevailing perception that the Arabs and their supporters alone have 'politicised' UNESCO.

SUMMARY AND CONCLUSIONS

This chapter has shown that there are reasonable grounds for viewing the decision by UNESCO's Executive Board in 1967 to submit Arab State textbooks used in the UNRWA/UNESCO education programme to intergovernmentally-sponsored scrutiny as (a) a response to developments 'extraneous' to UNESCO; (b) a reversal both of established non-interventionist policy in the sphere of education, and of long-standing UNRWA/UNESCO practice; (c) an infringement of Arab national sovereignty in the field of education; and (d) an exercise of selective morality. The decision could thus be seen as corresponding to the concept of 'politicisation' dominant in the West; in this instance, however, it was not the new majority but rather Israel and the Western States which were to emerge as the 'politicising' agents.

It has also been shown that the capacity of the Palestinians, as those most affected, to influence proceedings was minimal, insofar as their point of view was represented neither directly at the level of policy-makers on the Executive Board, nor indirectly through media cover-age at the level of Western publics.

The absence of any sustained discussion, in the wider debate on 'politicisation' of UNESCO, of the decision to screen the Arab textbooks is significant in that it may be seen to have truncated and, to that extent, distorted the debate.

9 UNESCO and Regulation of Science and Culture

INTRODUCTION

By way of comparison with outcomes in relation to recent UNESCO texts bearing centrally upon mass communications, the present chapter will examine the outcomes of debates on standard-setting texts adopted by the General Conference during the same period in the fields of science and culture.

The texts in question are the Recommendation on the Status of Scientific Researchers (1974), the Recommendation on participation by the people at large in cultural life and their contribution to it (1976) and the Recommendation concerning the Status of the Artist (1980).

We shall look at the way these instruments deal with the goals of knowledge in the various fields, and with the rights and responsibilities of practitioners and/or of States; and also at any prescriptions bearing upon mass media. We shall then consider how far the outcomes may be explained in terms of the relative strength of the different interests involved.

1. THE RECOMMENDATION ON THE STATUS OF SCIENTIFIC RESEARCHERS (UNESCO, 1974)

The Recommendation on the Status of Scientific Researchers,[1] adopted by the General Conference of UNESCO in 1974, is replete with statements of the 'responsibilities' of scientists and of the use of scientific knowledge by States in the interests of peace, justice and human welfare. Reference to responsibilities is in fact placed, throughout the text, before reference to rights.[2]

At first glance, it appears surprising that a text endowed with greater normative force (i.e. a Recommendation) and systematically stressing the 'responsibilities' of practitioners and the proper end-uses of science should have been adopted four years before the Media Declaration, and before what is widely regarded as the post-1974 era of 'politicisation' marked by the 'Israel resolutions' and the election of a Third World national as Director-General. A number of factors would seem to account for this outcome. First, those most directly affected, namely scientific researchers themselves, were not opposed to international codification of scientific responsibility.

The two international non-governmental organisations (NGOs) mainly concerned were the International Council of Scientific Unions (ICSU) and the World Federation of Scientific Workers (WFSW). Both would have been somewhat handicapped in resisting adoption of the Recommendation, had they been so minded. Indeed the former, while powerfully represented in UNESCO and national scientific councils, was limited by a self-proclaimed 'nonpolitical tradition' to the less visible (albeit not necessarily less effective) methods of lobbying.[3] The latter not only suffered from weaker administrative structures and less familiarity with UNESCO procedures, but was compromised in Western eyes by a 'radical' reputation. As can be discerned from periodic Secretariat reports on NGO activities, the WFSW enjoys far less favourable standing in UNESCO circles than ICSU.[4]

In fact, however, the histories of both ICSU and its affiliates (e.g. the Royal Society in the UK) and WFSW reveal a decades-old concern with questions of responsibility in science and, as a corollary, with the restriction of scientists' rights arising from the fact that most scientific research has for some time been conducted under military and/or commercial auspices.[5]

Similarly the Secretariat, notably in the person of the British official directly in charge of preparatory work on the Recommendation, was convinced of the need to stress accountability.[6] The initial moves in 1968 towards drafting an international instrument emerged from a generalised concern for the promotion of science in society. While this aim was seen to require incentives to scientists and to that extent an emphasis on rights, the Secretariat considered it essential also to stress responsibility, if only for purely pragmatic reasons (the need to maintain or restore public support and funding for scientific research at a time of some disenchantment with the products and by-products of science).[7]

For scientists and Secretariat, the main duty of scientific researchers was to ensure that the goals and methods of scientific research were humane and also socially and ecologically responsible. Effective exercise of these duties was seen to entail as preconditions a number of rights, chief among them freedom of expression and publication, participation in determining the aims and means of research, a right of reasoned disagreement from given programmes or projects, and measures to counteract the relatively weak bargaining position of scientific researchers in national economies vis-à-vis employers. The preliminary Secretariat report on which Member States were consulted, reflecting these positions, sought to minimise restriction and to maximise protection of scientific researchers.[8]

Secondly, Member States of both East and West favoured codification of scientific responsibility at the international level. However, as against scientists' understanding of the concept as outlined above, governments defined it more particularly in terms of national security. Soviet bloc States, while generally commending the stress placed on responsibility in the Secretariat draft, suggested in their written comments that the instrument itself refer explicitly to what they saw as the duties of the researcher to his home country and to the safeguarding of national sovereignty, international peace and peaceful coexistence.[9]

Western States, for their part, questioned the wisdom of including ethical considerations in the Recommendation and of 'overemphasising' the harnessing of science and technology to peaceful ends. In addition to restrictions advocated in the name of national security, Western States (especially Japan, France, the UK and the USA), stressed the rights of employers of scientific researchers in the private sector,[10] defined by the UK as 'the legitimate commercial interests of employers'.[11]

The interest of Third World States in the instrument was confined almost entirely to the question of the 'brain drain'[12] although, at Peruvian initiative,[13] reference to the role of scientists in 'making the world a better place' was amended to that of setting up 'a more humane and really just international society'.[14]

Thus, unlike the case of the Media Declaration, where Western States and mass media were broadly united against the Soviet bloc and others favourable to setting some limits on freedom of expression and publication, the alignment in this instance could more accurately be characterised as scientists and Secretariat seeking to minimise restrictions, versus employers of scientists – whether governments of East or West, or the private sector – supporting a greater measure of restriction.

Thirdly mass media, which might conceivably have rallied in support of greater freedom of expression, would seem to have played little part in the overall process. No press accreditation register is available for

1974, but the Secretariat was at no point conscious of any significant press attention to the Recommendation.[15] Media interests were not directly affected by the text; moreover, the latter's adoption by the General Conference at its 18th session coincided with the 'Israel resolutions' and election of the new Director-General, on which most press attention was concentrated.

The various positions were confronted at an intergovernmental expert meeting in April 1974 convened to finalise, for submission to the General Conference, the draft Recommendation prepared by the Secretariat[16] in the light of written comments from Member States.[17] Four-fifths of the draft amendments tabled on this occasion[18] (120 out of some 150) were sponsored by Western delegates, and in particular by two States with highly developed science sectors, namely the USA (38 amendments) and Japan (33), followed by France (18) and the UK (9).*

The outcome was a revised draft[19] in which the rights of publication and reasoned disagreement were substantially qualified in favour of the employers of scientific researchers, whether governmental or other.[20] For example, under initial Secretariat proposals, Member States 'should regard it as the norm that scientific researchers be at liberty to publish the results of R&D they perform', any curtailment of such liberty being on an exceptional and temporary basis, and subject to strict conditions and a right of appeal.[21] Under the provisions of the text as revised, it was recommended only that Member States should 'seek to regard' freedom of publication as the norm and should 'seek' to minimise restrictions 'consistent with public interest and the rights of their employers and fellow-workers', while the conditions attaching to restriction of the right to publish were also weakened.[22] The text as reworked by the April meeting was subsequently adopted by the General Conference, after only minor modification in Programme Commission,[23] by 82:0:4.[24]

2. THE RECOMMENDATION ON PARTICIPATION BY THE PEOPLE AT LARGE IN CULTURAL LIFE AND THEIR CONTRIBUTION TO IT (UNESCO, 1976)

The above Recommendation,[25] designed to 'guarantee as human rights those rights bearing on access to and participation in cultural life',

---

* Note that West Germany constituted an exception to this response, no doubt for historical reasons. It submitted no written comments on the preliminary report and tabled only five draft amendments at the April 1974 meeting.

contains a number of provisions relating to mass media. In its general thrust, the Recommendation may be seen as challenging 'cultural élitism' and concentration of control over access to the means of producing and disseminating culture at national and global levels, and thus among other things over mass media.

More specifically, the Recommendation stipulates that

> mass media . . . *should not* threaten the authenticity of cultures or impair their quality; they *ought not* to act as instruments of cultural domination *but serve* mutual understanding and peace.[26] (Emphases added)

It further recommends that Member States or the appropriate authorities should

> encourage the communication media . . . to enhance the cultural quality of programmes intended for the public at large . . . to give preference to material which serves the purposes of information and education, rather than those of propaganda and publicity and to pay special attention to the protection of national cultures from potentially harmful influences of some types of mass production.[27]

Similarly, Member States or the appropriate authorities should

> . . . encourage the *use of communication media*, including telecommunication satellites, *to promote the ideals* of peace, human rights and fundamental freedoms, friendship among men and international understanding and cooperation, and thus create the necessary conditions to enable their national cultures to resist ideas of hatred between peoples, war, force and racism . . .[28] (Emphases added)

The Recommendation also refers explicitly to questions of commercialism and profit-seeking in the field of culture. At Soviet initiative,[29] the preamble speaks of 'taking measures against the harmful effect of "commercial mass culture"';[30] while an operative section entitled 'Cultural Industries', inserted on a Swedish proposal,[31] recommends that Member States or the appropriate authorities

> should make sure that the criterion of profit-making does not exert a decisive influence on cultural activities . . .[32]

Earlier drafts of most of the above provisions[33] had been reworked, to some extent at least, in the direction of more 'positive' or permissive wordings, at the initiative of the leading Western States (Australia,

Canada, West Germany, Japan, the Netherlands, Sweden, Switzerland, the UK and the USA).[34] Nevertheless, the provisions relating to mass media in this text are clearly more prescriptive than those contained in the Media Declaration adopted two years later, and it is worth considering the possible reasons for this outcome.

The Recommendation as a whole in fact encountered a fair degree of opposition from Western States. Of the 349 draft amendments[35] tabled at an intergovernmental expert meeting in April 1976 to the text drawn up by an Algerian staff member on the basis of Member States' written comments, 296 were authored by Western delegates.[36] Apart from criticisms with respect to style, the principal reservations expressed on this occasion and at the General Conference by Western States, notably West Germany, Japan, Switzerland, Canada and the USA, bore upon the term 'people at large' (in French, *les masses populaires*); the preambular reference to 'commercial mass culture', including its 'negative' form; and a more generally-expressed concern that implementation of the instrument might lead to restrictions on freedom of expression and on the independence of the media.[37]

The strongest opposition was registered by the USA which, as home of some of the world's largest 'cultural industries', possibly regarded itself as the prime target of the Recommendation. The USA asserted a belief from the outset that access to and participation in cultural life were not fit subjects for international regulation, took minimal part in the drafting process, sent no delegation to the intergovernmental meeting, urged the General Conference to turn down the proposed text and, after its adoption, announced that it had no intention of transmitting the Recommendation to the relevant authorities or institutions in the USA.[38]

Certain other Western States, such as West Germany, Japan and Switzerland, although voicing doubts similar to those of the USA, played a greater part in negotiations on the text. Nevertheless, when the draft came before the plenary of the General Conference, these States maintained that the basis for adoption by consensus was insufficient and, with a view to rejecting the text, endorsed a Canadian proposal that it be put to the vote.[39] On the other hand, the positions of certain Western States (notably French-speaking and Nordic countries, post-Salazar Portugal, post-Franco Spain, and Italy) were more shaded.[40]

Third World countries, for their part, contributed relatively little to the preparation of the instrument. But viewing the question of participation at the global level, and seeing themselves as recipients on a disproportionate scale of foreign and/or 'commercial' culture, those which commented on the draft (chiefly Algeria, Argentina, Egypt, India, Niger, Oman, Senegal and Singapore) were to support the text as a whole.[41] For Soviet bloc States, work on the text provided opportunities to indict, in the name of the less privileged, what were portrayed as commercial excesses, bourgeois élitism and inequalities in the cultural field in the West.[42]

Meanwhile, the 'cultural industries', as those most directly challenged by the Recommendation, would seem to have been barely involved in work on the instrument. National industries, having no consultative status with UNESCO, may well have been unaware that a standard-setting text in this field was being drafted. On the other hand, the main international NGO representing owners' interests, the International Film and Television Council (IFTC), was ill-placed to present a united front since it grouped beneath its umbrella not only the larger film industries but also amateurs, actors, authors, critics, film-clubs and producers of specialist and sectarian films.[43] According to the Secretariat officials concerned, the IFTC did not seek to influence the course of events, and an interview at IFTC offices at UNESCO Headquarters yielded neither written nor verbal sources of enlightenment as to its position with respect to the Recommendation.[44] Input, if any, by the 'cultural industries', can thus only have taken the form of lobbying of national authorities.

Last but not least, the mass media would seem to have made no effort to affect outcomes. The UNESCO press register for the period shows no accreditation of journalists to the meeting of April 1976, and the Secretariat was conscious of virtually no media interest or attendance at debates on the subject.[45]

Two particular considerations may account for the lack of media attention. First, although as we have seen mass media stood to be adversely affected by the general burden and specific provisions of the Recommendation, they were not the central concern of the text nor did they apear in its title. Secondly, and arguably more important, the session of the General Conference to which the draft Recommendation was submitted for adoption was the 19th session in Nairobi in 1976. As shown in Chapter 5, this was the session at which the attention of the mass media to UNESCO's involvement in the sphere of mass communications, and in particular to the draft Declaration on Mass Media, was first brought fully to bear, and it is unlikely that much press attention would have been diverted on that occasion to a text less directly concerned with mass media.

These circumstances may explain why, despite the vocal opposition of a number of leading Western States, the General Conference adopted, by a vote of 62:5:15,[46] a Recommendation which was considerably more prescriptive in relation to the mass media than the Media Declaration itself.

3. THE RECOMMENDATION CONCERNING THE STATUS OF THE ARTIST (UNESCO, 1980)

The above instrument,[47] adopted by the General Conference of UNESCO in 1980, arose out of UNESCO's general programme and a number of ministerial conferences on cultural policy. The Recommendation addresses the problems of the artist in an era of declining private patronage, increasingly powerful 'cultural industries' and constant change – seen as damaging to the artist – in reproduction and communications media.

The drafting of this instrument overlapped with the resurgence of Western vigilance in connection with UNESCO standard-setting activities in the wake of the mass media debates. Leading Western States (above all Japan, but also the USA, UK, France and West Germany) at first opposed proposals for international regulation in this sphere and secured delays in the drafting process.[48] Central to the objections expressed by these and other Western Members in debate and in writing[49] was the principle of artistic freedom: according to Western States, the possibility that the artist might be defined as such not by himself but by the State, and the question of the 'responsibilities' he might be assigned in the process, threatened that freedom.

The French staff member responsible for work on the Recommendation, Alexandre Blokh, recalls that representatives of France, Japan and the USA initially sought to win him over to these views in the course of vigorous lobbying visits to Secretariat offices, although French and American positions at least evolved substantially (see below).[50] 'Cultural industries', taking in this instance the form of the International Federation of Producers of Phonograms and Videograms (IFPPV) (and on one occasion the Mexican Camera Nacional de la Industria de la Radio y la Televisión) also aired reservations in the name of artistic freedom with respect to regulation.[51]

However, a different view of the matter was held by the NGOs representing those engaged in the various fields of artistic endeavour, notably the International Association of Art (IAA), the International Federation of Authors and Composers (IFAC), the International Federation of Musicians (IFM), the International Federation of Actors (IFA) and the International Confederation of Professional and Intellectual Workers (ICPIW). Spokesmen for these bodies proved to be chiefly and actively concerned to secure codification of the status of artists as 'cultural workers' in the hope of improving their material conditions of existence. Artists would certainly have been worse placed than scientists to resist any proposals to restrict their freedom: the social organisation of artists (whether as a result of the individualism of their calling or of the circumstances of self-employment, part-time employment, unemployment or 'secondary employment') is notoriously weak. But in fact artists' representatives tended to devote relatively little of their eloquence to questions of artistic freedom which they were increasingly inclined to equate with 'freedom to starve'.[52] The NGOs concerned were repeatedly to stress their support for urgent adoption of an international instrument; and in so doing were also regularly to proclaim not only the duties of industry towards artists, but their own readiness to accept reference to artistic responsibility.[53]

Western States and 'cultural industries' therefore appeared, somewhat untenably, as stauncher advocates of artistic freedom than those directly concerned. In the circumstances, the States in question relinquished their opposition of principle, mostly also pronouncing themselves reassured by the general tenor of the Secretariat's preliminary draft, and in some cases (e.g. Sweden[54]) announcing that they had come to perceive a position need for regulation.[55] The shift in the US stance, in particular, was evidenced by a number of draft amendments proclaiming the necessity of government help in creating material conditions conducive to the release and flowering of artistic talent.[56]

Thereafter, Western States turned their attention to detailed consideration of the Secretariat's preliminary draft.[57] Specifically, they concentrated on (a) references in the draft to duties and responsibilities (in the event stated in very general terms) and to the role of artistic activity in society;[58] and (b) questions of compensation for the unfavourable effects of technological change on the situation of artists, and the role of cultural industries and States in this connection.[59]

Meanwhile Soviet bloc States supported the principle of regulation, although claiming that the provisions envisaged fell short of those prevailing in their own countries, and although also urging stronger formulation of the 'social and political responsibilities' of the artist.[60] However, these States did not pursue questions of responsibility as vigorously in the case of artists as they did in relation to mass media. This may have been for a number of reasons: the instrument was not a Soviet bloc initiative; insistence on imposing duties or restrictions, given the strength of initial Western opposition to the instrument, might have resulted in the latter's abandonment, an outcome which would scarcely have redounded to Soviet bloc credit in the eyes of impecunious artists; and, perhaps most basically, the potential impact and reach of art and artists, whether for good or evil, could be seen as considerably less than those of scientists or mass media.

For their part, Third World States submitted comparatively few written comments or amendments. But from these and related sources, it can be seen that they favoured international regulation as a means of protecting traditional forms of art against imported culture, exodus of talent, and/or commercialisation, although they were to claim that the final text took insufficient account of the position of the artist in developing countries.[61]

The Secretariat official concerned, in private life a writer and after retirement from UNESCO a staff-member of International PEN, was generally sympathetic to the position of artists.[62]

Meanwhile, as far as can be ascertained from an interview with this official and from consultation of the UNESCO press register, mass media paid minimal attention to the Recommendation: journalists from only two press organs, both of a specialist nature (*France Culture* and *Tribune juive*) were accredited to the intergovernmental expert meeting held in February–March 1980 to finalise a draft for submission to the General Conference.[63]

Some 84 draft amendments[64] were tabled at the intergovernmental meeting, of which 56 by Western Member States. The outcome was a text in which references to 'responsibilities' were reduced to a single preambular mention, reworded to accord more closely with Western conceptions (i.e. the responsibilities of the artist being those of any citizen); provisions dealing with compensation of artists in respect of technological advance and with the contribution of the industries concerned were diluted; and several of the specific recommendations to States were revised in more tentative form, the word 'should' being replaced by the phrase 'are invited to'.[65]

This text was adopted by consensus by the intergovernmental meeting[66] and (after inclusion of a Canadian-sponsored reference to child artists[67]) by the 21st session of the General Conference.[68]

SUMMARY AND CONCLUSIONS

The three instruments considered in this chapter are all Recommendations, that is, texts enjoying higher normative status than a Declaration
such as was adopted in 1978 in the case of mass media. Any proposals
for restriction of freedom of expression in these texts could therefore
have been expected to attract correspondingly greater resistance on
the part of traditional opponents of such restrictions, including
Western States, media, and the interests or practitioners concerned.
The findings of the present chapter are interesting in that the level of
prescription and restrictiveness of the three texts examined prove to be
in inverse proportion to the relative strength of the material interests
affected.

The 1976 Recommendation on participation in cultural life emerges
as the most prescriptive text with respect to the responsibilities of
practitioners, although the 'cultural industries' and mass media, as the
interests most directly challenged, may be seen as those commanding
the greatest material resources of those concerned in this chapter.
However, not only were both Third World and Soviet bloc States
pressing for the prescriptions in question, but direct representation of
the 'cultural industries' was in the event weak and the attention of mass
media was at the time focussed on another text (the Media Declaration) which affected their interests more centrally.

The Recommendation on the Status of Scientific Researchers
adopted two years earlier could be seen as next in order of restrictiveness and in frequency of reference to practitioner responsibility of the
texts considered here, and certainly as more so than the 1978 Media
Declaration. While the relevant scientific interests were only able and
willing to resist restriction within certain limits, and while mass media
took no position on the debate, leading Western countries in this
instance combined tacitly with Soviet bloc States to qualify the
freedoms of expression, publication and reasoned disagreement
sought by scientists. For although scientists may be seen to derive
power from their knowledge and skills, the knowledge in question is of
a type (militarily and/or commercially relevant) whose use States in
general and powerful employers have an interest in controlling.

Finally, despite the relative weakness of artists as organised
interests, and despite the absence once again of mass media attention,
the 1980 Recommendation on the Status of the Artist appears as the
least prescriptive of the three with respect to practitioner responsibility
and the goals of communication. The fact that Soviet bloc States,

which were virtually alone in suggesting greater emphasis on the 'social and political responsibilities' of artists, pressed the point with only minimal insistence may be attributed in part to the intensity of the initial opposition by newly vigilant Western States, but more especially to the relatively less significant type of activity and reach of artists as compared with either scientists or the mass media.

The conclusion to which the above findings point is that the extent of restriction on freedom of expression in UNESCO standard-setting instruments is a function not so much of the legal status of the particular text, but rather of the importance of the type of information at issue to different groups of States, the strength of the interests concerned and of their response relative to that of the States seeking restriction, and the degree of media mobilisation or non-mobilisation.

10 'Information' Outcomes in 'Race' Contexts

INTRODUCTION

This chapter is concerned with provisions for regulation of information content adopted by the UN and UNESCO from the 1960s onward in contexts which focussed primarily not on information but on race.

By the 1960s, the Third World constituted a majority on full-membership organs of the UN system. At that time, Third World policy with regard to the sphere of mass communications as a whole was still largely uncoordinated. But at a more specific level, a majority of African, Asian and Caribbean countries maintained a focussed concern with information as it impinged upon matters of racial (and to a lesser extent religious) discrimination, and were to direct their attempts at regulation mainly towards this limited aspect of information content. In so doing, they were generally able to count on Soviet bloc support. Conversely, not being centrally concerned with mass media, the proceedings in question were to attract little press coverage.

The purpose of the present chapter will be to consider how far outcomes bearing on information in 'race' contexts differed from those in 'information' contexts proper, and the reasons for the differences.

1. THE INTERNATIONAL COVENANT ON CIVIL AND POLITICAL RIGHTS (UN, 1966), ARTICLE 20

In December 1966, the UN General Assembly adopted the two International Human Rights Covenants. Initially designed to express in binding form the principles contained in the Universal Declaration of Human Rights of 1948, the two instruments took nearly twenty years to draft and, in the event, differed from the earlier text in certain important respects.[1]

Of particular note in this connection is Article 20 (restriction of certain types of expression) of the International Covenant on Civil and Political Rights (ICCPR),[2] adopted by the Third Committee of the General Assembly in 1961. Of the 27 substantive articles, this article (along with Article 19 concerning freedom of expression) was among

172

the most hotly debated and among the last to be adopted by the Committee.[3]

Article 20, which attracted especially hostile Western reactions, provides for certain mandatory legal restrictions on information flow:

1. Any propaganda for war shall be prohibited by law.
2. Any advocacy of national, racial or religious hatred that constitutes incitement to discrimination, hostility or violence shall be prohibited by law.

Although it does not provide for punishment of such expressions, this article is broader in scope than any previously adopted in the UN system with respect to information. It includes incitement to discrimination or hostility as such, not only where linked to violence, and it requires no subjective intent to incite the phenomena in question.

Article 20 was not based on any parallel provision in the 1948 Universal Declaration. Instead, the principle of providing for prohibition of such categories of expression was recommended by an arena concerned primarily with 'race' issues, namely the Sub-Commission on Prevention of Discrimination and Protection of Minorities (SCPDPM) of the Commission on Human Rights (CHR), where it was conceived in the context of an article on minority rights.[4]

The rationale for Western opposition to Article 20, as expressed notably by the Nordic countries, the Netherlands and the UK in written comments on the draft as well as in proposals for deletion and in subsequent explanations of vote, was not only that 'it proclaimed no individual right' – and as such had no place in a Covenant on Human Rights – but also that 'on the contrary it authorises and requires repressive legislation'.[5] An earlier CHR draft,[6] reflecting Western positions more closely, had provided for a narrower ban: advocacy of national, racial or religious hostility would be prohibited only where inciting to both hatred and violence.

The wording adopted by the Assembly was based on an amendment to the CHR text by a coalition of fourteen Third World and two East European States.[7]

The article was adopted by the Third Committee in 1961 by a roll-call vote of 52:19:12, with most leading Western States opposing and France abstaining.[8] Votes on particular sections of the article yielded similar results: paragraph 1 (war propaganda) was adopted by a recorded vote of 53:21:9, with the West opposing; the expression 'discrimination, hostility or', extending the scope of the ban in paragraph 2, was adopted by a roll-call vote of 43:21:19 over Western objections; and that paragraph, as a whole as amended, was adopted by 50:18:15.[9]

The Covenant in its entirety, embodying Article 20 as approved by the Third Committee in 1961, was adopted unanimously by the latter[10] as well as by the plenary of the General Assembly five years later, in 1966.[11]

By the late 1970s, most Western States had signed and/or ratified the Covenants.[12] In so doing, however, a number of them, notably the Nordic countries, had entered specific reservations or declarations with respect to Article 20.[13] It should be noted that in most cases the reservation applied only to the first paragraph (war propaganda), which reflected a more traditional Soviet bloc preoccupation, and not to the second (incitement to racial discrimination), which catered more directly for Third World concerns.

The UK, however, registered a reservation to the article in its entirety, announcing that it would be interpreted by the UK as consistent with the freedoms provided for elsewhere in the Covenant, and reserving the right not to introduce further domestic legislation on the subject.[14]

The USA, by 1977, had signed but not ratified the Covenant. While, for domestic political reasons, it had not taken part in earlier stages of drafting,[15] the USA had resumed active participation by the time of adoption in the General Assembly. The American delegation expressed satisfaction at the general tenor of the two human rights Covenants, but like the UK aired specific reservations with regard to ICCPR Article 20 as a whole.[16] Recommending congressional ratification of the ICCPR and certain other human rights instruments in 1977, President Carter suggested a reservation to this particular article.[17]

The above pronouncements are significant insofar as the number of substantive articles to elicit Western reservations was generally low – between 3 and 6 out of a total of 27.[18] The legitimacy of the reservations has in fact since been questioned by Third World representatives.[19] (Exceptions to the general Western response were Italy, West Germany and Japan, none of which entered formal reservations to these provisions.[20])

2.   THE INTERNATIONAL CONVENTION ON THE ELIMINATION OF ALL FORMS OF RACIAL DISCRIMINATION (UN, 1965), ARTICLE 4

Article 4 of the 1965 Race Convention[21] dealt with incitement, and contained the broadest provisions for regulating freedom of expression adopted up to that point by the United Nations. It required States Parties to ban not only racial incitement by State and/or public authorities, but also incitement to racial discrimination by any individual, group or organisation. Under the two paragraphs of Article 4 concerning bodies other than public authorities, States Parties:

(a) Shall declare an offence punishable by law all dissemination of ideas based on racial superiority or hatred, incitement to racial discrimination, as well as all acts of violence or incitement to such acts against any race or group of persons of another colour or ethnic origin . . .

(b) Shall declare illegal and prohibit organisations, and also organised and all other propaganda activities, which promote and incite racial discrimination, and shall recognise participation in such organisations or activities as an offence punishable by law.[22]

Article 4 was held by several delegates, including those of the UK, the Netherlands and the USSR, to be the key element of the Convention,[23] and the debates surrounding it at every stage of drafting were heated and lengthy.[24] The USA explicitly stressed the importance it attached to the issues addressed by the article, which it took an active part in drafting.[25] In the Assembly, it was one of only two articles of the text adopted by the Commission on Human Rights (CHR) – apart from the inherently contentious definitional article – to be redrafted, and the last to be adopted by the Third Committee. It was also the only article to which amendments were submitted in plenary.[26]

The Assembly debate was based on Article 4 as drafted by the CHR,[27] with which the USA, UK and France had pronounced themselves generally satisfied.[28] The Third World, and especially African and Asian countries, had at the time been under-represented on the CHR relative to the West in terms of overall strengths in the Assembly;[29] and this political balance had enabled the West to reduce the restrictions envisaged in an earlier draft submitted to the CHR by the Sub-Commission on Prevention of Discrimination and Protection of Minorities.[30]

In the Assembly, by contrast, voting strength was unambiguously on the side of the Third World (taken here on the basis of voting behaviour as including Israel but not Japan), with 82 out of 118 votes.[31] Of these the African, Asian and Caribbean States which, for historical reasons, might be assumed to be most directly interested in an international convention against racism, commanded an absolute majority of 66 seats. Meanwhile the Soviet bloc, whose interest in the matter was conceivably more instrumental, accounted for 10 additional votes.

The wording of paragraphs (a) and (b) as quoted above was based on amendments to the CHR text sponsored separately by three African States[32] and by Czechoslovakia,[33] and backed in debate[34] by a cross-section of Members including Israel, Italy, Uruguay and Czechoslovakia.[35] As amended, the two paragraphs were adopted by votes of 63:1:25 and 66:1:16 respectively, with the leading Western States abstaining in both cases on the ground that the provisions in question went beyond their domestic legislation on incitement to racism.[36] A Latin American amendment in plenary[37] proposing to narrow the restrictions again was rejected by 54:25:23.[38]

However, the General Assembly also adopted certain Western-backed safeguards relating to Article 4. It did so, moreover, with the active support of African and Caribbean States, whose concern to win Western endorsement of a major instrument against racism would seem to have favoured receptiveness to Western arguments.[39]

Thus the Third Committee inserted a check into the introductory paragraph of Article 4 in the form of a 'due regard' clause which refers explicitly to the freedoms set forth in the Universal Declaration of Human Rights and in Article 5 of the Convention itself.[40] A Nordic initiative,[41] orally sub-amended by France,[42] this clause was subsequently incorporated in a compromise text tabled by Nigeria[43] and adopted by a comfortable majority of 76:1:14.[44] Thus amended, Article 4 as a whole was adopted in Third Committee by 88:0:5.[45]

The plenary, meanwhile, at the instigation of 33 African and Caribbean States,[46] amended the Convention further to include a reservations clause (Article 20) whose relevance was expected to relate primarily to Article 4. An article of this sort had been rejected in Third Committee (by a vote of 25:19:34)[47] with the result that, as the Ghanaian delegate remarked, adoption of the convention itself appeared to be jeopardised.[48] Even so, the West (notably France, Greece, the UK and the USA) objected strongly to the form in which the clause was ultimately adopted – by unrecorded votes, on the parts and on the whole, of 62:18:27, 76:13:15 and 82:4:21 –[49] since it left the admissibility of reservations open to political rather than juridical determination.[50]

The General Assembly adopted the Race Convention by unanimity in 1965[51] and most Western States have since ratified it.[52] However, not all were fully reassured by the safeguards described above. Some of their number, notably Australia, Belgium, France and the UK, consequently appended declarations to their instruments of ratification to the effect that they understood or intended to interpret Article 4 as imposing no obligation on States Parties to take action impairing the freedoms of speech and association.[53] The USA, for its part, had signed but not ratified the text by 1979. Recommending ratification by Congress, President Carter suggested in 1977 that the USA enter a reservation to that particular article.[54] (Once again, certain Western States diverged somewhat from the general Western position, either by advocating broader restrictions or, more passively, by not entering reservations upon ratification. Such was the stance of Italy and West Germany, 'ex-enemy' States and, conversely, of Israel.[55])

3. THE INTERNATIONAL CONVENTION ON THE SUPPRESSION AND PUNISHMENT OF THE CRIME OF *APARTHEID* (UN, 1973), ARTICLES III AND IV

Article III of the *Apartheid* Convention establishes international criminal responsibility applying to individuals, members of organisations and institutions, and representatives of the State whenever, among other things, they 'directly incite or encourage' *apartheid* and related policies or practices as defined under Article II.[56] Under Article IV, States Parties undertake to adopt legislation or other measures necessary to suppress and to prevent any encouragement of *apartheid* so defined. The provisions go still further than those of the Race Convention both by criminalising incitement and by calling for its 'suppression' and 'prevention' (which imply prior censorship) as distinct from its prohibition.

In the event, however, it is hard to draw any clear conclusions regarding Western responses to these specific provisions. Indeed, all the major Western powers objected to the Convention as a whole in the form in which was tabled, most notably on account of the categorisation of *apartheid* as a crime against humanity, and of proposals for extraterritorial jurisdiction.[57] Western States failed to secure referral to a legal organ for closer scrutiny of the draft, announced that they would abstain throughout the voting, and tabled no amendments in the plenary of the General Assembly.[58]

The substantive articles and the Convention as a whole were all adopted by a four-fifths majority, with token opposition (Portugal, and on occasion the USA), and one-fifth – Western States – abstaining systematically.[59] Some Western delegates voted in favour of a Latin

American amendment[60] (which was to be rejected by a recorded vote of 48:20:40) to reduce the restrictions under Article III, but others abstained in this instance too.[61]

As at 1981, no Western States had signed or ratified the Convention.[62] Insofar as the sponsors identify Western powers as a, if not the, major source of support to the *apartheid* régime, Western non-ratification may be assumed to render the instrument largely ineffectual in their eyes.

4. THE DECLARATION ON RACE AND RACIAL PREJUDICE (UNESCO, 1978), ARTICLES 5–7

The above instrument[63] constituted UNESCO's major contribution to the UN Decade for Action to Combat Racism and Racial Discrimination. It aimed to provide more comprehensive accounts of concepts associated with race and of the causes of racism than were to be found in previous instruments on the subject, as well as to spell out the application of such texts to UNESCO's spheres of competence.[64]

The text adopted by the General Conference in December 1978 was in fact the same as the draft approved in March that year[65] by an intergovernmental expert meeting attended by representatives of one hundred States.[66] On both occasions, the African, Asian and Caribbean States together commanded a majority of the votes, while the Third World as a whole, combined with the Soviet bloc, accounted for some four-fifths of the membership.[67]

While both meetings were also attended by observers from the Commonwealth Press Union,[68] the attention of Western journalists during the 1978 General Conference, as mentioned earlier, was directed in the main to the draft Declaration on mass media. (The UNESCO press accreditation register for the period 1976–81 contains no entry for the March 1978 intergovernmental expert meeting on the Race Declaration. This fact could be taken to indicate either incompleteness of the register, or absence of journalists, or both; but in any case would suggest that the press was not present in great strength.)

Three articles of the Race Declaration are devoted to 'responsibilities' in the spheres of education, culture and mass communication. Article 5(3) addresses the media:

. . . the mass media and those who control or serve them, as well as all organised groups within national communities, are urged . . . to promote understanding, tolerance and friendship among individuals and groups and to contribute to the eradication of racism, racial discrimination, and racial prejudice . . .

The role of the State is dealt with in Article 6:

. . . the State should take all appropriate steps, *inter alia* by legislation, particularly in the spheres of education, culture and communication, to prevent, prohibit and eradicate racism, racist propaganda, racial segregation and *apartheid* . . .

Article 7, meanwhile, concerns the role of law:

. . . law is one of the principal means of curbing any propaganda, any form of organisation or any practice which is based on ideas or theories referring to the alleged superiority of racial or ethnic groups or which seeks to justify or encourage racial hatred and discrimination in any form. States should adopt such legislation as is appropriate to this end . . . [69]

It should be noted that each of these provisions is qualified by a safeguard clause based on domestic constitutions or the Universal Declaration of Human Rights (referring specifically to Article 19 on freedom of expression) and inserted at the initiative of Western States (e.g. Austria, Italy, Japan, Sweden, the UK and the USA).[70] Nevertheless, the Race Decalaration goes further than the Media Declaration in that it 'urges' mass media to behave in prescribed ways, uses 'prohibitive' vocabulary and envisages the possibility of measures being taken by the State and/or by law against racist propaganda.

In written comments,[71] none of the Western powers had demonstrated great enthusiasm for the Race Declaration, whose adoption they had succeeded in postponing at the previous session of the General Conference.[72] Western misgivings regarding the above provisions and other aspects of the Race Declaration remained at the time of its adoption by the 20th session of the General Conference and were to be aired in explanations of vote.[73] The United Kingdom delegate, in particular, hoped that the Explanatory Statement (which, it may be noted, tended to support an interventionist reading of the articles quoted above)[74] would be treated – in the customary manner – as having only transitory value.[75]

But such reservations notwithstanding, Western delegations refrained from tabling amendments to the draft declaration at the General Conference, and joined in its adoption by acclamation.[76]

(The USA, however, did not take part in the March 1978 meeting of governmental experts where the text was finalised, on the grounds that the Decade for Action to Combat Racism – to which the Declaration was a contribution – was still linked to the UN resolution identifying zionism with racism.[77] If present during adoption of the text by the General Conference, the US delegation did not take the floor to indicate what position it would take or had taken on the Declaration.)

5.   WESTERN MEDIA COVERAGE

For none of the texts considered in this chapter was the level of press interest, as registered at any rate in the indexes to leading English-language newspapers, especially marked. Neither *The Times Index* nor the *New York Times Index*, for instance, despite detailed breakdowns of coverage under the heading of the United Nations by organ and subject, contain any separate or explicit reference in their entries under the UN rubric for 1965, 1966 and 1973 respectively to the International Covenant on Civil and Political Rights, to the Race Convention, or to the *Apartheid* Convention, or more specifically to the information provisions of these instruments.[78] Meanwhile, the 1978 Race Declaration was to be largely eclipsed in terms of press coverage by the UNESCO Media Declaration, adopted the same year, and by related communications issues: the *New York Times Index* for 1978 makes no mention of the Race Declaration, while *The Times Index* for 1978 refers once to that text but 24 times to communications questions.[79]

SUMMARY AND CONCLUSIONS

The brief review in this chapter has shown that Third World numbers and cohesion sufficed as early as the 1960s to yield some successes, at the formal level at least, in regulating information in the case of texts drafted in a 'race' context.

In three of the four cases examined, the relevant provisions are expressed both in mandatory and prohibitive form, and in instruments which are legally binding on States Parties (namely Article 20 of the 1966 International Covenant on Civil and Political Rights (ICCPR); Article 4 of the 1965 Race Convention; and Articles III and IV of the 1973 *Apartheid* Convention).

Such an outcome is surprising partly because these texts were all adopted before – and in some cases many years prior to the 1978 UNESCO Media Declaration. But it is also surprising insofar as the normative rank of such instruments might have led one to expect stronger and still more effective resistance on the part of opponents of regulation than in the case of a non-binding Declaration as adopted by UNESCO in the case of the media.

The provisions of the 1978 UNESCO Race Declaration bearing upon information content, meanwhile, are not worded in a mandatory manner, nor is the instrument itself of a legally-binding character. Nevertheless, the relevant provisions are more prescriptive than corresponding parts of the Media Declaration, adopted the same year and by the same organ of UNESCO but with maximum press coverage.

How then should we account for the difference in formal outcomes with respect to regulation of content as adopted in 'race' and 'information' contexts respectively? In part, it would seem to be attributable to the strength and cohesiveness of the new majority and the importance they attached to the issues involved in the former case. It may also be due, to some extent at least, to the fact that Third World appeals for curbs on 'racist propaganda' could count on readier sympathy among Western spokesmen than Soviet bloc calls for restriction of 'war propaganda': witness the Western tendency to abstain rather than oppose in votes on the former, and indeed the provisions dealing with incitement in domestic race legislation introduced subsequently in certain Western States.

But it remains that Western States objected to the specific provisions embodied in the various instruments with regard to information and the media. We would therefore conclude that the difference is explained most crucially by the fact that media interests were not centrally affected by the 'race' instruments, and consequently engaged in little if any effort to influence proceedings.

Meanwhile, gains by the new majority at the level of formal outcomes concerning information content in 'race' contexts should not be overrated. As we have seen, the significance of such achievements was to a large extent, and in a variety of ways, to be undermined in practice by Western powers. The means involved ranged, at the mildest end of the scale, from explanations of vote construing texts in *laissez-faire* terms (as with the UNESCO Race Declaration), through the entering of reservations to offending portions of instruments (as with the ICCPR and the Race Convention), to non-ratification of the instrument as a whole (e.g. the Apartheid Convention). Indeed, the prospect of such responses, and Third World concern to secure Western adherence to the Race Convention, in particular, would seem on occasion to have encouraged accommodation to Western positions at the drafting stage – witness African and Caribbean support for insertion of safeguard and reservations clauses in the latter instrument.

11 Conclusions: 'Politicisation' in Context

The proposition we set out to test in this study was that the outcomes of debate on any given subject within the UN system would be a function largely of the relative power of the established and the challenging interests involved, including the capacity to shape public perceptions of the debate, where both sides decide to stand firm.

We have examined this proposition in relation to debates on the regulation of knowledge within UNESCO and the United Nations, in light of the positions of the West, the Soviet bloc and the Third World as set out in Chapter 2.

In Chapter 3 we showed that, while retaining unquestioned jurisdiction with respect to 'education for peace', narrowly understood, UNESCO had by the early 1950s for all practical purposes surrendered to the UN that portion of its constitutional mandate bearing upon 'information for peace' defined more broadly to include news and the press. This pragmatic, inter-institutional division of labour was shown to have been brought about principally by the UNESCO Secretariat, seeking in the process to protect the Agency from the type of negative publicity which had attended postwar UN debates on freedom of information and which might have had the effect of jeopardising public support for UNESCO as a whole. Among other things, the informal shift in effective jurisdiction was to give rise to the now conventional view that UNESCO was endowed with no competence with respect to information content. Postwar 'consensus' within UNESCO in the information field was thus shown to have been achieved not so much spontaneously as through the referral of controversial questions of information policy to the United Nations. The loss of policy autonomy involved was interpreted here as 'technicisation' of UNESCO in the information field through the deterrent effect of media coverage.

Chapter 4, examining the substantive postwar debate on freedom of information, showed that the latter had been introduced into the UN system by the USA with a view to adoption of the concept of 'free flow

183

of information' as a principle of international law, and that this move was considered by some to have been inspired by political motives (Cold War considerations and/or concern to preserve and legitimise American predominance in the communications field). It also showed that, even in the 1940s, the scale of opposition to a *laissez-faire* policy in this field had precluded adoption of any legally-binding instrument endorsing the principle of international free flow of information. At the same time, the opposition was at that point too eclectic in source and nature, and too dependent on the USA in other respects, to secure adoption of any alternative policy. We showed that American success in the postwar era had been confined largely to the level of agendas and mandates, but that the achievement at this level was not without significance: after the USA, backed by certain other Western States and Western media, had secured effective closure of debates on the subject in the United Nations, the concept of 'free flow' was to remain the controlling frame of reference for subsequent activity and discourse in the information field in the UN system.

Chapter 5, dealing with the contemporary information debate, showed that where the opposition of Western Member States and mass media to initiatives of the new majority was less than full scale (e.g. in regional contexts where Western States had only observer status, or where Western media interest was less than fully aroused), outcomes were prescriptive and in many respects distasteful from the Western point of view.

But where resistance was more thoroughly mobilised by Western interests, results were generally more acceptable from the latter's perspective. The most conclusive trials of strength occurred with respect to debates within the full-membership General Conference of UNESCO, and with the full attention of Western media, concerning Soviet bloc initiatives for codification of the use of mass media and Third World proposals for a 'new world information and communication order'(NWICO).

Western States were to prove, over time, more sympathetic to Third World positions than were the mass media, or at least the leading Anglo-Saxon press organs. Nevertheless, and no doubt to an important extent as a result of the degree of concern demonstrated by Western media over the issue, Western powers granted the Third World little normative leeway and organised to confine the challenge from this quarter to the more manageable technical level.

The principal method by which Western States sought to contain the new majority in these debates consisted in recourse to minority-based procedures and in what could be seen as a general attempt to undermine if not delegitimise majoritarian principles. This approach was evidenced in the referral of proposals to increasingly exclusive arenas, often created for the purpose, and in appeals for 'consensus', where the latter concept could be seen to imply something other or more than a majority. It was also visible in Western questioning of UNESCO standard-setting activities more generally and in reversal of the earlier Western preference for normative approaches to the topic in favour of more 'technical' solutions. These measures were accompanied by warnings of still stronger measures, notably budgetary withholding, and culminated in US and British withdrawals from membership of UNESCO in 1985 and 1986 respectively.

On the part of Western media, acting in the circumstances (albeit of necessity) as judges in their own cause, the responses of Western States were reinforced by coverage of a scale and nature to be seen by many, including certain Western observers, as living up less than fully to liberal ideals of objectivity.

The result, as we showed, was that the standard-setting initiatives not only of the Soviet bloc minority but of the Third World majority were largely neutralised: the 1978 UNESCO Media Declaration emerged from negotiations void of prescriptive content, while the normative aspects of Third World proposals for a NWICO were for the most part discouraged in favour of more technical remedies. By the early 1980s, no legally-binding text endorsing the concept or any definition of a NWICO had been adopted either by the UN or by UNESCO.

As the obverse of our argument that the resistance of Western States was stiffened by Western media concern, this outcome may be attributable at least in part to the nature of existing Soviet and Third World alternatives to Western media. The fact that these are recognised, even in the countries concerned, as being for the most part inferior and unattractive no doubt helped to weaken further the position of Eastern and Southern States in debates on the subject.

It remains, nevertheless, that Western interests have so far succeeded in preserving a determining say for the minority in the field of information policy. In the process, Western media could be seen to have been, in effect, enfranchised, while the new majority, by contrast, could be seen to have been for practical purposes disenfranchised.

Chapter 6, examining parallel debates in the sphere of education, showed that postwar proposals by East European and Third World countries both for worldwide textbook revision under UNESCO auspices and for international regulation with respect to school programmes more generally had been unsuccessful. Failure of these proposals was attributed largely to lack of active support from the then pro-Western majority and Secretariat. UNESCO's commitment to 'education for peace' was shown not to have entailed, in Western eyes, any binding requirement to monitor the content of education systems on a universal basis for compatibility with the ideals of peace and international understanding, although such intervention might be envisaged in selected instances (notably in the case of UNESCO involvement in Allied 're-education' of Germany).

Chapter 7 showed that somewhat greater headway in regulating the content of education had been made in the debates of the 1970s, and that the instruments in question, adopted with minimal publicity, not only all enjoyed higher normative rank as Recommendations than the 1978 Media Declaration, but were also all more prescriptive with respect to the goals of knowledge than the latter text. At the same time, they remained liberal in form and, with one or two marginal exceptions, the content of prescription remained acceptable to leading Western States. However, these outcomes were explained not so much in terms of any demonstration of strength by the interests involved, or by mass media on their behalf, but rather in terms of the self-restraint exercised, for varying reasons, by the Soviet bloc and the Third World with regard to these instruments.

Chapter 8 examined the decision by the Executive Board of UNESCO in 1967–8 to submit to intergovernmentally-sponsored screening the Arab State textbooks used in UNRWA/UNESCO schools for Palestinian refugees. It showed that there were reasonable grounds for interpreting the decision as a precedent for 'politicisation', as that term is understood in the West, but that in this instance Israel and the leading Western States rather than the new majority had emerged as the 'politicising' agents. The particular significance of the precedent in the context of the 'politicisation' debate was shown to lie not only in its relationship to the Middle East conflict, but in the fact that it had received so little publicity as compared with subsequent developments in the UN system less favourable to Israel.

Chapter 9 examined further parallels with information debates in the spheres of culture and science. Somewhat paradoxically, the level of prescription and restrictiveness of the three Recommendations involved proved to vary inversely with the strength of the material interests affected. A 1976 Recommendation in which the 'cultural industries' and mass media were those most directly affected emerged as the most prescriptive text with respect to practitioner 'responsibilities'. The next most prescriptive text in this regard was a Recommendation on the Status of Scientific Researchers, adopted in 1974. The least prescriptive and restrictive was a Recommendation on the Status of Artists adopted in 1980.

These results were explained by a combination of factors. In the case of the former text, 'cultural industries' happened to be weakly represented at debates, while press attention was focussed on the Media Declaration which stood to affect media interests more centrally. In the case of scientific researchers, not only did the latter accept the principle of codification, but Western and Soviet bloc States, as well as private employers, could be seen to share an interest in determining the uses of scientific knowledge whether in the context of national security or of commercial interest. Meanwhile the fact that Soviet bloc States pressed the case for codifying the social and political 'duties' of the artist only minimally was explained by the inferior reach and thus power of artists relative to mass media. The power of the media compared with that of artists could thus be seen in this instance to have weighed indirectly rather than directly in the calculations of States.

Finally, Chapter 10 examined outcomes with respect to regulation of information in contexts where the central focus was not information but race and where, in consequence, media interest was slighter. It showed that, as early as the 1960s, Third World numbers and cohesion had sufficed to yield some successes, at the level of formal outcomes, in regulating information in the context of 'race' texts, not least in legally-binding instruments. It also showed that the 1978 UNESCO Race Declaration, although not legally binding, was more prescriptive with regard to information content than the Media Declaration, adopted by the same session of the General Conference but with maximum publicity. Nevertheless, however, it showed that at the level of implementation Western States were, in practice, to undermine these gains at the level of formal outcomes by a number of means, most notably by appending explicit reservations to offending provisions of an instrument upon ratification, or by non-ratification of an instrument as a whole.

———————

These findings may be taken to illustrate the proposition that it is not so much the number of States or the subject matter involved as the relative power of the contending interests which determines the extent to which a given issue becomes or is perceived as 'politicised'. The failure of the Soviet bloc in the postwar era and the Third World more recently to secure some measure of regulation of mass media; Soviet bloc failure to prevent UNESCO involvement in postwar German 're-education'; the inability of scientists in the 1970s to prevent the adoption of certain restrictions on their freedoms; and the practical incapacity of the Arab States to prevent scrutiny of their school textbooks – all point in this direction. The fact that tactics of the sort used by the present-day Western minority failed, when used by the various earlier minorities, to secure their ends, is a measure of the inequality between the different minorities. Walk-outs, threats of or actual withdrawal from membership, and failure to ratify normative instruments simply cannot be said to carry the same weight when practised by the Soviet bloc or by the new majority as when employed by Western States. The effectiveness of reprisals by the Western minority must, ultimately, be explained in terms of the power which that minority derives from its control over relevant material resources and finance.

A particularly significant dimension of the inequality of the various interests is relative command over the means of shaping public perceptions of the debates in question, including the extent to which these are defined as constituting 'politicisation'.

Those perceiving an Agency as 'politicised' at any given point are likely to be those who feel that it fails to advance their interests adequately, or even that it actively damages those interests. While definitions of that which is politicised or, conversely, consensual are thus likely to remain relative, the question of which definition prevails may itself become an important determinant of outcomes.

As has been shown, opposition to Western policies within the United Nations system has always existed. But the positions expressed by other States, and in particular their views on what they may regard as past and present 'politicisation' of the Specialised Agencies by Western States, have on the whole failed to reach Western publics.

In the case of debates on freedom of information and mass media, opposition to *laissez-faire* policies at the international level, in the postwar era as now, has been interpreted to Western publics by the interests most directly affected, that is, by Western mass media. The Non-Aligned countries, as the principal source of challenge, lack comparable means to make their positions in the debate known to Western publics.

The singular power of the media, where they have regarded their interests as centrally challenged and where they have mobilised in consequence to influence outcomes, was demonstrated by the fact that UNESCO's surrender of policy autonomy or 'technicisation' in the postwar era occurred in the field of 'information' (understood as news and the press) alone, not in those of education, science or culture.

It was also illustrated by comparison with outcomes in relation to regulation of other areas of knowledge (notably science) and with respect of regulation of information in contexts where media interests have been less centrally affected and where they have accordingly offered less resistance, notably in the case of instruments dealing primarily with racial matters.

Similarly, our findings illustrate the unequal capacity of, on the one hand, pro-Israeli and pro-Zionist opinion, and, on the other hand, pro-Palestinian and pro-Arab opinion, to secure a hearing at the level of Western publics. While recent developments unfavourable to Israel have been brought forcefully to Western attention, Arab and Palestinian positions in the debate on the textbooks used in UNRWA/UNESCO schools found minimal if any Western outlet, and only the former developments were defined as constituting 'politicisation'.

By the same token, although the issue in the debates both on Arab textbooks and on mass media was freedom or regulation of knowledge, only the latter debate received coverage on any scale in the Western press and was to be presented as 'politicisation'.

In conclusion, the results of our research into debates on the regulation of knowledge within the UN and UNESCO bear out the hypothesis that the principal determinant of outcomes, either at the level of formal decisions or at that of implementation, will be the relative strength of the contending interests, understood in terms not only of formal voting power but of material resources and of capacity to ensure that particular definitions of the debate – including definitions of 'politicisation' – prevail. The position of mass media as the principal interest challenged in the media debate and, at the same time, as the principal source of public information on that debate, may be regarded as uniquely strong. Equally, it may explain why UNESCO has been portrayed as more 'politicised' than most other United Nations Specialised Agencies: the interests challenged by the new majority in the framework of UNESCO may be seen as more powerful and better able to organise resistance than those challenged elsewhere.

What then is the outlook for the future of UNESCO? Clearly there are important substantive divergences within the Agency on certain subjects, notably mass communication, and personalisation of the issues through attacks on the current Director-General should not obscure the fact. Pressures for reform of existing international arrangements in the mass communication field were underway before M'Bow's term of office and are sure to continue long after it. M'Bow probably did as much as could have been expected of one with his particular electoral base to steer the African delegations along lines acceptable to the West during debates on communications policy. The departure of Mr M'Bow – whether or not he is prevailed upon to resign before his term of office expires in 1987 – may have cathartic value for those who have come to regard him as the symbol of UNESCO's problems, and to that extent may help to defuse the tension generated around UNESCO in the last decade, but it seems unlikely to have much bearing on the heart of the matter.

In the immediate, meanwhile, several conservative-led Western States have announced or hinted that they might follow the US lead and withdraw from membership of UNESCO in the next year or two. If they do, as well they may, the budget crisis facing UNESCO would obviously worsen, as would the effects on the Agency's work.

But in fact the withdrawal of America and more recently Britain would of itself probably suffice to bring about the desired reforms. This is not to say that the underlying conflicts would have been resolved: inequalities in the mass communication field remain and are likely not only to persist for the foreseeable future but to grow. In addition, there will doubtless be some resentment among the new majority at what will have been perceived as a victory of might over right.

On the other hand, as we have argued, the Third World has every interest in the survival of UNESCO as a universal organisation, that is to say one in which all the leading Western States participate. In any case, as we also saw, well-placed observers in America and Britain had noted what seemed to them to be steps in the right direction even before the withdrawals of these two countries were announced.

This being the case, and given also the opposition already registered by various governmental and non-governmental circles in the USA and Britain to the withdrawal decisions, there is every likelihood that the USA, the UK and such other Western States as might in the meantime have left the Agency will resume active membership.

On the other hand, if the decision of the Reagan and Thatcher

Administrations were motivated by political considerations largely extraneous to UNESCO, then little that the Members of the Organisation or its Director-General can do will be likely to affect the situation much. It may be that the USA and the UK will only re-enter UNESCO under new Administrations.

But on balance it may be assumed that in the fairly short term the Western States concerned will resume full membership and a Director-General more amenable to Western influence, or at least better placed to contain the new majority, will take office. What can then be anticipated is a moratorium during which the new majority will exercise a measure of self-censorship and during which in consequence debate in the field of mass communications will be handled at a strictly technical level, in accordance with Western preferences.

But if at some later stage Third World countries find that, as in earlier decades, technical assistance programmes fail to yield sufficient incremental change, and if as a result they remain unconvinced of any genuine Western commitment to reducing inequalities in this field, then it is to be expected that they will seek to reopen the normative debate. Much will thus no doubt depend on the extent to which Western States and media interests are willing to fulfill their pledges of substantially enhanced aid to the communications-poor countries.

Underlying all the substantive debates, the central issue remains the institutional structures which, within UNESCO as in other Agencies, make possible the registering of Third World challenges to the existing order. It is conceivable that proposals may be made by the West to modify the 'one state, one vote' arrangements, although it is hard to imagine that formal amendments to the rules of procedure along these lines would be endorsed by the new majority. But if the rules are not officially changed, then restricted-membership bodies such as the Drafting and Negotiation Group at UNESCO, designed to neutralise behind the scenes those moves by the new majority which are uncongenial to the West, are likely to become institutional fixtures.

While challenge-containing mechanisms of this sort will be seen by some as an essential and necessary means of reconciling purse power with voting power, they will no doubt be regarded by others as instruments for disenfranchisement of the weaker by the stronger.

Appendices

APPENDIX I: UNESCO RES 4/9.3/2 (MEDIA DECLARATION)

4/9.3/2 DECLARATION ON FUNDAMENTAL PRINCIPLES
CONCERNING THE CONTRIBUTION OF THE MASS MEDIA
TO STRENGTHENING PEACE AND INTERNATIONAL
UNDERSTANDING, TO THE PROMOTION OF HUMAN
RIGHTS AND TO COUNTERING RACIALISM, APARTHEID
AND INCITEMENT TO WAR

Preamble

The General Conference

Recalling that by virtue of its Constitution the purpose of Unesco is to 'contribute to peace and security by promoting collaboration among the nations through education, science and culture in order to further universal respect for justice, for the rule of law and for the human rights and fundamental freedoms' (Art. I, 1), and that to realize this purpose the Organization will strive 'to promote the free flow of ideas by word and image' (Art. I, 2),

Further recalling that under the Constitution the Member States of Unesco, 'believing in full and equal opportunities for education for all, in the unrestricted pursuit of objective truth, and in the free exchange of ideas and knowledge, are agreed and determined to develop and to increase the means of communication between their peoples and to employ these means for the purposes of mutual understanding and a truer and more perfect knowledge of each other's lives' (sixth preambular paragraph),

Recalling the purposes and principles of the United Nations, as specified in its Charter.

Recalling the Universal Declaration of Human Rights, adopted by the General Assembly of the United Nations in 1948 and particularly Article 19 thereof, which provides that 'everyone

Source: UNESCO 20 C/*Resolutions* at 100.

has the right to freedom of opinion and expression; this right includes freedom to hold opinions without interference and to seek, receive and impart information and ideas through any media and regardless of frontiers'; and the International Covenant on Civil and Political Rights, adopted by the General Assembly of the United Nations in 1966, Article 19 of which proclaims the same principles and Article 20 of which condemns incitement to war, the advocacy of national, racial or religious hatred and any form of discrimination, hostility or violence,

Recalling Article 4 of the International Convention on the Elimination of all Forms of Racial Discrimination, adopted by the General Assembly of the United Nations in 1965, and the International Convention on the Suppression and Punishment of the Crime of Apartheid, adopted by the General Assembly of the United Nations in 1973, whereby the States acceding to these Conventions undertook to adopt immediate and positive measures designed to eradicate all incitement to, or acts of, racial discrimination, and agreed to prevent any encouragement of the crime of apartheid and similar segregationist policies or their manifestations,

Recalling the Declaration on the Promotion among Youth of the Ideals of Peace, Mutual Respect and Understanding between Peoples, adopted by the General Assembly of the United Nations in 1965,

Recalling the declarations and resolutions adopted by the various organs of the United Nations concerning the establishment of a new international economic order and the role Unesco is called upon to play in this respect,

Recalling the Declaration of the Principles of International Cultural Co-operation, adopted by the General Conference of Unesco in 1966,

Recalling Resolution 59(I) of the General Assembly of the United Nations, adopted in 1946 and declaring:

'Freedom of information is a fundamental human right and is the touchstone of all the freedoms to which the United Nations is consecrated;

. . . .

'Freedom of information requires as an indispensable element the willingness and capacity to employ its privileges without abuse. It requires as a basic discipline the moral obligation to seek the facts without prejudice and to spread knowledge without malicious intent;

. . . .'

Recalling Resolution 110(II) of the General Assembly of the United Nations, adopted in 1947, condemning all forms of propaganda which are designed or likely to provoke or encourage any threat to the peace, breach of the peace, or act of aggression,

Recalling resolution 127(II), also adopted by the General Assembly in 1947, which invites Member States to take measures, within the limits of constitutional procedures, to combat the diffusion of false or distorted reports likely to injure friendly relations between States, as well as the other resolutions of the General Assembly concerning the mass media and their contribution to strengthening peace, trust and friendly relations among States,

Recalling resolution 9.12 adopted by the General Conference of Unesco in 1968, reiterating Unesco's objective to help to eradicate colonialism and racialism, and resolution 12.1 adopted by the General Conference in 1976, which proclaims that colonialism, neo-colonialism and racialism in all its forms and manifestations are incompatible with the fundamental aims of Unesco,

Recalling resolution 4.301 adopted in 1970 by the General Conference of Unesco on the contribution of the information media to furthering international understanding and co-operation in the interests of peace and human welfare, and to countering propaganda on behalf of war, racialism, apartheid and hatred among nations, and *aware* of the fundamental contribution that mass media can make to the realization of these objectives,

Recalling the Declaration on Race and Racial Prejudice adopted by the General Conference of Unesco at its twentieth session,

Conscious of the complexity of the problems of information in modern society, of the diversity of solutions which have been offered to them, as evidenced in particular by the consideration given to them within Unesco, and of the legitimate desire of all parties concerned that their aspirations, points of view and cultural identity be taken into due consideration,

Conscious of the aspirations of the developing countries for the establishment of a new, more just and more effective world

information and communication order,
Proclaims on this twenty-eighth day of November 1978 this
Declaration on Fundamental Principles concerning the Con-
tribution of the Mass Media to Strengthening Peace and
International Understanding to the Promotion of Human
Rights and to Countering Racialism, Apartheid and Incite-
ment to War.

Article I

The strengthening of peace and international understanding, the
promotion of human rights and the countering of racialism,
apartheid and incitement to war demand a free flow and a
wider and better balanced dissemination of information. To
this end, the mass media have a leading contribution to
make. This contribution will be the more effective to the
extent that the information reflects the different aspects of
the subject dealt with.

Article II

1. The exercise of freedom of opinion, expression and information, recognized as an integral part of human rights and
   fundamental freedoms, is a vital factor in the strengthening
   of peace and international understanding.
2. Access by the public to information should be guaranteed by the
   diversity of the sources and means of information available to
   it, thus enabling each individual to check the accuracy of facts
   and to appraise events objectively. To this end, journalists
   must have freedom to report and the fullest possible facilities
   of access to information. Similarly, it is important that the
   mass media be responsive to concerns of peoples and
   individuals, thus promoting the participation of the public in
   the elaboration of information.
3. With a view to the strengthening of peace and international
   understanding, to promoting human rights and to countering racialism, apartheid and incitement to war, the mass
   media throughout the world, by reason of their role,
   contribute to promoting human rights, in particular by
   giving expression to oppressed peoples who struggle against
   colonialism, neo-colonialism, foreign occupation and all

forms of racial discrimination and oppression and who are unable to make their voices heard within their own territories.

4. If the mass media are to be in a position to promote the principles of this Declaration in their activities, it is essential that journalists and other agents of the mass media, in their own country or abroad, be assured of protection guaranteeing them the best conditions for the exercise of their profession.

Article III

1. The mass media have an important contribution to make to the strengthening of peace and international understanding and in countering racialism, apartheid and incitement to war.

2. In countering aggressive war, racialism, apartheid and other violations of human rights which are *inter alia* spawned by prejudice and ignorance, the mass media, by disseminating information on the aims, aspirations, cultures and needs of all peoples, contribute to eliminate ignorance and misunderstanding between peoples, to make nationals of a country sensitive to the needs and desires of others, to ensure the respect of the rights and dignity of all nations, all peoples and all individuals without distinction of race, sex, language, religion or nationality and to draw attention to the great evils which afflict humanity, such as poverty, malnutrition and diseases, thereby promoting the formulation by States of the policies best able to promote the reduction of international tension and the peaceful and equitable settlement of international disputes.

Article IV

The mass media have an essential part to play in the education of young people in a spirit of peace, justice, freedom, mutual respect and understanding, in order to promote human rights, equality of rights as between all human beings and all nations, and economic and social progress. Equally, they have an important role to play in making known the views and aspirations of the younger generation.

Article V

In order to respect freedom of opinion, expression and information and in order that information may reflect all points of view, it is important that the points of view presented by those who consider that the information published or disseminated about them has seriously prejudiced their effort to strengthen peace and international understanding, to promote human rights or to counter racialism, apartheid and incitement to war be disseminated.

Article VI

For the establishment of a new equilibrium and greater reciprocity in the flow of information, which will be conducive to the institution of a just and lasting peace and to the economic and political independence of the developing countries, it is necessary to correct the inequalities in the flow of information to and from developing countries, and between those countries. To this end, it is essential that their mass media should have conditions and resources enabling them to gain strength and expand, and to co-operate both among themselves and with the mass media in developed countries.

Article VII

By disseminating more widely all of the information concerning the universally accepted objectives and principles which are the bases of the resolutions adopted by the different organs of the United Nations, the mass media contribute effectively to the strenghtening of peace and international understanding, to the promotion of human rights, and to the establishment of a more just and equitable international economic order.

Article VIII

Professional organizations, and people who participate in the professional training of journalists and other agents of the mass media and who assist them in performing their functions in a responsible manner should attach special

importance to the principles of this Declaration when drawing up and ensuring application of their codes of ethics.

Article IX

In the spirit of this Declaration, it is for the international community to contribute to the creation of the conditions for a free
flow and wider and more balanced dissemination of information, and of the conditions for the protection, in the exercise
of their functions, of journalists and other agents of the mass
media. Unesco is well placed to make a valuable contribution
in this respect.

Article X

1. With due respect for constitutional provisions designed to
   guarantee freedom of information and for the applicable
   international instruments and agreements, it is indispensable to create and maintain throughout the world the
   conditions which make it possible for the organizations and
   persons professionally involved in the dissemination of
   information to achieve the objectives of this Declaration.
2. It is important that a free flow and wider and better balanced
   dissemination of information be encouraged.
3. To this end, it is necessary that States facilitate the procurement
   by the mass media in the developing countries of adequate
   conditions and resources enabling them to gain strength and
   expand, and that they support co-operation by the latter both
   among themselves and with the mass media in developed
   countries.
4. Similarly, on a basis of equality of rights, mutual advantage and
   respect for the diversity of the cultures which go to make up
   the common heritage of mankind, it is essential that bilateral
   and multilateral exchanges of information among all States,
   and in particular between those which have different economic and social systems, be encouraged and developed.

Article XI

For this Declaration to be fully effective it is necessary, with due
respect for the legislative and administrative provisions and

the other obligations of Member States, to guarantee the existence of favourable conditions for the operation of the mass media, in conformity with the provisions of the Universal Declaration of Human Rights and with the corresponding principles proclaimed in the International Covenant on Civil and Political Rights adopted by the General Assembly of the United Nations in 1966.

APPENDIX II: UNESCO 21 C/RES. 4/19 (MACBRIDE COMMISSION AND NWICO)

4/19   **International Commission for the Study of Communication Problems**

The General Conference

Reaffirming its attachment to the principles proclaimed in the Charter of the United Nations, the Universal Declaration of Human Rights, the International Covenant on Civil and Political Rights, the Constitution of Unesco and the Declaration on Fundamental Principles concerning the Contribution of the Mass Media to Strengthening Peace and International Understanding, to the Promotion of Human Rights and to Countering Racialism, Apartheid and Incitement to War,

Recalling more particularly Article 19 of the Universal Declaration of Human Rights which provides that 'Everyone has the right to freedom of opinion and expression; this right includes freedom to hold opinions without interference and to seek, receive and impart information and ideas through any media and regardless of frontiers' and Article 29, which stipulates that, like all others, 'These rights and freedoms may in no case be exercised contrary to the purposes and principles of the United Nations',

Recalling also Articles 19 and 20 of the International Covenant on Civil and Political Rights,

Recalling also the declaration in the Constitution of Unesco that 'the States Parties to this Constitution, believing in . . . the unrestricted pursuit of objective truth, and in the free exchange of ideas and knowledge, are agreed and deter-

Source: UNESCO 21 C/*Resolutions* at 68.

mined to develop and to increase the means of communication between their peoples and to employ these means for the purpose of mutual understanding and a truer and more perfect knowledge of each other's lives',

Recalling moreover that the purpose of Unesco is 'to contribute to peace and security by promoting collaboration among the nations through education, science and culture in order to further universal respect for justice, for the rule of law and for the human rights and fundamental freedoms which are affirmed for the peoples of the world, without distinction of race, sex, language or religion, by the Charter of the United Nations' (Article 1 of the Constitution),

Reaffirming the responsibilities of Unesco and its role in the field of communication and recalling previous General Conference debates on this subject, including resolutions 4/9.1/2 and 4/9.1/3 adopted at its twentieth session (1978),

Noting the increasing attention devoted to communication problems and needs by other inter-governmental organizations, both regional and international, notably the Movement of Non-Aligned Countries which, in the Declaration of the Colombo Summit (1976), stated that 'a new international order in the fields of information and mass communications is as vital as a new international economic order' and, in the Declaration of the Havana Summit (1979), noting progress in the development of national information media, stressed that 'co-operation in the field of information is an integral part of the struggle for the creation of new international relations in general and a new international information order in particular',

Recalling that the Director-General, in pursuance of resolution 100 adopted by the General Conference at its nineteenth session (Nairobi, 1976), set up the International Commission for the Study of Communication Problems, composed of sixteen eminent persons acting in an individual capacity, that the Commission was able to carry out its work in total independence and that it prepared a final report published under the title *Many Voices, One World*,

Considering that the publication by Unesco of the Report of the International Commission for the Study of Communication Problems is not only stimulating a discussion of considerable breadth and intensity, but is, at the same time, encouraging professional circles and the general public to join in the debate,

Noting with satisfaction that the report of the Director-General on the findings of the International Commission for the Study of Communication Problems (21C/85) has greatly facilitated the discussions devoted to communication problems and to the different aspects of the Organization's programme related to them,

Conscious that communication among individuals, nations and peoples, as well as among national minorities and different social, ethnic and cultural groups can and must, provided that its means are increased and its practices improved, make a greater contribution to individual and collective development, the strengthening of national and cultural identity, the consolidation of democracy and the advancement of education, science and culture, as well as to the positive transformation of international relations and the expansion of international co-operation,

I

1. *Expresses* its thanks to the Director-General for having put at the disposal of the International Commission for the Study of Communication Problems the means necessary for its work;
2. *Addresses* its appreciation and thanks to the Chairman, Mr Sean MacBride, and to the members of the International Commission for the Study of Communication Problems, and congratulates them on the quality of the work carried out, the breadth of vision they have shown and the praiseworthy efforts they have made to fulfil their mandate in the allotted time;

II

3. *Considers* the publication of the Report of the International Commission for the study of Communication Problems as a valuable contribution to the study of information and communication problems;
4. *Recognizes* that that Report has succeeded in identifying a large number of the most significant information and communication problems, examining certain questions posed in this field at different levels and pointing to a number of directions

in which action with a view to settling those questions in the short, medium and long term might be taken;

5. *Emphasizes* that the debate to which the Report has given rise up to now shows that the international community is becoming aware of the universality of the problems of information and communication, of the growing interdependence of countries and of the community of interests in this field;

6. *Hopes* that this debate will continue and become more searching, drawing in all those to whom the Report's recommendations were addressed, including 'governments and international organizations, policy-makers and planners, the media and professional organizations, researchers, communication practitioners, organized social groups and the public at large', bearing in mind that communication takes diverse forms and involves large sectors of all societies;

7. *Welcomes* the steps taken by the Director-General to ensure the widest possible distribution of the Final Report of the International Commission for the Study of Communication Problems;

8. *Approves* the comments of the Director-General concerning the Final Report of the Commission, notably those in which he affirms that 'it should be possible to give effect to some' of its recommendations 'in the immediate future, whereas others call for resources or studies which would take varying lengths of time to provide';

9. *Considers* that the Report and its recommendations also constitute valuable encouragement for the continuing examination, analysis and study of information and communication problems within the Secretariat, and in Member States and professional associations;

III

10. *Invites* Member States:
    (a) to circulate the Report widely and to study the conclusions and recommendations approved by the Commission, which merit the attention of all Member States;
    (b) to study the Final Report in detail, particularly the recommendations it contains, and to communicate their comments and observations on those recommendations to the Director-General of Unesco in time for him to be able to make use of

them in the preparation of the second Medium-Term Plan (1984–1989);

(c) to take the Commission's recommendations into considera- tion in the preparation and strengthening of their national communication capabilities, without losing sight of the fact that differing social, cultural and economic circumstances call for a variety of approaches to the definition and implementation of national policies and systems and to the identification and overcoming of the obstacles to develop- ment in the field of information and communication;

(d) to bear in mind also the fundamental need to safeguard freedom of opinion, expression and information; to ensure that the peoples are given the widest and most democratic access possible to the functioning of the mass media; and to make communication an integral part of all development strategy;

(e) to further the development of communication infrastruc- tures, paying special attention to the establishment of fairer telecommunication, postal and other tariffs, and to define in liaison with the International Telecommunication Union and other competent organizations of the United Nations system the conditions necessary for a more equitable utilization of limited natural resources such as the electromagnetic spec- trum and geostationary orbits;

IV

11. *Invites* interested international and regional intergovern- mental, non-governmental and professional organizations:

(a) to take note of the recommendations approved by the International Commission for the Study of Communication Problems and to convey their comments and observations to the Director-General;

(b) particularly if they belong to the United Nations system, to expand their co-operation so as to contribute to the solution of the most pressing information and communication prob- lems;

V

12. *Reaffirms* that Unesco, which has been particularly active in the field of information and communication within the United

Nations system, plays a major role in the examination and solution of problems in this domain;

13. *Invites* the Director-General to take the necessary measures to follow up the suggestions presented in his report on the findings of the International Commission for the Study of Communication Problems, and in particular:

(a) to continue to promote dissemination of the Commission's Report, within the limits of the regular programme and budget, by providing assistance for this purpose to countries which request it;

(b) to communicate the Commission's Final Report and recommendations to the international and regional intergovernmental and non-governmental organizations concerned in order that they may examine measures that they might be able to carry out;

(c) to take into consideration to the greatest possible extent, in implementing the Programme for 1981–1983, those recommendations of the Commission that lend themselves to rapid application;

(d) to provide in forthcoming programmes for the continuation of studies on those problems of communication about which data are still incomplete, which did not receive sufficient attention from the Commission, or which deserve attention as a possible basis for procedures for implementing national, regional and international action;

(e) to examine how Unesco could help professional journalists to acquire a better knowledge of the cultures and the economic, political and social realities of different Member States, for instance by holding seminars for journalists on the cultures, societies and history of these countries;

(f) to examine the possibility of giving the programme sector concerned a place and a position in keeping with the growing importance which Member States appear to be attaching to it;

(g) to take into account as far as possible in the preparation of the next Medium-Term Plan the comments and observations made by Member States and international intergovernmental and non-governmental organizations on the conclusions and recommendations of the International Commission for the Study of Communication Problems and any other suggestions received from other organizations professionally concerned with communication problems;

(h) to undertake or sponsor, in particular, the studies and analyses necessary for the formulation of specific and practical proposals for the establishment of a new world information and communication order, and to convene an international meeting of experts for that purpose;

VI

14. *Considers* that:
   (a) this new world information and communication order could be based, among other considerations, on:
      (i) elimination of the imbalances and inequalities which characterize the present situation;
      (ii) elimination of the negative effects of certain monopolies, public or private, and excessive concentrations;
      (iii) removal of the internal and external obstacles to a free flow and wider and better balanced dissemination of information and ideas;
      (iv) plurality of sources and channels of information;
      (v) freedom of the press and information;
      (vi) the freedom of journalists and all professionals in the communication media, a freedom inseparable from responsibility;
      (vii) the capacity of developing countries to achieve improvement of their own situations, notably by providing their own equipment, by training their personnel, by improving their infrastructures and by making their information and communication media suitable to their needs and aspirations;
      (viii) the sincere will of developed countries to help them attain these objectives;
      (ix) respect for each people's cultural identity and for the right of each nation to inform the world public about its interests, its aspirations and its social and cultural values;
      (x) respect for the right of all peoples to participate in international exchanges of information on the basis of equality, justice and mutual benefit;
      (xi) respect for the right of the public, of ethnic and social groups and of individuals to have access to information sources and to participate actively in the communication process;

> (b) this new world information and communication order
> should be based on the fundamental principles of inter-
> national law, as laid down in the Charter of the United
> Nations;
> (c) diverse solutions to information and communication prob-
> lems are required because social, political, cultural and
> economic problems differ from one country to another and,
> within a given country, from one group to another;
> 15. *Expresses the wish* that Unesco demonstrate its willingness in its
> short-term and medium-term activities to contribute to the
> clarification, elaboration and application of the concept of a
> new world information and communication order.

APPENDIX III: UNESCO 77 EX/DEC. 6.8: CO-OPERATION WITH THE UNITED NATIONS RELIEF AND WORKS AGENCY (UNRWA) (3 DECEMBER 1967)

> *The Executive Board,*
> 1. *Having examined* the report of the Director-General on co-
> operation with the United Nations Relief and Works Agency
> (UNRWA) (77 EX/34),
> 2. *Conscious* of the enhanced importance of this co-operation in
> present circumstances and of the educational work in
> question on humanitarian grounds and in the interests of
> peace,
> 3. *Authorizes* the Director-General to co-operate with UNRWA in
> educational matters wherever UNRWA educational estab-
> lishments may be available with observance of the principles
> of international law regarding occupied territories and in the
> spirit of the agreement signed between Unesco and UNRWA
> on 26 January 1967 and on the basis of the following
> principles:
> (a) the ethical ideals laid down in the Unesco Constitution and in
> Article 26, dealing with education, of the Universal Declara-
> tion of Human Rights, paragraph (2) of which provides that
> 'Education shall be directed to the full development of the
> human personality and to the strengthening of respect for
> human rights and fundamental freedoms. It shall promote
> understanding, tolerance and friendship among all nations,
> racial or religious groups, and shall further the activities of
> the United Nations for the maintenance of peace', while

Source: UNESCO 77 EX/*Decisions*, p. 31.

paragraph (3) stipulates that 'Parents have a prior right to choose the kind of education that shall be given to their children',

(b) the directives adopted in resolution 7.81 by the General Conference at its ninth session (1956) which required in particular that the necessary measures be adopted to 'ensure that everywhere education shall respect the national, religious and linguistic traditions of the inhabitants, and that its nature shall not be altered for political reasons',

(c) the demand for unity in any system of education which implies that students shall be able later to pursue their studies in establishments at a higher level of the system to which the establishment they are attending belong, or of a system having the same socio-cultural, and particularly linguistic, characteristics;

4. *Invites* the Director-General to submit a report to the Executive Board at its next session on the implementation of this resolution, with any specific proposals by which he may consider it necessary or desirable to obtain the approval or authorisation of the Board.

APPENDIX IV: MEMBERSHIP OF THE EXECUTIVE BOARD OF UNESCO AT ITS 77TH AND 78TH SESSIONS

No. of States	Region*	Member States
7	Western Europe	Federal Republic of Germany, Finland, France, Italy, Netherlands, Switzerland, UK.
7	Africa	Cameroon, Ivory Coast, Mali, Nigeria, Senegal, Tanzania, Zambia.
6	Latin America	Argentina, Brazil, Chile, Costa Rica, Panama, Peru.
3	Asia	India, Iran, Japan.
3	Eastern Europe	Hungary, Rumania, USSR.
2	Arab States	Egypt (UAR), Lebanon.
2	Other	Israel, USA.

* The classification used here does not correspond to the five regional groupings established for purposes of election to the Executive Board.

Sources: UNESCO Docs. 77 EX/SR.1 (1967) and 78 EX/SR.1 (1968).

References

1. Concepts of 'Politicisation'

1. Quoted in M. Nerfín, 'Is a Democratic United Nations Possible?', *Development Dialogue* (1976:2) p. 86.
2. Ibid., pp. 80–1.
3. David A. Kay, 'On the Reform of International Institutions: A Comment', *Int. Org.*, 30:3 (1976) pp. 533–4.
4. David A. Kay (ed.), *The Changing United Nations: Options for the United States* (New York: Academy of Political Science, 1977) p. 12.
5. John Holmes, 'A Non-American Perspective', in Kay (ed.), *The Changing United Nations*, op. cit., p. 37.
6. 'US brushes aside Western pleas to stay in Unesco', *The Times*, 30 December 1983. See also R. Righter, 'Inside the court of 'dictator' M'Bow', *ST*, 8 January 1984.
7. Richard Hoggart, *An Idea and its Servants: UNESCO from within* (London: Chatto & Windus, 1978) p. 58.
8. Ibid., p. 75.
9. See UNESCO 18 C/Res. 13 of 23 November 1974 (UNESCO 18 C/*Resolutions* at 123).
10. See UNESCO 18 C/Res. 3.427 of 20 November 1974 (UNESCO 18 C/*Resolutions* at 61).
11. See UNESCO 18 C/Res. 46.1 of 21 November 1974 (UNESCO 18 C/*Resolutions* at 192).
12. See 'Déclaration au Journal "Le Monde" de Monsieur Amadou-Mahtar M'Bow, Directeur Général de l'Unesco, relative aux décisions de la dix-huitième session de la Conférence générale concernant Israël', UNESCO *Press Release* of 7 December 1974. See also Association Franco-arabe de juristes, *L'UNESCO et Israël: ce qui s'est réellement passé* (Paris: Imp. Inter Compos Montmartre, undated).
13. E.g. William Korey, 'UNESCO and Israel', *Midstream: A Monthly Jewish Review* (Feb. 1975) pp. 7–17, esp. pp. 8–11 and 14; Jacob Katz, 'Zionism versus Anti-Semitism', *Commentary*, 67:4 (1979) pp. 46–52; Bernard Lewis, 'The Anti-Zionist Resolution', *Foreign Affairs*, 55:1 (1976) pp. 54–64; and Abba Eban, 'Israel, Anti-Semitism and the United Nations', *Jerusalem Quarterly*, 1 (Fall 1976) pp. 110–20. In the same spirit, see also Daniel P. Moynihan, 'The US in Opposition', *Commentary*, 59:3 (1975) pp. 31–44.
14. See Gene Lyons, David Baldwin and Donald McNemar, 'The "Politicization" Issue in the UN Specialized Agencies', in Kay (ed.), *The Changing United Nations*, op. cit., p. 88.
15. Ibid. p. 89
16. Robert Gregg, 'The Apportioning of Political Power', in Kay (ed.), *The Changing United Nations*, op. cit., p. 76.
17. E.g. Robert Cox and Harold Jacobson (eds), *The Anatomy of Influence*

(New Haven: Yale University Press, 1973) pp. 405 and 419–23; see esp. Jacobson, 'WHO: Medicine, Regionalism and Managed Politics'; and Jacobson, 'ITU: A Potpourri of Bureaucrats and Industrialists'. See also Hoggart, *An Idea and its Servants*, op. cit., p. 55.

18. See e.g. Jacobson, 'ITU. . .', op. cit., p. 67; and Lawrence Scheinman, 'IAEA: Atomic Condominium?', in Cox & Jacobson (eds), *The Anatomy of Influence*, op. cit., pp. 243–4.
19. Jacobson, 'ITU. . .', op. cit., pp. 59 and 63.
20. Lyons, Baldwin & McNemar, 'The "Politicization" Issue', op. cit., p. 90. See also Scheinman, 'IAEA. . .' op. cit., p. 244.
21. Gregg, 'The Apportioning of Political Power', op. cit., p. 80.
22. Ibid. p. 72.
23. Holmes, 'A Non-American Perspective', op. cit., p. 39.
24. David Mitrany, *A Working Peace System* (Chicago: Quadrangle Books, 1966).
25. See Scheinman, 'IAEA. . .', op. cit., pp. 229–35.
26. Jacobson, 'WHO. . .', op. cit.
27. See Susan Strange, 'IMF: Monetary Managers', in Cox & Jacobson (eds), *The Anatomy of Influence*, op. cit.; David Baldwin, 'The International Bank in Political Perspective', *World Politics*, 18:1 (1965) pp. 68–81; and Theodore Cohn, 'Politics in the World Bank Group: the Question of Loans to the Asian Giants', *Int. Org.*, 28 (1974) pp. 561–71.
28. See subsequent chapters.
29. For background material on the Specialised Agencies, we have drawn mainly on the studies in Cox & Jacobson (eds), *The Anatomy of Influence*, op. cit.
30. Ibid.
31. For a discussion of the questions of national sovereignty and domestic jurisdiction in the UN system, see Inis L. Claude Jr., *Swords into Plowshares* (New York: Random House, 1956) pp. 181–92.
32. Ibid.
33. For development of this theme, see e.g. Robert Tucker, *The Inequality of Nations* (Oxford: Martin Robertson, 1977).
34. See e.g. Hoggart, *An Idea and its Servants*, op. cit., pp. 66 and 138; and James P. Sewell, 'UNESCO: Pluralism Rampant', in Cox & Jacobson (eds), *The Anatomy of Influence*, op. cit., pp. 162–8. See also Chapter 3, section 5 below.
35. Jacobson, 'ITU. . .', op. cit.
36. Ibid., pp. 73 and 81.
37. For an analysis of the politics of membership, see Claude, *Swords into Plowshares*, op. cit., pp. 99–110.
38. On the status of Indian membership, see T. T. Poulouse, 'India as an Anomalous International Person', *B.Y.I.L.*, 64 (1970) pp. 201–12.
39. On this point in relation to UNESCO, see Jean Thomas, *U.N.E.S.C.O.* (Paris: Gallimard, 1962) pp. 134–5.
40. See e.g. George N. Shuster, *UNESCO: Assessment and Promise* (New York: Harper & Row, 1963) pp. 69 ff.
41. On Soviet bloc non-participation in UN Specialised Agencies, see W. Morawiecki, 'Institutional and Political Conditions of Participation of

Socialist States in International Organisations', *Int. Org.*, 22:2 (1968) pp. 494–507.

42. Scheinman, 'IAEA. . .', op. cit., pp. 226–8.
43. UNESCO 3 C/*Proceedings*, pp. 39–46.
44. Walter H. C. Laves and Charles A. Thomson, *UNESCO: Purpose, Progress, Prospects* (Bloomington: Indiana University Press, 1957) p. 407 note 23.
45. This section draws on studies in Cox & Jacobson (ed.), *The Anatomy of Influence*, op. cit.
46. Scheinman, 'IAEA. . .', op. cit.
47. Jacobson, 'ITU. . .', op. cit., p. 82.
48. See Scheinman, 'IAEA. . .', op. cit., p. 229; also 'Politicking dogs atom agency', *Guardian*, 28 September 1981.
49. David Fishlock, 'U.S. and Britain quit IAEA conference' and 'UN faces crisis over Arab move against Israel', *FT*, 25 September and 18 October 1982.
50. See figures supplied in Cox & Jacobson (eds), *The Anatomy of Influence*, op. cit., pp. 62, 65, 144–5, 181 and 220–1.
51. See e.g. Cox & Jacobson (eds), *The Anatomy of Influence*, op. cit., pp. 78–80, 158, 228 and 253; also Nerfín on 'the third veto', 'Is a Democratic UN Possible?', op. cit., pp. 88–92.
52. Details of UNESCO staffing as at mid-1978 are derived from data in UNESCO Doc. 20 C/54 (1978). For subsequent adjustments, see UNESCO Docs. 21 C/52 (1980) and 22 C/56 & Add. (1983). For a more detailed study of UNESCO staffing by this writer, see C. Wells, "The UNESCO Secretariat Decolonised?: Geographical Distribution of the Staff, 1972–84", in T. Weiss and D. Pitt (eds), *The Nature of United Nations Bureaucracies*, (London: Croom Helm, 1986).
53. Hoggart, *An Idea and its Servants*, op. cit., p. 90.
54. Strange, 'IMF. . .', op. cit., p. 269; and Jacobson, 'ITU. . .', op. cit., p. 80.
55. See e.g. T. G. Weiss and R. S. Jordan, *The World Food Conference and Global Problem-Solving* (New York: Praeger, 1976); and Barry Buzan, 'Negotiating by Consensus: Developments in Technique at the United Nations Conference on the Law of the Sea', *A.J.I.L.*, 75:2 (1981) pp. 324–48.
56. Gregg, 'The Apportioning of Political Power', op. cit., p. 77.
57. Strange, 'IMF. . .', op. cit., e.g. pp. 270–1.
58. See UNESCO Doc. DG/78/01 (1978); and Chapter 5, section 5 below.
59. For a sample of the coverage of challenges to Israel within UNESCO, see UNESCO *Press Reviews* from September 1974 to October 1976.
60. For an account of the sanctions, see Korey, 'UNESCO and Israel' op. cit., pp. 15–16.
61. See e.g. in Chapters 5 and 10.
62. See UNESCO *Press Reviews* of 5 May 1976 and of 30 September to 4 October 1976.
63. Ibid.
64. See e.g. 'Israel back in Unesco', *Guardian*, 23 November 1976; I. Guest, 'ILO hoping to impress America', *Guardian*, 7 June 1978; R. Kilian, 'US

gets ready to rejoin ILO', *Guardian*, 7 June 1979; K. Harper, 'US may rejoin new-style ILO', *Guardina*, 20 June 1979; and 'Russia's cruel union farce', *Guardian*, 4 March 1978.
65. Ibid.; and UNESCO 19 C/Res. 37 of 8 November 1976 (UNESCO 19 C/*Resolutions* at 115).

2. Conceptual Issues in the Information Debate

1. John Stuart Mill, 'On Liberty of Thought and Discussion', *On Liberty* (Harmondsworth: Penguin, 1978). For a development of liberal theory with particular reference to the information aspects, see Warren Breed, *The Self-Guiding Society* (New York: Free Press Paperback, 1971).
2. Mill, 'On Liberty of Thought and Discussion', op. cit., pp. 79–80 and 98.
3. Ibid., pp. 80–1.
4. Ibid., pp. 90–4, 111 and 115.
5. Ibid., p. 99.
6. Ibid., p. 111.
7. See e.g. Wilbur Schramm, *Responsibility in Mass Communication* (New York: Harper & Bros, 1967) p. 71 ff.; and Charles M. Wiltse, *The Jeffersonian Tradition in American Democracy* (University of North Carolina Press, 1935) pp. 139–50.
8. Wilbur Schramm, *Mass Media and National Development* (Paris: UNESCO, 1964).
9. Schramm, *Responsibility in Mass Communication*, op. cit., pp. 74–5.
10. Ibid., pp. 86–97.
11. Ibid.
12. For discussions of the issues involved in recent international debates on freedom of information and the press, see e.g. article by the Head of the AP Paris Bureau, Mort A. Rosenblum, 'Reporting from the Third World', *Foreign Affairs*, 55 (July 1977) pp. 815–35; Antony Smith, *The Politics of Information* (London: Macmillan Press, 1978); Rosemary Righter, *Whose News? Politics, the Press and the Third World* (London: Burnett Books, 1978) and 'Newsflow International', *The Political Quarterly*, 5:3 (1979) pp. 302–15; Colin Legum and John Cornwell, *A Free and Balanced Flow* (Mass.: Lexington Books, 1978); Richard Hoggart, *The Mass Media: A New Colonialism?* (London: 8th STC Communication Lecture, 1978); Leonard R. Sussman, *Mass Media and Third World Challenge* (Washington D.C.: Georgetown University, 1977); and Jeffrey St. John, 'The Third World and the Free Enterprise Press', *Policy Review* 5 (1978) pp. 59–70.
13. *Constitution* of UNESCO, adopted on 16 November 1945, *UNTS* 4 at 275; preamble, 1st recital.
14. See Doc. ECO/CONF./29 (1946) e.g. pp. 20–7; and UNESCO 1 C/*Proceedings*, pp. 19, 24–5, 44–5 and 61–4.
15. William G. Harley, 'The Mass Media and Society: An American Viewpoint', *The UNESCO Courier* (April 1977) pp. 28–31.
16. For the major postwar debates on the subject in the UN, see UN GAOR 2, C.1, 79–86 mtg (22–7 October 1947) pp. 179–248; C.3, 68–72 mtg (24–

9 October 1947) pp. 126–59; Plen 108 mtg (3 November 1947) p. 745, and Plen 115 mtg (15 November 1947) pp. 956–9; and UN GAOR 3(II), C.3, 181–226 mtg (6 April–11 May 1949) pp. 2–419. See also UN Docs E/CN.4/Sub.1/151 (1951) and Add.1 (1952) and E/CONF.6/10 (1948). For briefer parallel debates within UNESCO, see esp. UNESCO 1 C/*Proceedings*, pp. 157–61, and 2 C/*Proceedings*, pp. 96–100, 127–36 and 142–50.

17. For the contemporary debate, we have drawn mainly on the summary or verbatim records of discussions reproduced in the following UNESCO documents: *Summary of Interventions made in Programme Commission III of the Nineteenth Session of the General Conference*, UNESCO Doc. CC.77/WS/21 (April 1977); *Records* of the International Colloquium on the Free and Balanced Flow of Information between Developed and Developing Countries, Florence, 18–20 April 1977, UNESCO Doc. PI/VI/432 (undated typescript); UNESCO 20 C/*Proceedings*, pp. 1063–117; and documents produced by UNESCO's International Commission for the Study of Communication Problems (ICSCP), notably the *Monographs* on Associated Press, United Press International, Reuter and TASS in ICSCP Docs 13 and 15 (undated). The monographs were prepared on the basis of data supplied by the news agencies themselves, with the exception of Reuter for which material was collated from existing works. We have also drawn on Righter, *Whose News?* and other secondary sources cited in note 12 above.

18. See e.g. UNESCO Doc. PI/VI/432, note 17 above, p. 10.

19. *Government Pressures on the Press* (Zurich: IPI, 1955). For the companion volume, see *The Press in Authoritarian Countries* (Zurich: IPI, 1959). For other studies by Western newsmen of political restrictions on the press in liberal democracies, see e.g. Henry Wickham Steed, *The Press* (London: Penguin Special, 1938); Francis Williams, *Press, Parliament and People* (London: Heinemann, 1946) and *The Right to Know* (London: Longmans, 1969); and Harold Evans, 'The Half-Free Press', *The Freedom of the Press* (London: Hart-Davis MacGibbon, 1974).

20. IPI, *Government Pressures on the Press*, op. cit., pp. 13–15, 19, 38–9 and 45–7.

21. Ibid., p. 89.

22. See e.g. UNESCO Doc. CC.77/WS/21, note 17 above, pp. 20–1; UNESCO 20 C/*Proceedings*, pp. 1099, 1103–4, 1107–8 and 1112; and UNESCO Doc. PI/VI/432, note 17 above. Also Gunnar Garbo, 'Freedom of the Press: Media Structure and Control', *Bulletin of Peace Proposals*, 8:3 (1977) 233–5; UNESCO ICSCP Doc. 11 (undated) p. 14; and K. Nordenstreng and T. Varis, *Television Traffic: A One-Way Street?* (UNESCO, Reports and Papers in Mass Communication No. 70, Paris, 1974) pp. 43–5.

23. UNESCO ICSCP Doc. 19 (undated) Ann.V; and UNESCO Doc. PI/VI/432, note 17 above, pp. 14 and 27.

24. See UNESCO ICSCP Doc. 13, pp. 19 and 25 and ICSCP Doc. 15, pp. 144 and 158 (French versions); and UNESCO Doc. PI/VI/432, note 17 above, pp. 7–8, 11 and 23.

25. Legum & Cornwall, *A Free and Balanced Flow*, op. cit., p. 33. See also

UNESCO ICSCP Doc. 15, pp. 115–16 (French version); and Righter, *Whose News?* op. cit., pp. 182–5.

26. UNESCO Doc. PI/VI/432, note 17 above, statement by J. Wilson (BBC), pp. 25–6.
27. Ibid., p. 11; Righter, *Whose News?*, op. cit., p. 61; and Legum & Cornwell, *A Free and Balanced Flow*, op. cit., p. 27.
28. Ibid. See also AP statistics quoted in Righter, *Whose News?* op. cit., p. 27.
29. See UNESCO ICSCP Doc. 13, pp. 25–6, and ICSCP Doc. 15, pp. 8, 9, 155 and 157; UNESCO Doc. PI/VI/432, note 17 above, pp. 13–14 and 18–19; and Rosenblum, 'Reporting from the Third World', op. cit., pp. 823–4.
30. See Chapter 5 below.
31. For a recent statement of Soviet views, see Y. N. Zasursky and Y. I. Kashlev, 'The Mass Media and Society: A Soviet Viewpoint', *The UNESCO Courier* (April 1977) pp. 24–7. See also UNESCO Doc. CC.77/WS/21, note 17 above, pp. 4–5, 8–11, 15–16, 18–20 and 24; and UNESCO ICSCP Doc. 15, pp. 132–40 (French version).
32. UNESCO ICSCP Doc. 15, p. 134.
33. See e.g. UNESCO Doc. CC.77/WS/21, note 17 above, pp. 18–19.
34. Zasursky & Kashlev, 'The Mass Media and Society', op. cit., p. 26.
35. UNESCO Doc. CC.77/WS/21, note 17 above, p. 18.
36. See e.g. UN Docs E/CN.4/Sub.1/28 (1947) and E/CN.4/Sub.1/54 (1948); also statements by Soviet bloc delegates in debates cited in notes 16–17 above.
37. For background and debates, see UN Docs E/CN.4/Sub.1/104 (1950); E/AC.7/SR.261–8 and SR.271–4 (14–20 and 27–9 April 1954); A/C.3/L.447 (1954); UN GAOR 9, C.3, 599–616 mtg (30 November–11 December 1954) and Plen 514 mtg (17 December 1954); and UN GA Res. 841(IX) of same date (UN GAOR 9 Supp. 21 at 22).
38. For text, see International Convention concerning the Use of Broadcasting in the Cause of Peace, Geneva, 1936; *LNTS* 4.319, v. 186, at 302.
39. See Doc. ECO/CONF./29, pp. 32–4, 50–99 and 194, and UNESCO 2 C/*Proceedings*, pp. 104–7 and 347.
40. See e.g. UN GAOR 2, C.1, 79–86 mtg (22–7 October 1947) pp. 179–248.
41. Ibid. Also UN GAOR 2, C.3, 68 mtg (24 October 1947) pp. 136 and 157.
42. See Un Docs E/CN.4/Sub.1/51 and 66 (1948); UNESCO 1 C/*Proceedings*, pp. 160–1; and UN GAOR 2, C.3, 68 mtg (24 October 1947) p. 131.
43. As notes 38–9 above. Also James P. Sewell, *UNESCO and World Politics* (Princeton University Press, 1977) p. 99.
44. Unless otherwise specified, this section draws on the classic statement of Non-Aligned policy published by the Tunisian Secretariat of State for Information, *The New World Order for Information* (Tunis, 1977) and a more polished study from the same source reproduced as UN Doc. A/SPC/33/L.5 Annex (1978); R. Najar, 'A Voice from the Third World: Towards a "New World Order of Information"', *The UNESCO Courier* (April 1977) 21–3; and a paper by B. Osolnik, Yugoslav member of the MacBride Commission, *Aims and Approaches to a New International Communication Order*, UNESCO ICSCP Doc. 32 (undated).
45. See comment by Elihu Katz, former Director of Israel Television, in

Cross-Cultural Broadcasting (UNESCO, Reports and Papers in Mass Communication No. 77, Paris, 1976) p. 37; also Righter, *Whose News?*, op. cit., pp. 222–3.

46. On this point see also Righter, *Whose News?*, op. cit., p. 52.
47. See UNESCO Doc. CC.77/WS/21, note 17 above, pp. 10, 17, 31 and 36.
48. See esp. *Development Dialogue* (1976:2) and 1977:1); and Report of the Dag Hammarskjöld Institute for 1975, *What Now? Another Development*.
49. See e.g. UNESCO Doc. CC.77/WS/21, note 17 above, pp. 13–18, 26, 29, 31 and 36–7.
50. E.g. Fred Hirsch and David Gordon, *Newspaper Money* (London: Hutchinson, 1975); Ralph Miliband, *The State in Capitalist Society* (London: Quartet Books, 1973) esp. ch. 8; Paul Hoch, *The Newspaper Game* (London: Calder & Boyars, 1974); and Jeremy Tunstall, *The Media are American* (New York: Columbia University Press, 1977).
51. E.g. Herbert Schiller, *Mass Communications and American Empire* (New York: Augustus Kelly, 1969); Denis Stairs, 'The press and foreign policy in Canada' and other articles in *International Journal*, 31:2 (1976); and T. Varis, *The Impact of Transnational Corporations on Communication*, available as UNESCO Doc. SHC-76/CONF.635/7.
52. See e.g. US Congress, Senate, Select Committee to Study Governmental Operations with respect to Intelligence Activities; *Hearings*, Volume 7: Covert Action. 94th Congress, 1st Session, 1975, pp. 174–5.
53. See Tunisia, *The New World Order for Information*, op. cit., p. 15.
54. Ibid., p. 45; Najar, 'A Voice from the Third World', op. cit., p. 23; also UNESCO Doc. CC.77/WS/21, note 17 above, pp. 14, 16–17, 20 and 26; and UNESCO ICSCP Doc. 32, pp. 13–16.
55. See UNESCO Doc. CC.77/WS/21, note 17 above, pp. 14, 18 and 24.
56. Tunisia, *The New World Order for Information*, op. cit., e.g. pp. 13, 16–17 and 20. See also UN Doc. A/SPC/33/L.5 Annex (1978) pp. 16–21.
57. UN Doc. A/SPC/33/L.5 Annex (1978) pp. 16 and 20.
58. See UNESCO Doc. CC.77/WS/21, pp. 13, 22 and 35–6. See also similar statements by Bulgaria and Byelorussia, ibid. pp. 8 and 15.

3. Postwar Information Debate: UNESCO 'Technicised'?

1. E.g. Righter, *Whose News?*, op. cit., esp. pp. 140–3 and 180.
2. *Constitution* of UNESCO, op. cit., Art. IV.
3. Ibid., Art. X.
4. *Agreement* between the United Nations and the United Nations Educational, Scientific and Cultural Organization, reproduced in UNESCO *Manual of the General Conference* (1984 edition) at 115.
5. UNESCO *Constitution*, op. cit., preamble, 1st recital.
6. Ibid., preamble, 3rd to 5th recitals.
7. Ibid., Art. I(1).
8. Ibid., Art. I(2).
9. Doc. ECO/CONF./29, pp. 23–8 and 91–3; and UNESCO 1 C/*Proceedings*, pp. 19–27.

10. UNESCO 1 C/*Proceedings*, pp. 63–4; and US proposal reproduced in Doc. ECO/CONF./29 p. 68

11. On this point, see e.g. T.V. Sathyamurthy, *The Politics of International Co-operation: Contrasting Conceptions of UNESCO* (Geneva: Droz, 1964).

12. For a discussion of the issues, see Chapter 2 above.

13. Doc. ECO/CONF./29, pp. 21–5; and UNESCO 1 C/*Proceedings*, pp. 63–4.

14. UNESCO 1 C/*Proceedings*, pp. 63–4.

15. *Charter* of the United Nations, UN Doc. DPI/511–175(2–80), Arts I, IX and X.

16. See e.g. UN Docs E/1891, pp. 1–3 and 6, and p. 14 para. 36; and E/AC.34/L.10/Add.1 (1951).

17. See e.g. Laves & Thomson, *UNESCO: Purpose, Progress and Prospects*, op. cit., p. 133; Tor Gjesdal, 'The Right to Information', *UNESCO Chronicle*, 6 (Nov. 1960) p. 420; Thomas, *U.N.E.S.C.O.*, op. cit., p. 119; J. Behrstock, 'News, Politics, and Unesco's Wrong Turn', *IHT*, 8 November 1978; and UNESCO Docs. 2 C/83 (1947) p. 2 and 3 C/PRG/2.2 (1948) p. 2.

18. See UN, *For Fundamental Human Rights*, op. cit., ch. VIII, p. 37; and Carroll Binder, 'Freedom of Information and the United Nations', *Int. Org.*, 6:2 (1952) pp. 221–2.

19. UNESCO 1 C/*Proceedings*, pp. 158–61.

20. See Chapter 4 below.

21. See UNESCO 1 C/*Proceedings*, p. 227; and *Note* by René Maheu dated 22 January 1947 (hereafter *Maheu Note*) in UNESCO C.R. File 001 A 3/82 "66" Part I.

22. UNESCO 1 C/*Proceedings*, pp. 192 and 239.

23. UNESCO 2 C/*Proceedings*, p. 293.

24. Ibid. p. 294. For an account of American positions, see Byron Dexter, 'Yardstick for UNESCO', *Foreign Affairs*, 28:1 (1949) 56–67.

25. See e.g. UNESCO 1 C/*Proceedings*, pp. 82–3, 157 and 160–1; and 2 C/*Proceedings*, pp. 99–100, 130–6, 142–50 and 255–8.

26. On this point see Chapter 4 below; and e.g. Binder, 'Freedom of Information and the UN', op. cit., pp. 223–4. Also Foreign Office draft submission of 25 May 1951 to Mr E. Davies, Paper US 1451/68, Public Record Office File FO 371/95833.

27. See UN Docs E/CONF.6/C.4/6/Rev.1 (1948) and E/CONF.6/SR.9 (19 April 1948), statement by Mr Benton, pp. 5–6.

28. See confidential staff report by R. Maheu, *U.N.E.S.C.O. and the United Nations Conference on Freedom of Information*, 3 May 1948, in UNESCO C.R. File 001 A 3/82 "66" Part I (hereafter *Maheu Report*), pp. 25–6 para. 27; and p. 28.

29. The relevant UNESCO Central Registry files (001 A 3/82 "66" Parts I–IV) are very incomplete. Many key papers are also missing from the Foreign and Cabinet Office records held by the Public Record Office (PRO); in addition, the classification system for these records changed twice between 1945 and 1952. The relevant PRO files are FO 924/299 to 304; FO 924/598; FO 924/642; FO 371/72774 to 72778; FO 371/78894 to

78908; FO 371/88722 and 88723; FO 371/88776 and 88777; FO 371/88909; FO 371/95832 to 95836; FO 371/95885; FO 371/101423 to 101425; CAB 134/388 and 389; CAB 134/396 to 399; CAB 134/404 to 412; CAB 134/422 to 426; and CAB 134/973.

30. UNESCO Doc. 3 C/PRG/2.2 (1948) p. 2; also *Maheu Report*, note 28 above, p. 5.
31. Ibid.
32. See UN Conference on Freedom of Information, Geneva, March–April 1948, *Final Act*, UN Doc. E/CONF.6/79 (1948), Res. 39.
33. UN ESC Res. 197(VIII) of 24 February 1949 (UN GAOR 8 Supp.1).
34. UNESCO 1 C/*Proceedings*, pp. 276–7.
35. UNESCO 3 C/Res. 7.2212 of 11 December 1948 (UNESCO 3 C/*Resolutions* at 31) and 4 C/Res. 7.225 of 5 October 1949 (UNESCO 4 C/*Resolutions* at 33).
36. See e.g. UNESCO 3 C/*Proceedings*, pp. 292 and 296; and UN ESCOR 6, Plen 163 mtg (4 March 1948) p. 353.
37. See e.g. *Freedom of Information: An Aspect of UNO-UNESCO Relationship*, Doc. UNESCO/Prep.Comm./15 (1946); *Maheu Note*, note 21 above; 'Spreading of Educational, Scientific and Cultural News', UNESCO *Press Release 340* of 14 October 1947, and 'Unesco Commission Advises on Free Flow of Information: Proposes Wider Distribution of Cultural News', UNESCO *Press Release 352* of 29 October 1947, both in UNESCO C.R. File 001 A 3/82 "66" Part I; *Commission of experts on the Free Flow of Information, 13–18 October 1947*, UNESCO Doc. 2 C/83 (1947) p. 3; *Interests and responsibilities of UNESCO in the Field of Freedom of Information: Document submitted by the UNESCO Representative*, UN Doc. E/CONF.6/22 (1948); *Maheu Report*, note 28 above; *Unesco's Contribution to the Free Flow of Information in Cooperation with other Organs of the United Nations*, UNESCO Doc. 3 C/PRG/2.2 (1948); *Coordination of the Activities of the United Nations and UNESCO relating to Freedom of Information: Report by the Secretary-General of the United Nations, prepared in collaboration with the Director-General of UNESCO*, UN Doc. E/1891 (1951); UN Doc. E/AC.34/L.10/Add.1 (1951); and secondary accounts cited in note 17 above.
38. See Doc. ECO/CONF./29, pp. 40–1; and UNESCO/Prep.Comm./15, op. cit., p. 2.
39. E.g. UNESCO 3 C/*Proceedings*, p. 292, Secretariat statement; UNESCO Doc. 18 EX/3 (1949); and UNESCO Doc. 18 EX/SR.9 (30 November 1949) pp. 6–9, Secretariat statement.
40. E.g. UNESCO Docs 2 C/83, 3 C/PRG/2.2, and 3 C/*Proceedings*, p. 293; *Maheu Report*, note 28 above; and UN Doc. E/1891 (1951).
41. UNESCO 2 C/*Proceedings*, p. 375.
42. See Chapter 4 below.
43. Compare e.g. *Maheu Report*, note 28 above, with UN Doc. E/AC.7/SR.179 (6 March 1951) p. 9, statement by Chile.
44. See Chapter 4 below.
45. *Maheu Report*, note 28 above, pp. 3–4; also René Maheu, 'Quel peut être notre rôle dans un débat politique?', *Le Courrier de l'UNESCO* (June 1948) pp. 7–8.

46. E.g. UNESCO Docs 2 C/83, 3 C/PRG/2.2, and 4 C/PRG/4.
47. UNESCO Docs 18 EX/SR.19 (30 November 1949) and 3 C/*Proceedings*, pp. 292–7.
48. See e.g. UNESCO/MCG *Memo*. No. 93 of 8 April 1948 from Farr to DDG, UNESCO C.R. File 001 A 3/82 "66" Part I; UNESCO Docs 3 C/PRG/2.2, p. 2, and 3 C/*Proceedings*, p. 292; ODG *Memo*. of 6 June 1950 from Maheu to Schneider, UNESCO C.R. File 001 A 3/82 "66" Part III; and UN Doc. E/1891 (1951) paras 33–8.
49. *Maheu Report*, note 28 above, pp. 18–23.
50. Insights gained from interview with Mr J. Behrstock, US national and former Head of UNESCO Division of Free Flow of Information, on 21 March 1983.
51. *Maheu Note* and *Maheu Report*, notes 21 and 28 above resp.
52. See UN Docs E/AC.7/SR.135 and 136 (12–13 July 1950).
53. UN Doc. E/1891 (1951).
54. See e.g. UN ESCOR 13, Plen 555 mtg (17 September 1951) p. 708; and UN Doc. E/AC.7/SR.179 (6 March 1951) p. 8. See also *letter* MC 162801 of 2 June 1950 from Farr to Behrstock and MC *Memo* No. 661 of 29 June 1950 from Farr to ODG, both in UNESCO C.R. File 001 A 3/82 "66" Part III.
55. Binder, 'Freedom of Information and the UN', op. cit. pp. 219–20.
56. See UN Docs E/AC.7/SR.135 and 136 (12–13 July 1950).
57. See UN ESCOR 13, Plen 555 mtg (17 September 1951); UN Docs E/AC.7/SR.214 to 219 (4–10 June 1950); UN ESCOR 14, Plen 603 mtg (12 June 1952); and UN Docs E/2178 and Add.1–8 (1952).
58. See esp. following briefs for UK delegations to UN meetings: Paper I.O.C.(59)109 of 6 June 1950, para.16, Public Record Office (PRO) File CAB 134/405; Paper I.O.C.(50)132 of 26 June 1950, PRO File CAB 134/406; and Paper I.O.C.(FI)(51)8 of 21 June 1951, PRO File CAB 134/426. Also *letter* from Foreign Office (Boothby) to UK Delegation to UN (Hoare), April 1950, Paper US 1451/18, PRO File FO 371/88722; and *letter* of 25 January 1952 from UK Delegation to General Assembly (Howard) to Foreign Office (Butler), Paper US 1451/1, PRO File FO 371/101423.
59. Commonwealth Relations Office *telegram* to Commonwealth Governments (undated), Paper US 1451/10, PRO File FO 371/101423.
60. For correspondence, see PRO File FO 371/78896, Papers UNE 1075/96, UNE 1107/1451/96 and UNE 1130/1451/96; PRO File FO 371/78898, Paper UNE 1584; PRO File FO 371/78906, Papers UNE 3016 & 3092; PRO File FO 371/78907, Papers UNE 3409, 3568 & 3819; PRO File FO 371/88722, Paper US 1451/8; and PRO File FO 371/95833, Papers US 1451/54, 56 and 62–3.
61. On this point see e.g. Sewell, 'UNESCO: Pluralism Rampant' op. cit., pp. 162–8.
62. For debates, see UN Docs E/AC.7/SR.179 to 180 (6 and 9 March 1951); and UN ESCOR 12, Plen 467 mtg (13 March 1951) pp. 252–3.
63. See e.g. UN ESCOR 13, Plen 517 mtg (24 August 1951) pp. 353–4.
64. See UNESCO staff report, *Memo* NY-6039 of 24 May 1951 from UNESCO New York Office (Arnaldo) to Berkeley & Behrstock at Paris

HQ, UNESCO C.R. File 001 A 3/82 "66" Part IV.

65. See UN Doc. E/AC.34/L.10/Add.1 (1951) in UNESCO C.R. File 001 A 3/82 "66" Part IV. The UNESCO file copy shows in handwriting the amendments adopted by the *ad hoc* Committee on 27 June 1951.

66. Ibid.

67. See report by UNESCO New York Office (Arnaldo) to Berkeley & Behrstock at Paris HQ on the *ad hoc* Committee meeting, *Memo*. NY-6223 of 27 June 1951, UNESCO C.R. File 001 A 3/82 "66" Part IV.

68. Ibid.

69. Ibid.

70. UN Docs E/AC.34/L.10/Add.1 and E/1995 and Add.1 (1951).

71. UN ESC Res. 414(XIII) B.I. of 18 September 1951 (UN ESCOR 13 Supp.1 at 80) and UN GA Res. 632(VII) of 16 December 1952 (UN GAOR 7 Supp.20 at 22).

72. See e.g. UNESCO Doc. 17 C/76 (1972) Part I para. 6.

73. See *Memos*. from Behrstock to Carnes, MRD/1966/75 of 8 January 1951; Maheu to Behrstock, 16 February 1951; and Behrstock to Carnes, 27 February 1952, pp. 4–5, all in UNESCO C.R. File 001 A 3/82 "66" Part IV: and Schneider to Carnes, 13 November 1952, ibid., Part V. See also wording of UNESCO Doc. 3 C/PRG/2.2, p. 2, Section 2A, para. 3.

74. Tor Gjesdal, 'The Right to Information', *UNESCO Chronicle*, 6 (Nov. 1960) p. 420.

75. Interviews with Mr J. Behrstock on 21 March 1983 and Mr P. Navaux on 28 April 1983.

76. See e.g. UNESCO Docs COM/CS/68/1/4 (1967) pp. 2–3 and 5–6; DG/74/4 (1974) p. 4; and 17 C/*Proceedings*, pp. 1012–13.

4. Postwar Information Debate: A Consensus?

1. E.g. Righter, *Whose News?*, op. cit.; and Hoggart, *An Idea and its Servants*, op. cit.

2. E.g. Binder, 'Freedom of Information and the UN', op. cit.; Laves & Thomson, *UNESCO: Purpose, Progress and Prospects*, op. cit., esp. pp. 43 and 116–19; and Herbert Schiller, 'Libre Circulation de l'Information et Domination mondiale', *Le Monde Diplomatique*, September 1975.

3. UN, *For Fundamental Freedoms*, op. cit., ch. VIII; and *These Rights and Freedoms*, op. cit., ch. VI.

4. For contrasting accounts of the background to US policy, see e.g. Binder, 'Freedom of Information and the UN', op. cit., and Schiller, 'Libre Circulation de l'Information' op. cit.

5. See UN Docs A/BUR/2 (undated) (UN GAOR 1(I), Gen.C., Annex 1a at 32); A/BUR/24 (1946) (UN GAOR 1(I), Gen.C., Annex 12 at 59); and A/C.3/76 (1946) (UN GAOR 1(II), C.3, Annex 16 at 406).

6. Doc. ECO/CONF./29 (1946) p. 58.

7. For debates, see UN GAOR 1(I), Gen.C. 12 mtg (7 February 1946) pp. 19–20 and 32–3; Plen 26 mtg (9 February 1946) p. 365; and UN GAOR 1(II), C.3, 28 mtg (30 November 1946) pp. 163–8.

8. Ibid.

9. Compare original motions cited in note 5 above with oral UK proposals and UN GA Res. 59(I) of 14 December 1946, esp. preamble, 3rd recital, and operative para. 2(a).

10. UN GA Res. 59(I) of 14 December 1946, preamble.

11. See UN Docs A/C.3/157 and Add.1 (1947) (UN GAOR 2 Annex 5 at 239); UN GAOR 2, C.3, 57–60 mtg (2, 3, 6 and 7 October 1947) pp. 49–81; Plen 117 mtg (17 November 1947) pp. 1023–4; and UN GA Res. 132(II) of 17 November 1947 (UN GAOR 2, *Resolutions*).

12. UN GAOR 1(II), C.3, 28 mtg (20 November 1946) p. 164.

13. UN GA Res. 59(I) (1946), para. 2(b).

14. UN Doc. E/CONF.6/79 (1948).

15. Binder, 'Freedom of Information and the UN', op. cit., pp. 222–3.

16. Ibid., pp. 223–4.

17. UN ESC Res. 9(2) of 21 June 1946 (UN ESCOR 2 Annex 14 at 400) para. 8.

18. UN ESC Res. 197(VIII) of 24 February 1949 (UN ESCOR 8 Supp.1).

19. On the background to the IPI, see Rosemary Righter, *IPI The Undivided Word: A History of the International Press Insitute 1951–1976* (Zurich: IPI, 1976) pp. 13–17. For UNESCO discussions, see UNESCO 2 C/*Proceedings*, pp. 371–4; 3 C/*Proceedings*, pp. 260 and 293–5; and 4 C/*Proceedings*, pp. 303–11.

20. Righter, *IPI The Undivided Word*, op. cit., p. 15 and ch. 4.

21. Ibid., pp. 16–17.

22. Laves & Thomson, *UNESCO: Purpose, Progress, Prospects*, op. cit., pp. 22–3, 43 and 116–19. See also Doc. ECO/CONF./29, pp. 40–1 and 68–9; UNESCO 1 C/*Proceedings*, pp. 63–4 and 157; and Sewell, *UNESCO and World Politics*, op. cit., p. 97.

23. UNESCO 1 C/*Proceedings*, p. 157.

24. Ibid., p. 276.

25. For debates on this project and on a British proposal for an 'Ideas Bureau', see UNESCO 1 C/*Proceedings*, pp. 157–61 and 277; 2 C/*Proceedings*, pp. 75–7, 228, 233, 385–6 and 404–8; 3 C/*Proceedings*, pp. 297–304; and 4 C/*Proceedings*, pp. 309–10.

26. Quoted in Sewell, *UNESCO and World Politics*, op. cit., pp. 97–9 and 149.

27. See UNESCO Docs 3 C/35 and 3 C/36 (1948).

28. Laves & Thomson, *UNESCO: Purpose, Progress, Prospects*, op. cit., p. 116. See also Sewell, *UNESCO and World Politics*, op. cit., pp. 97–9 and 149.

29. Sewell, *UNESCO and World Politics*, op. cit. pp. 97–9 and 225.

30. See Byron Dexter, 'Unesco Faces Two Worlds', *Foreign Affairs*, 25:3 (1947), esp. pp. 396–8 and 402–5.

31. For Foreign Office and Cabinet views on US policy, see esp. Papers LC 1818 and 1851, PRO File FO 924/300; Paper LC 4805, PRO File FO 924/302; Paper LC 5196, PRO File FO 924/303; and Paper I.O.C.(FI)(47)2 (Rev) of 26 April 1947, p. 3 para. 11, PRO File CAB 134/422.

32. See e.g. Papers LC 5595, PRO File FO 924/304; I.O.C.(FI)(48)4, PRO File CAB 134/433; LC 3764, PRO File FO 924/642; and I.O.C.(FI)(49)1, PRO File CAB 134/424.

33. See UNESCO 1 C/*Proceedings*, pp. 50–1, 80, 130 and 161.

34. See esp. *Minute* of 19 October 1946 by F. R. Cowell in Paper LC 4805, PRO File FO 924/302; and *Minute* of 3 November 1946 by Cowell in Paper LC 5035 and *Memo* of 6 November 1946 by Cowell, para. 3, in Paper LC 5196, both in PRO File FO 924/303.

35. On Soviet non-participation at this time, see e.g. Morawiecki, 'Institutional and Political Conditions of Participation of Socialist States . . .' op. cit., esp. pp. 504–5; and D. Mylonas, *La Genèse de l'UNESCO* (Brussels: Bruylant, 1976), esp. pp. 140–1 and 363–5; John Armstrong, 'The Soviet Attitude toward UNESCO' *Int. Org.*, 8:2 (1954) esp. pp. 232–3; and Dexter, 'Unesco Faces Two Worlds' op. cit.

36. See e.g. UN ESCOR 6, Plen 165 mtg (5 March 1948), statements by Messrs Katzsuchy (Poland) and Arutinian (USSR), pp. 368–9 and 374 resp.; UN ESCOR 7, Plen 212 mtg (24 August 1948), statement by Mr Altman (Poland), pp. 601–2; UN ESCOR 8, Plen 241 mtg (17 February 1949), statement by Mr Morozov (USSR) p. 147; and UN ESCOR 13, Plen 518 mtg (24 August 1951), statements by Mr Birecki (Poland) p. 352, and Mr Zonov (USSR) p. 355.

37. E.g. Doc. ECO/CONF./29, pp. 90–1; UNESCO 1 C/*Proceedings*, pp. 51–2 and 138; and UNESCO 2 C/*Proceedings*, pp. 97–100.

38. Doc. ECO/CONF./29, pp. 90–1.

39. UNESCO 2 C/*Proceedings*, p. 218.

40. Doc. ECO/CONF./29, pp. 60 and 107; and UNESCO 1 C/*Proceedings*, pp. 39–41 and 81–2.

41. See e.g. UNESCO 1 C/*Proceedings*, pp. 40–1 and 81–2; 5 C/*Proceedings*, pp. 304–5; and UNESCO 5 C/Res. F.33 of 17 June 1950 (UNESCO 5 C/*Resolutions* at 31).

42. On the concept and practice of 'uninstructed experts' in the UN system, see Inis L. Claude Jr., 'The Nature and Status of the Sub-Commission on Prevention of Discrimination and Protection of Minorities', *Int. Org.*, 5 (1951) pp. 300–12.

43. UN Doc. A/BUR/86 (1947) (UN GAOR 2, C.1, Annex 13a at 375).

44. Ibid.

45. UN Doc. A/BUR/SR.38 (21 September 1947).

46. UN GA Res. 110(II) of 3 November 1947 (UN GAOR 2, p. 14 (A/519)).

47. For debates and votes see UN GAOR 2, C.1, 79–86 mtg (22–7 October 1947) pp. 179–248.

48. For draft amendments, see UN Docs A/C.1/219–21 and 223–8 (1947) (UN GAOR 2, C.1, Annexes 13 b–j at 575).

49. UN GAOR 2, C.1, 86 mtg (27 October 1947) p. 239. See also UN GAOR 2, C.3, 69 and 72 mtg (24 and 29 October 1947) pp. 139 and 158 resp.

50. See Un Doc. A/C.3/162 (1947) (UN GAOR 2, C.3, Annex 11 at 256).

51. For draft resolutions, see UN Docs A/C.3/180, 185, 188 and 189 (1947) reproduced in relevant meeting records (see next note) and in UN GAOR 2, C.3, Annex 11a at 257.

52. UN GAOR 2, C.3, 68–72 mtg (24–9 October 1947) pp. 126–61, and Plen 115 mtg (15 November 1947) pp. 956–9.

53. UN GA Res. 127(II) of 15 November 1947 (UN GAOR 2 *Resolutions* at 38).

54. UN GAOR 2, Plen 108 mtg (3 November 1947) p. 745; and C.3, 72 mtg (29 October 1947) p. 158.
55. UN GAOR 5, C.1, 372–83 mtg (23 October–3 November 1950) and Plen 308 mtg (17 November 1950); GA Res. 381(V) of same date (UN GAOR 5 Supp.20 at 14); UN GAOR 7, C.3, 421–42 mtg (22 October–11 November 1952); UN Doc. A/2744 (1954) (UN GAOR 9 Annexes, Agenda item 69 at 1); UN GAOR 9, Gen.C. 96 mtg (19 October 1954); UN GAOR 9, ahPC 38–41 mtg (30 November–2 December 1954) and Plen 510 mtg (11 December 1954); UN Doc. A/2844 (1954) (UN GAOR 9 Annexes, Agenda item 69 at 2); and GA Res. 819(IX) of 11 December 1954 (UN GAOR 9 Supp.21 at 9).
56. UN Docs E/L.360 (1952) and E/AC.7/SR.214 to 216 (4–10 June 1952); and UN ESCOR 14, Plen 604 mtg (13 June 1952).
57. UN Doc. A/L.125 (1952).
58. UN GAOR 7, Plen 403 mtg (16 December 1952) pp. 357–67.
59. UN Doc. A/C.3/L.255/Rev.1 (1952) (UN GAOR 7 Annexes, Agenda item 29 at 31).
60. UN GAOR 7, C.3, 435 mtg (5 November 1952).
61. See UN Docs E/AC.7/SR.135 to 139 (12–17 July 1950); UN ESCOR 11, Plen 405 mtg (9 August 1950) pp. 265–70; UN ESC Res. 306(B)(XI) of same date (UN ESCOR 11 Supp.1 at 33); and UN GA Res. 424(V) of 14 December 1950 (UN GAOR 5 Supp.20 at 44).
62. Universal Declaration of Human Rights (hereafter UDHR) adopted by UN GA Res. 217(III)A of 10 December 1948 (UN GAOR 3(I)), Art. 19.
63. For debates and votes, see UN GAOR 3(I), C.3, 128–30 mtg (9–10 November 1948) pp. 408–29, and Plen 180–3 mtg (9–10 December 1948) pp. 852–912. (Note that Art. 19 was discussed in draft as Art. 17, adopted as Art. 20, and only later renumbered.)
64. UN Doc. A/784 (1948) (UN GAOR 3(I) Annexes, at 545).
65. UN GAOR 3(I), Plen 180–3 mtg (9–10 December 1948) pp. 852–912. (Note as for note 63 above.)
66. UDHR, note 62 above, Art. 29.
67. See UNESCO 3 C/*Proceedings*, pp. 203–5 and 294, and 4 C/*Proceedings*, p. 63.
68. For texts, see UNESCO Docs 2 C/BUR/2 (1947) and 2 C/*Proceedings*, p. 100.
69. UNESCO Docs 2 C/BUR/5 and 2 C/107 and Annex (1947).
70. UNESCO 2 C/Res. X,3 of 29 November 1947 (UNESCO 2 C/*Resolutions* at 63).
71. See UNESCO 2 C/*Proceedings*, pp. 100, 127–36 and 142–50.
72. See e.g. UN Doc. A/AC.42/7 (1951).
73. See UN Doc. E/CONF.6/79 (1948).
74. See UN, *For Fundamental Human Rights*, op. cit., p. 40; and *Maheu Report* cited in ch. 3 note 28 above, esp. p. 24.
75. UN GAOR 3(II), C.3, 181–226 mtg (6 April–11 May 1949) and summary in *YUN* [1948–9] pp. 553–77.
76. Ibid.
77. Ibid.
78. On this point see Binder, 'Freedom of Information and the UN', op. cit.,

p. 223; and UN, *These Rights and Freedoms*, op. cit., pp. 203–4.

79. See *Convention* on the International Transmission of News and the Right of Correction (hereafter CITNRC), adopted by UN GA Res. 277(III)C of 13 May 1949 (UN GAOR 3 *Resolutions* at 21) Arts. IX & XVIII.

80. Ibid., Art. I para. 4.

81. Ibid., Art. VII.

82. Ibid., Art. IX.

83. Ibid., Art. IX para. 1.

84. Ibid., Art. VIII para. 2; and Art. XII para. 5.

85. Ibid., Art. XVIII.

86. As note 75 above.

87. See UN Doc. A/C.3/495 Rev. 1 (1949).

88. As note 75 above.

89. Ibid.

90. UN Doc. A/C.3/L.5 (1949).

91. As note 75 above.

92. Ibid. and UN GA Res. 277(III)A and C of 13 May 1949 (UN GAOR 3 *Resolutions* at 21).

93. For voting record, see UN GAOR 3(II), C.3, 211–14 mtg (1949) pp. 293–324, esp. p. 316.

94. UN GA Res. 426(V) of 14 December 1950 (UN GAOR 5 Supp. 20 at 40). For procedural debate, see UN GAOR 5, C.3, 320–4 mtg (20–2 November 1950) pp. 302–27, and Plen 325 mtg (14 December 1950) pp. 666–7.

95. For the Committee's report, see UN Doc. A/AC.42/7 (1951) (UN GAOR 7 Annexes, Agenda item 29 at 4). For membership list, see *YUN* [1951] pp. 36–7.

96. UN Doc. A/AC.42/7 (1951) Annex A.

97. UN Doc. A/AC.42/7 (1951) pp. 26–7.

98. See e.g. UN Docs E/2031 and Add. 1–10 and E/AC.7/L.103 (1951); debate in ECOSOC, UN Docs E/AC.7/SR.199 to 204 (13–16 August 1951), and UN ESCOR 13, Plen 531 mtg (1 September 1951) pp. 469–76; and UN Docs A/C.3/L.5 (1949) and A/C.3/L.113 (1950).

99. UN GAOR 7, C.3, 430 mtg (1952) pp. 69–73.

100. See UN Doc. A/C.3/L.252 and Rev.1, Add.1 (1952) (UN GAOR 7 Annexes, Agenda item 29 at 31).

101. UN GAOR 7, C.3, 432 mtg (1952) pp. 79–85.

102. UN GAOR 7, Plen 403 mtg (16 December 1952) pp. 357–67. See UN GA Res. 630(VII) of same date (UN GAOR 7 Supp.20 at 22).

103. On this point see *Many Voices, One World* (Paris: UNESCO, 1980) pp. 248–9.

104. See *Multilateral Treaties deposited with the Secretary-General: Status as at 31 December 1982*, UN Doc. ST/LEG/SER.E/2 (1983) p. 521.

105. For debates in the Sub-Commission, see UN Docs E/CN.4/Sub.1/SR.69 to 84 (15–25 May 1950) and SR.87 to 112 (3–21 March 1952) and report, UN Doc. E/2190 and Annex A (1952). For debates in ECOSOC, see UN Docs E/AC.7/SR.138 (17 July 1950); UN ESCOR 11, Plen 405 mtg (9 August 1950) pp. 265–70; and E/AC.7/SR.214 p. 6 to SR.216 p. 19 (1952). For debates in General Assembly, see UN GAOR 7, C.3, 440–1

mtg (11 November 1952) pp. 129–42; UN GAOR 8, C.3, 513–16 mtg (4–6 and 9 November 1953) pp. 167–86, and Plen 460 mtg (28 November 1953) pp. 325–6.

106. Ibid.
107. See e.g. UN GAOR 2, C.1, 83 mtg (24 October 1947) p. 217.
108. UN Doc. E/CN.4/Sub.1/114 (1950).
109. UN Doc. E/CN.4/Sub.1/SR.77 (1950) p. 9.
110. UN Doc. E/CONF.6/79 (1948) pp. 44–5, Res. 35.
111. UN Doc. E/2190 (1952) Annex A.
112. UN Doc. E/L.360 (1952).
113. UN ESCOR 14, Plen 604 mtg (13 June 1952) pp. 259–61.
114. UN Doc. E/CONF.6/79 (1948) p. 45, Res. 36.
115. UN Doc. E/2190 (1952).
116. Ibid., Annex A.
117. For draft resolutions, see UN Docs A/C.3/L.263 and Revs 1,2 (UN GAOR 7 Annexes, Agenda item 29 at 31) and A/C.3/L.375 and Rev.2 (1953); for General Assembly debates, see note 105 above; and for resolutions, see UN GA Res. 635(VII) of 11 December 1952 (UN GAOR 7 Supp.20 at 22) and Res. 736(VIII) of 28 November 1953 (UN GAOR 8 Supp.17 at 17).
118. UN GA Res. 838(IX) of 17 December 1954 (UN GAOR 9 Supp.21 at 22).
119. CITNRC, note 79 above, preamble, 7th recital, and Art. IX. See also UN Doc. A/AC.42/7 (1951) pp. 34–5 and Annex A, p. 33, Art. 5.
120. See *Agreement* for Facilitating the Circulation of Visual and Auditory Materials of an Educational, Scientific and Cultural Character, adopted by UNESCO 3 C/Res. XIV(5) of 10 December 1948 (UNESCO 3 C/*Resolutions* at 113).
121. See e.g. UNESCO 1 C/*Proceedings*, pp. 157 and 160; 3 C/*Proceedings*, pp. 174–80, 295 and 301–8; and 4 C/*Proceedings*, p. 310.
122. UNESCO 3 C/*Proceedings*, pp. 306–8.
123. Ibid., pp. 174–80.
124. Ibid., pp. 178 and 180 resp.
125. UNESCO 1 C/*Proceedings*, p. 160.
126. UNESCO 3 C/*Proceedings*, p. 180.
127. Ibid., pp. 180 and 293.
128. See e.g. UNESCO 4 C/*Proceedings*, p. 306; and correspondence in UNESCO C.R. File 001 A 3/82 "66" Parts I–V.
129. See *Multilateral Treaties* . . ., note 104 above, pp. 485–6.
130. *Agreement* on Importation of Educational, Scientific and Cultural Materials, adopted on 17 June 1950 (UNESCO 5 C/*Resolutions*, Appendix, at 141).
131. UNESCO 5 C/*Proceedings*, pp. 223 and 457–60.
132. Ibid., p. 460.
133. See *Multilateral Treaties* . . ., op. cit., pp. 487–9.
134. See debates and resolutions on 'Information Facilities in Underdeveloped Regions of the World' and similar headings summarised in *YUN* [1948–9] p. 571; [1950] p. 556; [1952] pp. 467–70; [1954] pp. 233–4 and 239–40; [1955] pp. 166–70; [1957] pp. 214–16; [1958] pp. 226–31; [1959]

pp. 209 and 215; [1961] pp. 307–10; and [1962] pp. 341–4.

135. See esp. UN ESCOR 17, Plen 769–74 mtg (9–13 April 1954) pp. 92–108 and 117–30, and 788–9 mtg (29 April 1954) pp. 213–18; and UN Doc. E/CN.4/Sub.1/SR.66 (13 June 1947) p. 12, statement by Mr Binder (USA).

136. As note 134 above.

137. See *Mass Media in Developing Countries: A UNESCO Report to the United Nations* (UNESCO, Reports and Papers in Mass Communication No. 33, Paris, 1961); and UN Doc. E/3437 and Add.1 (1961) (UN GAOR 31 Annexes, Agenda item 10 (part I) at 1).

138. Ibid.

139. For summary of debates and decisions, see *YUN* [1961] pp. 307–10 and [1962] pp. 341–4.

140. Schramm, *Mass Communications and National Development*, op. cit.

141. UN GAOR 3(II), C.3, 181–226 mtg (6 April–11 May 1949) and Plen 209–11 mtg (12–13 May 1949).

142. See e.g. UN Docs A/C.3/L.5 (1949) and A/C.3/L.113 (1950).

143. On this point see e.g. Binder, 'Freedom of Information and the UN', op. cit., pp. 216–18. See also description of US press coverage in Chapter 3 above.

144. In this connexion see e.g. report by Salvador Lopez (Philippines), UN Doc. E/2426 and Add.1 (1954) (UN GAOR 17 Supp.12); comments by Member States, UN Doc. E/2427 and Add.1, 2 (1953) (UN GAOR 17 Annexes, Agenda item 12 at 11); debate in ECOSOC, UN Docs E/AC.7/SR.261 to 268 and SR.271 to 274 (14–20 and 27–9 April 1954). See also summary of resolutions and debates in *YUN* [1948–9] pp. 560–3 and 571–6; [1950] pp. 544–7 and 553; [1951] pp. 509–13; [1952] pp. 475–9; [1953] pp. 418–21; [1954] pp. 229–36 and 242; [1955] pp. 166–7; [1957] p. 213; and [1958] p. 227.

145. For views of the various States, see e.g. UN Docs E/2178 and Add.1–8 (1952) and A/3868 and Add.1–8 (1958).

146. UN GAOR 4, Plen 232 mtg (20 October 1949) pp. 106–17; and C.3, 233–4 mtg (27 September 1949) pp. 2–11; also UN Doc. A/C.3/L.6 (1949), and as note 144 above.

147. See UN Doc. E/2970 Rev.1 and Corr.1 (1957), ch. VII, Res. IX.

148. For report, see UN Doc. E/3088 (1958), ch. V.

149. For draft resolutions, see UN Docs E/L.824 (1959) (UN ESCOR 27 Annexes, Agenda item 10 at 17) and E/AC.7/L.388 adopted without change as UN ESC Res. 732(XXVIII) of 30 July 1959 (UN ESCOR 28 Supp.1 at 20).

150. For written comments of governments, see UN Docs E/3323 and Add.1–5 (1960).

151. For debates in Social Committee and plenary of ECOSOC, see UN Docs E/AC.7/SR.387 p. 3 to SR.388 p. 7 (both 21 April 1959); UN ESCOR 27, Plen 1061–2 and 1066 mtg (24 April 1959) pp. 85, 99 and 123–4 resp.; UN Docs E/AC.7/SR.405 and 406 (27–8 July 1959); and UN ESCOR 29, Plen 1095 and 1111 mtg (5 and 21 April 1960) pp. 5–8 and 98 resp.

152. For summaries of debates on the draft Declaration and draft Convention on freedom of information and procedural discussions on future work on these texts, see *YUN* [1959] pp. 210–14; [1960] pp. 333–7; [1961] p. 307; and [1962] pp. 342–3.

153. Ibid. For report on developments between 1954 and 1961, see UN Doc. E/3443 and Add.1, 2 (1961) (UN GAOR 31 Annexes, Agenda item 10 (Part II) at 1).
154. See UN Doc. A/4173 and Add. 1, 2 (1959).
155. As note 152 above; also *YUN* [1963] p. 359; [1964] pp. 360–1; [1965] pp. 488–9; [1966] pp. 480–1; etc.

5. The Contemporary Information Debate

1. See e.g debates on Art. 2 of the UN draft Convention on Freedom of Information, UN GAOR 15(I), C.3, 1028–45 and 1058 mtg (21 November–5 December and 16 December 1960) pp. 251–344 and 425–7, and UN GAOR 16(I), C.3, 1126–32 and 1134 mtg (6–12 and 14 December 1961); on Art. 19 of the ICCPR, UN GAOR 16(I), C.3, 1070–77 mtg (11–26 October 1961) pp. 55–91; on the *Declaration* on the Promotion among Youth of the Ideals of Peace, Mutual Respect and Understanding between Peoples, adopted by UN GA Res. 2037(XX) of 7 December 1965 (UN GAOR 20, Supp.14, at 40), summarised in *YUN* [1965] pp. 478–81; on the *Treaty* on principles governing the activities of States in the exploration and use of outer Space, including the moon and other celestial bodies (Outer Space Treaty) adopted on 19 December 1966 (UN GAOR 21 Supp.16 at 13), summarised in *YUN* [1966] pp. 32–43; on freedom of information, UN GAOR 23, C.3, 1639–40 and 1646 mtg (13 and 17 December 1968) and Plen 1748 mtg (19 December 1968), UN Doc. A/7433 (1968) (UN GAOR 23 Annexes, Agenda item 62 at 7) and UN GA Res. 2448 (XXIII) of 19 December 1968 (UN GAOR 23 Supp.18 at 52). Also debates within UNESCO on the *Declaration* on the Principles of International Cultural Co-operation, adopted by UNESCO 14 C/Res. 8.1 of 4 November 1966 (UNESCO 14 C/*Resolutions* at 86), UNESCO 14 C/*Proceedings*, item 18.4. See also debates in the United Nations on a Soviet bloc proposal for regulation of direct television broadcasting by satellite, UN Doc. A/8771 (1972) (UN GAOR 27 Annexes, Agenda items 28–9 and 37 at 1), and subsequent debates and resolutions summarised in *YUN* [1972] pp. 43–9; [1973] pp. 55–6, 60–2 and 66; [1975] pp. 80–4; [1976] pp. 61–6; [1977] pp. 68–71; [1978] pp. 130–2; [1979] pp. 102–6; and [1980] pp. 119–22.
2. See e.g. *Declaration* of Guiding Principles on the Use of Satellite Broadcasting for the Free Flow of Information, the Spread of Education and Greater Cultural Exchanges, adopted by UNESCO 17 C/Res. 4.111 of 15 November 1972 (UNESCO 17 C/*Resolutions* at 67) and debate, UNESCO 17 C/*Proceedings*, pp. 1012–21.
3. Righter, *Whose News?*, op. cit.
4. Roger Heacock, *UNESCO and the Media* (Geneva: Institut de Hautes Etudes Internationales,Etudes et Travaux No. 15, 1977).
5. Righter, *Whose News?*, op. cit., pp. 149 and 152.
6. Heacock, *UNESCO and the Media*, op. cit., p. 31
7. Righter, *Whose News?*, op. cit., pp. 151–2 and 154.
8. See Heacock, *UNESCO and the Media*, op. cit., esp. ch. IV.

9. See Righter, *Whose News?*, op. cit., esp. chs 4 and 5.
10. Righter, *Whose News?*, op. cit., p. 154, and Heacock, *UNESCO and the Media*, op. cit., p. 34.
11. Robert U. Brown, quoted in Jeffrey St. John, 'The Third World and the Free Enterprise Press', *Policy Review* 5 (1978) p. 62.
12. See Righter, *Whose News?*, op. cit., pp. 149, 152 and 154; and Heacock, *UNESCO and the Media*, op. cit., pp. 33, 34, 41 and 48–52.
13. For list of participants see *Final Report*, UNESCO Doc. COM/MD/38 (undated), Annex V.
14. Righter, *Whose News?*, op. cit., p. 154. For Director-General's speech, see UNESCO Doc. COM/MD/38 (undated) Annex II pp. 50–4. See also comments by Director-General in UNESCO Doc. 19 C/106 (1976) p. 2 para.3; and in UNESCO 19 C/*Proceedings* Part 1, p. 196.
15. UNESCO 19 C/*Proceedings* Part 1, e.g. statement by Guyana, p. 403.
16. For San José Declaration, see UNESCO Doc. COM/MD/38 (undated) pp. 23–4.
17. Righter, *Whose News?*, op. cit., p. 155.
18. For Recommendations see UNESCO Doc. COM/MD/38 (undated) pp. 25–45.
19. Ibid., Recommendation 1.
20. Ibid., esp. Recommendations 1, 2 and 4.
21. Ibid., esp. Recommendation 8; also Recommendation 6 para. 5(a), and Recommendation 24.
22. Ibid., e.g. Recommendation 1 para. 4, and Recommendations 4, 5, 9, 18 and 25(a).
23. Ibid., Recommendation 1 para. 3; and Righter, *Whose News?*, op. cit., pp. 155–6.
24. Heacock, *UNESCO and the Media*, op. cit., esp. pp. 33, 35 and 53.
25. Ibid., pp. 45 and 48–52.
26. Righter, *Whose News?*, op. cit., esp. ch. 4 and 5.
27. E.g. UNESCO 13 C/Res. 6.21 of 6 November 1964 (UNESCO 13 C/*Resolutions* at 88); 14 C/Res. 10 of 28 November 1966 (UNESCO 14 C/*Resolutions* at 92); 15 C/Res. 9 of 15 November 1968 (UNESCO 15 C/*Resolutions* at 88); 16 C/Res. 4.301 of 13 November 1970 and 16 C/Res. 8 of 7 November 1970 (UNESCO 16 C/*Resolutions* at 60 and 79 resp.).
28. Ibid. and UNESCO 17 C/Res. 4.113 of 15 November 1972 (UNESCO 17 C/*Resolutions* at 70); see also UNESCO Doc. 17 C/77 (1972).
29. UNESCO Doc. COM-74/CONF.616/3 (undated).
30. UNESCO Doc. COM-74/CONF.616/5 (25 April 1974) Annex I; and slightly altered text in UNESCO Doc. 18 C/35 (12 July 1974) Part II.
31. UNESCO Doc. 19 C/91 (1 July 1976) Annex I.
32. For background and meeting reports, see UNESCO Docs COM-74/CONF.616/5 (1974); 18 C/35 (1974) Part I; and 19 C/91 (1976) Annex II and Appendices 1 and 2.
33. UNESCO Doc. 18 C/35 (1974) Art. X.
34. For draft amendments, debate in Programme Commission, and decision, see UNESCO Docs. 18 C/COM/DR. 1–12 (1974); UNESCO 18 C/*Reports*, paras. 40–7 and 57; and UNESCO 18 C/Res. 4.111 of 20 November 1974 (UNESCO 18 C/*Resolutions* at 64).

35. For background report and draft amendments, see UNESCO Docs. COM-75/CONF.201/4 (1975) and COM-75/CONF.201/DR. 1–26 (1975); for report and attendance record, see UNESCO Doc. 19 C/91 (1976) Annex II and Appendix 2.
36. UNESCO Doc. 19 C/91 (1976) Annex I.
37. UNESCO Doc. 19 C/91 (1976) Annex II, p. 11.
38. UNESCO Doc. CC.77/WS/21 (1977) pp. 3–4 and 6–7.
39. See *letters* from relevant delegations reproduced in UNESCO Docs COM-75/CONF.201/INF. 4–10 (1975); and 19 C/91 (1976) Annex II pp. 5–6.
40. UNESCO 20 C/*Proceedings*, pp. 294–5. Also Righter, *Whose News?*, op. cit., p. 142.
41. See *The Times Index* [1972] pp. 112–13; [1974] p108; [1976] pp. 136–7; [1978] p. 393; and [1980] p. 351.
42. On US threats of further budgetary withholding, see note 101 below; also Righter, *Whose News?*, op. cit., p. 166; and Heacock, *UNESCO and the Media*, op. cit., p. 57.
43. For a sample of coverage, see UNESCO *Press Reviews*, September 1974 to October 1976. Note that the press reviews were previously held by the UNESCO Press Room but at the time of research were held by the Private Office of the Director-General.
44. UPI dispatch of 22 October 1976 cited in Heacock, *UNESCO and the Media*, op. cit., p. 57.
45. See AFP wire quoting Jean Mauriac, UNESCO *Press Review 189* of 27 October 1976.
46. See UNESCO 19 C/*Proceedings* Part 1, pp. 338, 404, 528, 591 and 603. See also J. Mauriac, AFP dispatch cited in note 45 above.
47. UNESCO 19 C/*Proceedings* Part 1, p. 286 para. 7.6.
48. Ibid., p. 297 para. 7.92.
49. UNESCO 19 C/*Proceedings* Part 1, pp. 495–8; also statement by Mr Kirkpatrick, Ibid., Part 2, pp. 458–9.
50. E.g. UNESCO 19 C/*Proceedings* Part 1, pp. 367–8, 482, 579, 594–5 and 631.
51. Ibid., pp. 496–8 paras. 16.16 to 16.17.
52. UNESCO 18 C/*Proceedings* Part 2, pp. 618–19 esp. paras. 97.4 to 97.8.
53. UNESCO 19 C/*Proceedings* Part 1, p. 367 para. 4.4.
54. Ibid., p. 473 para. 47.9; p. 499 para18.6; p. 579 para. 2.20; pp. 594–5 para. 10.13 and 10.19; and p. 631 para. 18.6.
55. UNESCO 19 C/*Proceedings* Part 2, pp. 226–7 esp. para. 76.12; and pp. 458–9 and 499. See also Mort A. Rosenblum, 'Reporting from the Third World', op. cit., p. 827.
56. See UNESCO Doc. CC.77/WS/21 (1977), pp. 4–5, 8–11, 13–20, 24, 26–7, 33 and 36–7; and UNESCO 19 C/*Proceedings* Part 1, pp. 648 and 650.
57. For debates in Programme Commission, see UNESCO Doc. CC.77/WS/21 cited in note 17 above. For general policy debate, see UNESCO 19 C/*Proceedings* Parts 1 and 2, 5th to 21st and 24th plenary meetings.
58. See UNESCO Doc. CC.77/WS/21, note 56 above, pp. 13–14, 20–1, 23–4, and 36–7.

59. For DNG terms of reference, see UNESCO Doc. 19 C/2 Add. (1976).
60. See UNESCO Doc. 19 C/2 (1976) pp. 6 and 11 and Add.
61. For DNG membership in 1976, see UNESCO 19 C/Res. 0.51 of 30 October 1976 (UNESCO 19 C/*Resolutions* at 14).
62. See UNESCO 19 C/*Resolutions*, Annex II at 63.
63. See UNESCO 19 C/*Proceedings* Part 2, p. 447 para. 54.1.
64. For DNG proposal, see UNESCO Doc. 19 C/PLEN/DR.20 (1976). For other draft resolutions and proposals, see UNESCO Docs 19 C/PRG.III/DR.2 and 3 and 19 C/INF.21 (1976).
65. UNESCO 19 C/Res. 4.143 of 29 November 1976 (UNESCO 19 C/*Resolutions* at 53).
66. Known as the 'September 1977 draft', in UNESCO C.R. File 659.3:323.1 INT.
67. For fuller details of this stage of drafting see September 1977 confidential *Aide-Mémoire*; *Memo.* of 29 November 1977 from G.C. Roque to ADG/CC; UNESCO *Memo.* CC/FCP/77/296 of 21 October 1977 from Kandil to ADG/CC and *Memo.* SJC/44/SF.1 of 3 November 1977 from Ansah to ADG/CC; and *letter* of 5 December 1977 from Harley (USA) to ADG/CC, all in UNESCO C.R. File 659.3:323.1 INT.
68. For details, see UNESCO Doc. 104 EX/28 (1978); UNESCO Doc. 20 C/20 (1978), Introduction, para. 7; and correspondence cited in note 67 above.
69. For summary of replies, see UNESCO Doc. 104 EX/28 (1978). For full text of replies, see UNESCO C.R. File 659.3:323.1 INT.
70. Ibid.
71. *Letter* of 5 December 1977 from William Harley to ADG/CC cited in note 6 above.
72. 'December 1977 draft', undated typescript, in UNESCO C.R. File 659.3:323.1 INT.
73. Ibid.
74. See UNESCO Doc. 104 EX/28 (1978) esp. paras. 4–6; and EX/SR.22 (31 May 1978) p. 206 paras. 8.5, 8.6 and 14.3. For debate, see UNESCO Docs. 104 EX/SR.22 to 24 and SR.34 and 35 (31 May and 1, 8–9 June 1978) pp. 205–29 and 305–9 resp.
75. Ibid.
76. See UNESCO Docs 104 EX/SR.23 and 24 (31 May and 1 June 1978), statements by Mr Garbo, pp. 213–14; Mr Warvariv, p. 215; Mr Hummel, p. 226; and Mr Valéry, p. 227.
77. See UNESCO Doc. 104 EX/SR.22 and 23 (31 May 1978), statements by Mr Uslar-Pietri, p. 207; Mr Gopel, p. 214 para. 4.2; and Mr Nsour. p. 216 para. 6.2.
78. See UNESCO Doc. 104 EX/Dec. 5.5.4 of 9 June 1978.
79. UNESCO Doc. 20 C/20 (1978).
80. UNESCO 20 C/*Proceedings*, pp. 648–53.
81. Ibid., pp. 496–9
82. Ibid., pp. 361–2 esp. paras. 16.16 to 16.25; and pp. 519–20 paras. 45.17 to 45.22.
83. Ibid., statements by Iceland, p. 415; Denmark, p. 449; UK, pp. 496–9; West Germany, pp. 528–9; Australia, p. 555; Netherlands, pp. 578–9;

USA, pp. 648–53; Switzerland, p. 750; IAPA, pp. 834–5; WPFC, pp. 867–8; and IAAB, p. 876.

84. For samples of coverage identifying M'Bow with the Declaration, see e.g. 'Unesco Head Backs Media-Control Draft', *IHT* 27 October 1978, quoting UPI dispatch; AFP dispatch of 26 October 1978 in UNESCO *Press Review 207*; UNESCO *Press Review 211*; and Peter Calvocoressi, 'Third World threat to the Truth', *ST*, 22 October 1978. On this theme, too, see Righter, *Whose News?*, op. cit., esp. ch. 4, e.g. p. 179.

85. UNESCO 20 C/*Proceedings*, pp. 288 and 1042.

86. Ibid., pp. 1063–117.

87. See UNESCO 20 C/Res. 0.61 of 25 October 1978 (UNESCO 20 C/*Resolutions* at 15); and debate, UNESCO 20 C/*Proceedings*, pp. 274–5.

88. For lists of attendance at the 18th to 20th sessions of the General Conference, see UNESCO 18 C/*Proceedings*, pp. XXI–LXXV; 19 C/*Proceedings* Part 1, pp. 21–64; and 20 C/*Proceedings*, pp. 85–90.

89. UNESCO, *Register of Cards Issued to Journalists, 2.4.76–27.5.81*, pp. 21–51. (The register is held by the UNESCO Press Room.)

90. Ibid., pp. 52–9.

91. E.g. statement by Barbados, UNESCO 20 C/*Proceedings*, pp. 1066–7.

92. A. H. Raskin, *Report on News Coverage of Belgrade UNESCO Conference* (New York: The National News Council, March 1981).

93. For list of journalists attending 21st session of General Conference in Belgrade, see UNESCO *Register of Cards Issued to Journalists*, note 89 above, typed list stapled to p. 67. The list shows 59 Yugoslav and 173 foreign journalists, of whom some 92 Western. (Entries are numbered to 176, but numbers 165–8 inclusive are missing.)

94. Raskin, *Report on News Coverage*, note 92 above, pp. 1–2.

95. Ibid., p. 10.

96. See e.g. *Tribune de Genève*, 1 November 1978.

97. See e.g. Paul Webster, 'News Row Splits Delegates to Unesco', *Guardian*, 23 October 1978.

98. AP dispatch reproduced in UNESCO *Press Review 203*, of 20 October 1978; also P. Chutkow, AP dispatch 'Impending Wrangle over the Organisation's initiatives in mass communications and international News', UNESCO *Press Review 206*, of 25 October 1978; Reuter dispatch of 26 October 1978; R. Righter, 'Free Press under threat from UNESCO', *ST*, 10 September 1978; etc.

99. Article by P. Calvocoressi in *ST*, 22 October 1978.

100. Article by I. Murray in *The Times*, 25 October 1978.

101. Compare e.g. P. Chutkow, AP dispatch in UNESCO *Press Review 213* of 4 November 1978, p.4, with Olivier Todd, 'Le Tiers Monde et l'Information', *L'Express*, 4 November 1978; and J. Nielsen and S. Sullivan, 'Pressure on the Press', *Newsweek*, 6 November 1978.

102. UPI dispatch of 26 October 1978 and *IHT*, 27 October 1978; and article by P. Calvocoressi in *The Times*, 30 October 1978. See also 'To Bar State Control in Third World, US offers to Help in Creating Media', *IHT*, 4 November 1978; 'A Simple No to Unesco', *NYT*, reproduced in *IHT*, 9 November 1978; and article in *The Economist* quoted in *Le Monde*, 24 October 1978.

103. See e.g. J. Power, 'The Unesco Debate on Role of Press', *IHT*, in UNESCO *Press Review 207* of 26 October 1978; J. Power, 'Unesco damming the flow?', *Guardian*, 23 October 1978; P. Webster, 'Unesco plan not meant to gag the press', *Guardian*, 27 October 1978; R. Cans, 'Le Rééquilibrage des Moyens d'Information', *Le Monde*, 24 October 1978; F. Giroud, 'Décoloniser l'Information', *Le Monde*, 9 November 1978; J. d'Ormesson, 'La chronique du temps qui passe', *Le Figaro Magazine*, 10 November 1978; and C. Legum, 'Press freedom battle goes on', *Observer*, 26 November 1978.
104. Righter, *Whose News?*, op. cit., pp. 178–80.
105. UNESCO 20 C/*Proceedings*, p. 294 para. 3.54, and p. 893 para. 3.49.
106. Ibid., p. 362 para. 12.23; p. 497 para. 14.5; and p. 520 para. 45.21.
107. Ibid., pp. 257 and 497.
108. Raskin, *Report on News Coverage*, note 89 above, pp. 2–3.
109. Ibid., pp. 3–4.
110. Ibid., p. 14.
111. See e.g. Colleen Roach, French Press Coverage of the Belgrade UNESCO Conference', *Journal of Communication* (Fall 1981) pp. 175–87; and Jules Gritti, *La Réunion sur la Protection des Journalistes, Paris, 16–18 février 1981: Analyse des Contenus de Presse*, UNESCO Doc. OPI–81/WS/11 (August 1981). (Gritti's study breaks coverage down into the following geographical regions: North America, Latin America, Africa, France, Europe minus France, and Japan.)
112. For text of the article and reference to *IHT* refusal to publish, see J. Behrstock, 'In defence of Unesco', *Opinion: UNESCO Staff Association Journal* (February–March 1980) pp. 48–50.
113. UNESCO Doc. 20 C/20 Rev. (1978).
114. See reports on this body in e.g. AFP dispatch of 6 November 1978 in UNESCO *Press Review 215* of 7 November 1978; *IHT*, 27 October and 8 November 1978); *The Times*, 24 October and 3 November 1978; R. Smyth, 'Bid for Unesco harmony', *Observer*, 5 November 1978; 'Compromis possible sur le problème de l'information', *L'Action*, Tunis, 4 November 1978; AFP dispatch, Paris, 3 November 1978; I. Murray, 'West eager to tone down Unesco stand on media', *The Times*, 17 November 1978; and R. Righter, 'Free press talks stay backstage', *ST*, 19 November 1978. See also Righter, 'Newsflow International', op. cit., p. 311.
115. Ibid.
116. UNESCO Doc. 20 C/20 Rev. (1978) of 21 November 1978, scheduled for adoption on 22 November 1978 (see UNESCO 20 C/*Journal*, 21 November 1978).
117. UNESCO 20 C/*Proceedings*, p. 980 paras. 7.1 to 7.4 and 9.1.
118. See UNESCO 20 C/*Reports*, pp. 153–4; and 20 C/*Proceedings*, p. 1060 paras. 53.46–48.
119. See *Declaration* on Fundamental Principles concerning the Contribution of the Mass Media to Strengthening Peace and International Understanding, to the Promotion of Human Rights and to Countering Racialism, *Apartheid* and Incitement to War, UNESCO 20 C/Res. 4/9.3/2 of 28 November 1978 (UNESCO 20 C/*Resolutions* at 100).

120. I am indebted to Mr Lloyd Sommerlad, former official of the Division of Free Flow of Information, and UNESCO Regional Communications Adviser for Asia at the time of the 20th session of the General Conference, for insights into the compromise reached.

121. See UNESCO Doc. 20 C/DR. 308 (1978) p. 2, last paragraph.

122. Interview with Mr V. D. Dratch, USSR Permanent Delegation to UNESCO. See also UNESCO 20 C/*Proceedings*, pp. 1080, 1093, 1095, 1097–9, 1100, 1102–4, 1112 and 1116–7.

123. Media Declaration, note 119 above, Art. II para. 3; and Art. III paras. 1 and 2.

124. For verbatim records of the Programme Commission debates, see UNESCO 20 C/*Proceedings*, pp. 1063–117.

125. Ibid., pp. 1078, 1087–8, 1091–2, 1096, 1101–2 and 1109–14.

126. Ibid., pp. 1072–3, 1079 and 1089–90 resp.

127. Ibid., pp. 1070 and 1092–3.

128. Righter, 'Newsflow International', op. cit., p. 310; Righter, 'Unesco's close shave for Press Freedom', *ST*, 26 November 1978; 'Pious Promises', *The Economist*, 25 November 1978; AP dispatch in UNESCO *Press Review 229* of 27 November 1978; Reuter dispatch of 22 November 1978; 'UNESCO relief over achievement', *New Scotsman*, 29 November 1978; etc. See also C. Roach, *The Reaction of the French Press to the Mass Media Declaration* (University of Paris, unpublished manuscript, March 1979).

129. On this point see Chapter 2 above; and Righter, *Whose News?*, op. cit., ch. 4, pp. 112, 166 and 172.

130. See UNESCO 19 C/Res. 100 of 29 November 1976 (UNESCO 19 C/*Resolutions* at 17) Part B paras. 22–3; and UNESCO Doc. 19C/4 (1976) Annex II, Guidance Notes on Objective 9.1.

131. For Commission mandate and membership, see UNESCO Doc. 20 C/94 (1978) pp. 2–3.

132. UNESCO Doc. 20 C/94 (1978).

133. Ibid., Section D, pp. 63–73.

134. Ibid., Section E, pp. 74–9.

135. UNESCO 20 C/*Proceedings*, p. 649 para. 8.9.

136. UNESCO Doc. 20 C/DR.305 (1978).

137. UNESCO Doc. 20 C/DR.307 (1978).

138. UNESCO 20 C/Res. 4/9.1/3 of 28 November 1978 (UNESCO 20 C/*Resolutions* at 99).

139. See *Many Voices, One World* (Paris: UNESCO, 1980); and *letter* of 30 November 1979 from Sean MacBride to Director-General, quoted in UNESCO Doc. 21 C/85 (1980) p. 11 para. 70.

140. R. Righter, 'Press Freedom row goes on', *ST*, 2 December 1979.

141. *Many Voices, One World*, op. cit., pp. 253–72.

142. On this point, Ibid., Part V para. 5, quoted in UNESCO Doc. 21 C/85 (1980) p. 11 paras. 64–5.

143. *Many Voices, One World*, op. cit., Recommendations 31–3.

144. Ibid., Recommendation 27.

145. Ibid., Recommendations 30 and 58.

146. Ibid., e.g. Recommendation 42.

147. Ibid., e.g. Recommendations 47, 52–3, 79–80 and 82.
148. Ibid., Recommendation 77.
149. Ibid., pp. 273–4.
150. See UNESCO Doc. 21 C/PRG.IV/DR.1 (1980).
151. *Many Voices, One World*, op. cit., pp. 279–80.
152. Ibid., pp. 280–1.
153. UNESCO Doc. 21 C/85 (1980). See also statement by representative of the Director-General, UNESCO 21 C/*Reports*, p. 181 paras. 493 and 495.
154. See notes 108–11 above; also R. Righter, 'Third World aim is to shackle the Fourth Estate', *ST*, 19 October 1980; 'News by order', *ST* editorial, 26 October 1980; and D. Spanier, 'Britain dismayed by Unesco threat to free flow of news', *The Times*, 28 October 1980.
155. UNESCO 21 C/*Proceedings*, pp. 500–1, 719–22, 838, 849, 1184–5, 1200–2 and 1353–4. Also UNESCO 21 C/*Reports*, pp. 178 and 182, and UNESCO Doc. 21 C/PRG.IV/DR.3 (1980).
156. Ibid.
157. UNESCO 21 C/*Proceedings*, p. 1230 para. 2.65.
158. UNESCO 21 C/Res. 4/19 of 27 October 1980 (UNESCO 21 C/*Resolutions* at 68); see also UNESCO Doc. 21 C/PRG.IV/DR.8 (1980).
159. UNESCO Doc. 21 C/PRG.IV/DR.4 (1980).
160. UNESCO 21 C/Res. 4/19, note 158 above, Section V para. h, and Section VI.
161. UNESCO 21 C/*Proceedings*, pp. 1358–60; and UNESCO 21 C/*Reports*, pp. 182–3.
162. UNESCO 20 C/DR.298 (1978).
163. UNESCO 20 C/Res. 4/9.4/2 of 28 November 1976 (UNESCO 20 C/*Resolutions* at 104).
164. For *Final Report* of the conference see UNESCO Doc. CC/MD/45 (1980) and for Director-General's report to the General Conference see UNESCO Doc. 21 C/86 (1980).
165. UNESCO Doc. CC/MD/45 (1980) Annex II esp. Section III.
166. UNESCO 21 C/Res. 4.21 of 27 October 1980 (UNESCO 21 C/*Resolutions* at 72).
167. Ibid.
168. UNESCO Doc. CC/MD/45 (1980) p. 6, and UNESCO 21 C/*Proceedings*, pp. 1230 and 1351.
169. UNESCO 21 C/*Proceedings*, pp. 655, 721–3, 838 and 849; and UNESCO 21 C/*Reports*, p. 172. See also statements by Gunnar Garbo, Chairman of the IPDC Intergovernmental Council (IGC), UNESCO Docs CC/MD/47 (1981) Annex VI pp. 5–6; and COM/MD/1 (1982) p. 6 para. 12.
170. UNESCO 21 C/*Proceedings*, p. 1353.
171. UNESCO Doc. CC/MD/47 (1981) p. 3.
172. Ibid.; and *Rules of Procedure* of Intergovernmental Council of the IPDC, UNESCO Doc. CC–81/WS/34 (1981), pp. 9–15.
173. On financial arrangements, see UNESCO Docs. CC/MD 47 (1981) esp. pp. 9–11 and Res. I; COM/MD/1 (1982) esp. pp. 6–8 and Annex III; also UNESCO 21 C/Res. 4/21 of 27 October 1980 (UNESCO 21 C/*Resolutions* at 72) esp. para. 4 (c) (e) and (f); and *Statutes* of the Intergovernmental Council of the IPDC, UNESCO Doc. CC–81/WS/34 (1981),

pp. 6–7, Art. 5(f) and (g).

174. On this point see e.g. R. Righter, 'Third World press pact hits snag', *ST*, 20 April 1980; R. Righter, 'US is lone man out over press pact', *ST*, 27 April 1980; and R. Berthoud, 'Carrington plea for wider news coverage', *The Times*, 10 June 1980.

175. Righter, 'US is lone man out over press pact', op. cit., and 'And now the bad news from Unesco', *The Times*, 18 June 1981.

176. See e.g. UNESCO Doc. CC/MD/47 (1981) p. 12 para. 82; UNESCO 21 C/*Reports*, p. 172 para. 403. Also 'Americans coy on Unesco cash', *The Times*, 20 January 1982, p. 5; and 'US refuses cash for Unesco media projects', *The Times*, 26 January 1982, p. 7.

177. See House of Lords, *Parliamentary Debates*, v. 426, 1 February 1982; and House of Commons, *Parliamentary Debates*, v. 29, 20 October 1982. Also Righter, 'The Third World tightens its hold over the media', *ST*, 26 October 1980.

178. For details of pledges, see UNESCO Docs. COM/MD/1 (1982) pp. 6–7 and Annex III, esp. pp. 11–12; and COM/MD/3 (1983) pp. 7–8 and Annex IV p. 3 para. 4.

179. UNESCO 21 C/*Reports*, p. 168 para. 349(a); also Ibid., p. 164 para. 311.

180. UNESCO 21 C/*Proceedings*, pp. 1353–5, and UNESCO 21 C/*Reports*, pp. 164–6 and 168.

181. UNESCO Doc. 21 C/5.

182. Ibid., e.g. paras. 4343, 4346, 4349–50, 4357, 4359 and 4370–1.

183. See UNESCO Doc. 21 C/5 Approved, paras. 4381, 4384, 4387–8, 4397–8 and 4409–10.

184. As note 178 above.

185. UNESCO Docs. COM/MD/1 (1982) Ann. III, p. 1. para. 3; and COM/MD/3, pp. 7–8.

186. UNESCO Doc. COM/MD/3 (1983) p. 6 para. 11.

187. As note 177 above; also J. Friendly, 'Unesco Shifts Approach on Press in Third World', *NYT*, 30 November 1981; A. Riding, 'U.S. Offers to Aid Journalism in Third World', *NYT*, 22 January 1982; and A. Riding, '"New Information Order": Debating Pragmatics', *NYT*, 24 January 1982; C. Hargrove, 'Face Saving formula at Unesco', *The Times*, 22 June 1981; S. Downer, 'Unesco tries to get cash for Third World media', *The Times*, 21 January 1982; and S. Downer, 'US refuses cash for Unesco media projects', *The Times*, 27 January 1982.

188. UN GA Res. 33/115 B of 18 December 1978 (UN GAOR 33 Supp.45 at 72).

189. UN Doc. A/SPC/33/L.22 (1978).

190. UN Doc. A/SPC/33/L.5 and Annex (1978).

191. UN Doc. A/SPC/33/SR. 38 (29 November 1978) p. 5 para. 11.

192. See e.g. UN Doc. A/SPC/33/L.5 Annex (1978) esp. ch. II p. 12 para. 4; pp. 13–14 para. 42 esp. indents 2, 4, 5, 7 and 9; p. 17 para. 47; p. 19 para. 49; and ch. III p. 24 last para., and p. 25, first two paragraphs and para. 59.

193. See UN Docs. A/BUR/33/SR.1 & SR.2 (20–1 September 1978) pp. 5–8 and 9–11 resp.

194. UN Docs. A/33/144 (1978) and A/SPC/33/SR.38, SR.41 to 46 and SR.48

(29 November and 1–8 December 1978).

195. UN Doc. A/SPC/33/SR.41 esp. pp. 8–9; SR.44 p. 12; and SR.45 p. 19 (1978).
196. UN Doc. A/SPC/33/SR.41 (1978) p. 9.
197. UN Doc. A/SPC/33/SR.48 (1978) p. 25 para. 118.
198. UN Doc. A/SPC/33/L.22 Rev.1 (1978).
199. For record of adoption see UN Doc. A/SPC/33/SR.48 (1978) p. 22; and report of the Special Political Committee, UN Doc. A/33/511 (1978) and draft Res. B; and UN GAOR 33, Plen 87 mtg (18 December 1978), p. 1536 para. 93, and pp. 1552–3 paras. 272–9.
200. UN Doc. A/SPC/33/SR.48 (1978) p. 12 paras. 124 and 127.
201. Ibid., p. 13 para. 127.
202. Ibid., p. 23 para. 123.
203. See UN Docs. A/SPC/33/L.23 rev.1 (1978) para. 2; A/SPC/33/SR.38, statements by Tunisia, p. 6; A/34/21 (1979) Annex I esp. paras. 13–14; and UN GA Res. 34/182 of 18 December 1979 (UN GAOR 34 Supp.46 at 82) Part I para. 2(a).
204. See UN Doc. A/SPC/33/L.23 Rev.1 (1978).
205. UN GA Res. 33/115 of 18 December 1978 (UN GAOR 33 Supp.45 at 72). For composition of the Committee, see *YUN* [1978] p. 1204 and [1979] p. 1357.
206. UN Doc. A/SPC/34/SR.25 (9 November 1979) p. 11 para. 36.
207. UN GA Res. 34/182, note 203 above, Section I para. 1.
208. UN Doc. A/SPC/34/L.18 and Rev. 1 (1979).
209. UN GA Res. 34/182, note 203 above.
210. See UN Docs A/34/808 (1979) and A/34/PV.107 (18 December 1979) pp. 38–42.
211. UN GA Res. 34/182, note 203 above, Section II para. 1(b).
212. Ibid., Section II para. 4.
213. Ibid., Section II para. 8.
214. Ibid., Section II para. 9.
215. Ibid., Section II para. 12.
216. UN Doc. A/SPC/34/SR.41 (4 December 1979) pp. 2 and 4. For debate in Special Political Committee, see UN Docs. A/SPC/34/SR.25 (9 November), SR.27 to 33 (12–15 November) and SR.40 and 41 (30 November–4 December 1979).
217. UN Doc. A/SPC/34/SR.30 p. 2 para. 5; see also France, UN Doc. A/SPC/34/SR.25 p. 8 para. 23 (1979).
218. UN Doc. A/SPC/34/SR.41 (1979) p. 5.
219. See UN Docs A/SPC/34/SR.31 (1979) p. 9, A/SPC/35/SR.33 (14 November 1980) p. 12 para. 42.
220. UN Doc. A/SPC/34/SR.41 (1979) pp. 2–3 and 5–6.
221. Ibid., p. 2.
222. See UN Doc. A/34/21 (1979) p. 15, and statement by UN Secretariat, UN Doc. A/SPC/34/SR.25 (1979) p. 3.
223. UN Docs A/SPC/33/SR.38 (1978) pp. 8–9 esp. paras. 31–3 and 36; A/SPC/33/SR.45 (1978) pp. 17–18; and A/SPC/34/SR.28 (1979) pp. 6–7 esp. para. 23.
224. UN Doc. A/SPC/33/SR.45 (1978) p. 18 paras. 75–81.

225. UN Docs A/SPC/34/SR.41 (1979) pp. 2–3, and A/SPC/35/SR.32 (1980) p. 8.

226. UN GA Res. 35/201 of 16 December 1980 (UN GAOR 35 Supp.48 at 93), Section III para. 10(d).

227. UNESCO Doc. 21 C/PLEN/DR.5 and Rev. (1980).

228. For alternative Western proposal, see UNESCO Doc. 21 C/PRG.IV/ DR.7 (1980). For debates, see UNESCO 21 C/*Reports*, pp. 188–9, and 21 C/*Proceedings*, p. 1351 para. 25.12, and p. 1366 paras. 106.2 to 106.3. For decision, see UNESCO 21 C/Res. 4/20 of 27 October 1980 (UNESCO 21 C/*Resolutions* at 71).

229. See e.g. UNESCO Doc. 20 C/77 (1978).

230. See UNESCO Docs. 99 EX/SR.4 (27 April 1976), statements by Messrs Smirnov, p. 24; Betancur Mejía, p. 26; and El-Wakil, p. 27; and 100 EX/ SR.8 (30 September 1976) statements by Messrs Ki-Zerbo, p.65; Messadi, p.67; Koutakov, pp. 68–9; Maser, p. 69; and Le Riverend, p. 70. See also UNESCO 19 C/*Proceedings* Part 1, p. 395 para. 16.16, p. 376 paras. 10.5 to 10.6, and pp. 404 and 475; and ibid., Part 2, pp. 442– 3.

231. See Chapter 1 above, and note 58.

232. E.g. R. Righter, 'West to fight back on press freedom', *ST*, 24 May 1981; 'US may quit Unesco', *The Times*, 8 June 1981, p. 1; Righter, 'And now the bad news from Unesco', *The Times*, 18 June 1981; N. Ashford, 'Pressures grow on Reagan to block Unesco's world information order', *The Times*, 20 July 1981; 'Washington protest on Unesco aid', *The Times*, 18 September 1981; 'Poison in the Media Pool', *The Times*, 23 November 1982; etc.

233. See UNESCO Docs. 20 C/22 (1978) and 21 C/26 (1980) and debates on agenda item 28 at the 20th and 21st sessions of the General Conference.

234. 'US brushes aside Western pleas to stay in Unesco', *The Times*, 30 December 1983.

235. 'UNESCO Begins Debate on Effects of U.S. Pullout', *IHT*, 13 February 1985.

236. 'Britain may quit Unesco to speed up reforms', *FT*, 23 November 1984.

237. A. Gavshon, 'Follow the red, white and blue', *Guardian*, 26 April 1985.

238. See Philip Webster, 'Unesco pull-out attacked by MPs', *The Times*, 6 December 1985.

239. See e.g. 'Le Japon menace de quitter l'Unesco', *Le Soir*, 15 February 1985.

240. N. Franck, 'La Suisse tente de sauver l'Unesco', *La Libre Belgique*, 21 April 1985.

241. H. Jackson, 'Leaked US memo reveals split on Unesco' and 'Campaign to reverse Unesco pullout', *Guardian* 24 and 30 January 1985 resp.; and J. P. Péroncel-Hugoz, 'Les Etats-Unis ont pris la décision de se retirer de l'UNESCO', *Le Monde*, 30 December 1983.

242. Details taken from report by Mr R. Beix, *The Activities of UNESCO and Co-operation with the Council of Europe*, Council of Europe Parliamentary Assembly Doc. AS/INF (84)4, pp. 8–11.

243. See René Lefort, 'La Crise? Quelle Crise?', *Le Matin*, 7 December 1984.

244. For the public debate in the UK, see ibid. and, for example, Nigel

Hawkes, 'Our unloved brainchild', *Observer*, 1 December 1985; Robert Mauthner, 'Reforms may not pass the Thatcher test', *FT*, 4 December 1985; 'Getting out for no good reason', *Guardian* editorial, 6 December 1985; James Naughtie and Hella Pick, 'Britain dismays EEC by leaving Unesco' and John Cunningham, 'Why it's goodbye to all that at Unesco', *Guardian*, 6 December 1985; and 'Bonn will not follow UK lead', *The Times*, 7 December 1985.

245. Ibid., and as note 237 above.

246. As note 237 above.

247. UNESCO *Register of Cards Issued to Journalists*, op. cit., and subsequent registers.

248. See 'The Rhetoric of Censorship', *The Times*, 19 May 1981; and R. Righter, 'West to fight back on press freedom', *ST*, 14 May 1981.

249. See e.g. letter from Gilles de Leiris, UNESCO Comptroller, 'UNESCO's $10 million', *IHT*, 26 February 1985; also as note 242 above.

250. I am grateful to Mr Hargrove for information on the report, supplied during interview on 25 March 1983.

6. Postwar Debate on Regulation of Education

1. For attendance records, see UNESCO 1 C/*Proceedings*, pp. 7–10; 2 C/*Proceedings*, pp. 7–12; 3 C/*Proceedings*, pp. 7–12; 4 C/*Proceedings*, pp. 9–14; 5 C/*Proceedings*, pp. 9–15; and 6 C/*Proceedings*, pp. 11–17.

2. E.g. Armstrong, 'The Soviet Attitude toward UNESCO' and Dexter 'Yardstick for UNESCO', op. cit.

3. For elections to the Executive Board for the first term and debate thereon, see UNESCO 1 C/*Proceedings*, pp. 66–8.

4. UNESCO 2 C/*Proceedings*, pp. 347 and 483.

5. Doc. ECO/CONF./29 (1946) p. 50.

6. Ibid., p. 60.

7. Ibid., pp. 31 and 103–4.

8. Doc. UNESCO/Prep.Comm./5th sess./PV 7(1) (7 July 1946) p. 4.

9. 'CAME proposals' in Doc. ECO/CONF./29 (1946) p. 1, Art. II, paras. 3–4.

10. See 'French proposals' in Doc. ECO/CONF./29 (1946) p. 6.

11. Doc. ECO/CONF./29, p. 100.

12. Doc. ECO/CONF./Com.I/18 in Doc. ECO/CONF./29, pp. 107–8; and summary of meeting, Doc. ECO/CONF./29, p. 101.

13. Compare 'CAME proposals' op. cit. (no explicit mention of domestic jurisdiction) and 'French proposals' op. cit., Art. 1 para. 2, with UNESCO *Constitution*, op. cit., Art. I para. 3.

14. UNESCO 1 C/*Proceedings*, p. 152.

15. Ibid., and p. 55

16. Ibid., p. 152

17. UNESCO 2 C/*Proceedings*, pp. 59, 110 and 438–4; 3 C/*Proceedings*, pp. 249, 254 and 311–16; and 4 C/*Proceedings*, esp. p. 275.

18. UNESCO 1 C/*Proceedings*, p. 152.

19. See Shuster, *UNESCO: Assessment and Promise*, op. cit., pp. 71–2. I am grateful to Mr Behrstock, former US official of UNESCO, for insights on this point.
20. See exchange of letters between Senator Benton and Luther Evans, cited in Laves & Thomson, *UNESCO: Purpose, Progress, Prospects*, op. cit., p. 230.
21. UNESCO 1 C/*Proceedings*, p. 152.
22. Ibid., p. 153.
23. Ibid.
24. Ibid.
25. UNESCO 1 C/*Proceedings* p. 224: Annex I, Section III, para. 3.
26. Ibid., Section III, para. 9.
27. Ibid., p. 221.
28. E.g. UNESCO 2 C/*Proceedings*, pp. 60, 84, 89–90 and 103; and 4 C/*Proceedings*, p. 64.
29. See UNESCO 1 C/*Proceedings*, pp. 271–2.
30. UNESCO 5 C/*Proceedings*, esp. 350; and 6 C/*Proceedings*, p. 284.
31. UNESCO 3 C/Res. 2.3 of 11 December 1948 (UNESCO 3 C/*Resolutions* at 18) and 4 C/Res. 2.3 of 5 October 1949 (UNESCO 4 C/*Resolutions* at 15).
32. UNESCO 6 C/Res. 1.316 of 10 July 1951 (UNESCO 6 C/*Resolutions* at 20).
33. UNESCO 7 C/Res. 1.331 of 11 December 1952 (UNESCO 7 C/*Resolutions* at 20).
34. *Handbook for the Improvement of Textbooks and Teaching Materials* (Paris: UNESCO, Publication No. 368, 1949).
35. UNESCO Doc. 4 C/3 (1949) p. 36.
36. UNESCO 5 C/Res. 1.324 of 17 June 1950 (UNESCO 5 C/*Resolutions*) and 6 C/Res. 1.315 of 10 July 1951 (UNESCO 6 C/*Resolutions* at 20).
37. See e.g. UNESCO series *Towards World Understanding* (1949–52); and Cyril Bibby, *Race, Prejudice and Education* (Paris: UNESCO, 1959).
38. UNESCO Doc. 2 C/102 (13 November 1947).
39. Ibid., p. 2, last paragraph.
40. UNESCO 2 C/*Proceedings*, pp. 483–4.
41. UNESCO Doc. 2 C/109 (19 November 1947).
42. Ibid., para. 1; and UNESCO 2 C/Res. 3.13 (UNESCO 2 C/*Resolutions* at 21). For debates see UNESCO 2 C/*Proceedings*, pp. 483–5.
43. UNESCO Doc. EX/4CP/SR.3 (27 April 1948) pp. 17–18.
44. Ibid.
45. UNESCO 3 C/Res. 2.514 of 11 December 1948 (UNESCO 3 C/*Resolutions* at 19).
46. See *Memo*. IU/105 of 19 May 1949 from C. E. Beeby to Director-General, UNESCO C.R. File 327.6.371.214A 182/064 (44) "49".
47. UNESCO Docs. 4 C/5 (1949) and 4 C/Res. 2.513 of 5 October 1949 (UNESCO 4 C/*Resolutions* at 16).
48. For Minutes of the meeting, see UNESCO Doc. 19 EX/12 (1950).
49. Ibid., p. 2.
50. Ibid., pp. 6–7, Section XI.
51. For text, ibid., pp. 8–12.

52. See *letter* ED 136.632 of 3 January 1950 from W. Laves to I. Kabbany Bey, Chairman of the expert meeting, UNESCO C.R. File cited in note 46 above.
53. See revised text in UNESCO Doc. 6 C/PRG/6 (1951) Part I, paras 1–2.
54. UNESCO Docs. 19 EX/SR.24 (25 February 1950) p. 9, and 19 EX/Dec. 5(g) (i) of same date.
55. For text of replies, see UNESCO Doc. 6 C/PRG/6 (1951).
56. Ibid.
57. Ibid., p. 3.
58. *Letter* ref. U.N.7 (7)/11 of 7 October 1949 from UK National Commission for UNESCO to the Director-General, in UNESCO File cited in note 46 above.
59. On this point see Thomas Buergenthal and Judith Torney, *International Human Rights and International Education* (Washington, D.C.: Dept of State, 1976), ch. 5.
60. UNESCO Doc. 6. C/PRG/6 (1951) p. 7, last para. For debate in Programme Committee of the Executive Board, see UNESCO Doc. 25 EX/CP/SR.1 and 2 (19–20 January 1951).
61. UNESCO Doc. 6 C/1/Rev. Annex I (1951) p. 4: item 8.7.1.3.
62. UNESCO 6 C/*Proceedings*, p. 284 paras 9–11. I am grateful to Mr Guiton, former official of the UNESCO Education Sector, for information provided during interview in November 1978.
63. For relevant UNESCO file, see note 46 above.
64. See UNESCO Doc. Cons.Exec./S.R.6 (9 December 1946) p. 7.
65. E.g. John Gimbel, *A German Community under American Occupation* (Stanford University Press, 1961) ch. 13; and Harold Zink, *The US in Germany, 1944–1945* (Princeton, N.J.: van Nostrand, 1957) ch. 13.
66. See UNESCO Docs. 6 EX/19 (1948) and 6 EX/SR.8 rev. (15 February 1948) pp. 2–6; 7 EX/5 (1948) and 7 EX/SR.2 to 4 rev. (2–4 April 1948); 10 EX/SR.2 prov. (14 September 1948) pp. 2–15; EX/5CP/SR.1 and 2 (16 September 1948) pp. 4–7 and 1–17 resp.; 11 EX/14 (1948) and 11 EX/SR.2 and 3 rev. (13–14 October 1948) pp. 3–7 and 2–18 resp.; and 16 EX/SR.11 rev. (15 June 1949) pp. 3–11.
67. See UNESCO Docs. 2 C/87 and 2 C/104 and Annex (1947); 2 C/*Proceedings*, pp. 171–6, 193–6 and 599–600; 3 C/*Proceedings*, pp. 415–6; and 4 C/*Proceedings*, pp. 185–201 and 413–8.
68. E.g. *Records* of the UNESCO Preparatory Commission, Education Committee, meetings of 24–5 May 1946, pp. 21 and 25 and pp. 3–4 resp; UNESCO Docs. 2 C/C2/9 (1947); 2 C/*Proceedings*, p. 599; 6 EX/SR.8 rev. (1948) statement by Mr Stoddard, p. 3; and 7 EX/SR.2 rev. (1948), statements by Messrs Hardman & Holland, pp. 7–8.
69. UNESCO 2 C/*Proceedings*, p. 599; and Docs. 6 EX/SR.8 rev (1948) p. 2 and 16 EX/SR.11 rev. (1949), statement by Mr Birecki (Poland) p. 5.
70. UNESCO Doc. 6 EX/SR.8 rev. (1948), statements by Messrs Birecki (Poland) and Opocensky (Czechoslovakia), pp. 3–4.
71. E.g. UNESCO 2 C/*Proceedings*, statement by Czechoslovakia, p. 196; 4 C/*Proceedings*, pp. 413–7; and UNESCO Docs. 7 EX/SR.2 & 4 rev. (1948), statements by Mr Birecki (Poland), pp. 4–6 and p. 4 resp.; EX/4CP/SR.4 (27 April 1948), statement by Mr Birecki, p. 15; 11 EX/SR.3

rev. (1948) statement by Prof. Arnold (Poland), p. 3; EX/5CP/SR.1 rev. (1948), statement by Mr Birecki, pp. 5–6; and 16 EX/23 (1949) Ann. III, statement by Mr Mencel (Poland), pp. 4–5.

72. Laves & Thomson, *UNESCO: Purpose, Progress, Prospects*, op. cit., p. 237.
73. See UNESCO 2 C/*Proceedings*, p. 599; and UNESCO Docs. 6 EX/SR.8 rev. (1948), statements by Messrs Stoddard, Cowell and Seydoux, p. 3, and by Director-General, p. 4; 7 EX/SR.2 rev. (1948), statements by Messrs Laves, Hardman, Holland and Huxley, pp. 2–3, 7–8 and 9–10; 11 EX/SR.2 rev. (1948), statement by Sir John Maud, p. 5 and 16 EX/SR.11 rev. (1948) statement by Mr de Blonay, p. 6.
74. See UNESCO Docs 9 EX/13 (1948) and 10 EX/SR.2 (prov.) (14 September 1948).
75. See UNESCO Doc. 11 EX/15 (1948) p. 5.
76. For programme resolutions, see UNESCO Docs 2 C/Res. IX. Ann. VII(6) of 3 December 1947 (UNESCO 2 C/*Resolutions* at 55); 7 EX/17 (1948); EX/CP/SC.1/3 (1948); 3 C/Res. XI Ann.V (I and II) of 6 December 1948 (UNESCO 3 C/*Resolutions* at 63); and 4 C/Res. 35 to 35.39 of 4 October 1949 (UNESCO 4 C/*Resolutions* at 75).
77. See e.g. UNESCO Docs. 10 EX/SR.2 (prov.) pp. 6–7; and 11 EX/SR.3 rev. (1948) pp. 6–7.
78. As note 76 above.
79. Ibid.

7. Contemporary Debate on Regulation of Education

1. *Recommendation* concerning education for international understanding, cooperation and peace and education relating to human rights and fundamental freedoms (hereafter *Recommendation on Ed. for IU*), adopted by UNESCO 19 C/Res. 38 of 19 November 1974 (UNESCO 19 C/*Resolutions* at 147).
2. See UNESCO Doc. 19 C/19 (1976) p. 11. For decision to study the question of preparing an instrument, see UNESCO 15 C/Res. 1.271 of 19 November 1968 (UNESCO 15 C/*Resolutions* at 26); and for a study of the pre-history of the subject, see UNESCO Doc. 89 EX/11 (1972).
3. E.g. UNESCO 13 C/Res. 6.21 of 6 November 1964 (UNESCO 13 C/*Resolutions* at 88); 14 C/Res. 10 of 28 November 1966 (UNESCO 14 C/*Resolutions* at 92); USSR, UNESCO Doc. 15 C/DR.93 (1968); Byelorussian SSR, UNESCO Doc. 16 C/DR.101 (1970); and UNESCO 16 C/Res. 8 of 7 November 1970 (UNESCO 16 C/*Resolutions* at 79).
4. See UNESCO Docs. 89 EX/SR.12 (27 June 1972), statement by Mr Haahr, p. 122. Also UNESCO 17 C/*Reports*, pp. 28–9.
5. See UNESCO Doc. 17 C/Res. 1.222 of 17 November 1972 (UNESCO 17 C/*Resolutions* at 24). See also UNESCO Doc. 17 C/19 (1972).
6. See UNESCO Docs ED/MD/32 (1974) Annex I, and ED/MD/32 Add., pp. 1–5 and 19–21.
7. UNESCO Doc. ED/MD/27 (1973). I am indebted to Messrs Guiton and Irvine for background information on the drafting of the instrument.

8. UNESCO Doc. ED/MD/32 Annex I and Add. and Add. 2–3 (1974).
9. UNESCO Doc. ED/MD/32 Annex III.
10. For full set of amendments, see UNESCO Docs. ED-74/CONF.208/ DR.1-167 (1974).
11. UNESCO Docs. ED-74/CONF.208/DR. 10, 45 and 59–60 (Switzerland); 11, 46–7, 107, 109, 126 and 137–45 (West Germany); 13, 27, 30, 58 and 125 (Belgium and/or Netherlands); 24–5 and 55 (France); 50–4, 127–34 and 147–8 (Nordic countries); and 69–70, 86–93 and 166 (Japan) (1974).
12. UNESCO Docs. ED-74/CONF.208/DR. 2, 4–5, 7, 36–42, 73–85 and 151–62 (1974).
13. UNESCO Docs. ED-74/CONF.208/DR. 8, 12, 16–18, 43, 56–7, 63, 72 and 149–50 (1974).
14. UNESCO Docs. ED/MD/32 Annex I, pp. 3–4 and 17–18; and ED/MD/ 32 Add., pp. 5–12, 15–17 and 20–1 (1974).
15. For attendance record, see UNESCO Doc. 18 C/24 (1974).
16. UNESCO Docs. ED-74/CONF.208/DR. 19–23, 31–35, 94–106 and 110–24; see also alternative Mexican draft in UNESCO Doc. ED/MD/32 Add. 3 (1974).
17. UNESCO Docs ED-74/CONF.208/DR. 1, 3 and 6 (Dahomey); 14 (Philippines); 15 and 44 (Chile); 26 and 48 (Iran); 28–9 (Liberia); 49 (Peru); 61–2, 64–7 and 135–6 (Sudan) and 108 (Senegal) (1974). See also written comments by Argentina, Guatemala, Mauritius and Singapore in UNESCO Doc. ED/MD/32 Annex I pp. 1–2, 8–9 and 12–14; India, Thailand and Zambia, UNESCO Doc. ED/MD/32 Add., pp. 17–19 and 25; and Egypt, UNESCO Doc. ED/MD/32 Add. 2 (1974).
18. UNESCO Doc. 18 C/24 (1974) Annex I.
19. UNESCO 18 C/*Proceedings* Part 2, p. 280 para. 24.
20. UNESCO Doc. 18 C/24 (1974) Annex I para. 3.
21. Ibid., para. 5.
22. Ibid., para. 6.
23. Ibid., para. 16.
24. Ibid., para. 11.
25. Ibid., para. 12.
26. Ibid., para. 33.
27. Ibid., para. 37.
28. Ibid., para. 43.
29. UNESCO Doc. ED-74/CONF.208/DR.165 (1974).
30. UNESCO Doc. 18 C/24 (1974) Annex I para. 36(b).
31. As note 6 above.
32. For record of debate, see UNESCO Doc. 18 C/24 (1974) Annex II.
33. UNESCO Doc. ED/MD/32 Add. (1974), p. 19.
34. UNESCO 18 C/*Reports*, p. 35 para. 240.
35. UNESCO Doc. 18 C/ED/DR.6 (1974).
36. See UNESCO 18 C/*Reports*, p. 35 paras 294 and 296; and UNESCO Doc. 18 C/118 (1974).
37. UNESCO Doc. 18 C/ED/DR.7 (1974).
38. See UNESCO 18 C/*Proceedings* Part 2, pp. 276–86, paras 11 to 73.2.
39. Ibid.

40. Ibid., p. 283.
41. Ibid., pp. 279–80 paras 22.1 to 22.3.
42. Ibid.
43. Ibid., p. 283.
44. *Recommendation on Ed. for IU*, op. cit., para. 6.
45. Interviews with Mr D. Irvine in November 1978 and March 1983; and with Mr A. Brock, UNESCO Dept. of Public Information, on 24 March 1983.
46. UNESCO 18 C/*Proceedings* Part 2, pp. 283–4.
47. For detail of opposing votes, see Buergenthal & Torney, *International Human Rights and International Education*, op. cit., p. 6.
48. UNESCO 18 C/*Proceedings* Part 2, pp. 285–6.
49. Ibid., p. 285.
50. Buergenthal & Torney, *International Human Rights & International Education*, op. cit., p. 6.
51. Note that the Buergenthal & Torney volume cited above was part of the US contribution to implementation of the instrument.
52. *Revised Recommendation* concerning Technical and Vocational Education (hereafter *Revised Recommendation*), adopted on 19 November 1974 (UNESCO 18 C/*Resolutions* at 154).
53. For background reports, see UNESCO Docs. 17 C/20 (1972) Annex; and ED/MD/28 (1973) Parts A & B.
54. UNESCO Doc. ED/MD/28 (1973) Part C.
55. UNESCO Docs. ED/MD/33 Annex I; and ED/MD/33 Add. and Add.2 (1974).
56. See UNESCO Docs ED/MD/33 Annex I, pp. 11, 12–16, 31 and 34–5; ED/MD/33 Add., p. 5; ED/MD/33 Add.2 p. 3; 18 C/25 Annex II; and 18 C/ED/DR.4 (1974).
57. UNESCO Docs. ED/MD/33 Annex I; and ED/MD/33 Add. 2 (1974).
58. Ibid.; and UNESCO Doc. ED/MD/33 Add. (1974).
59. See UNESCO Docs ED/MD/33 Annex I pp. 23 and 26–7; and ED/MD/33 Add., p. 7 (1974).
60. UNESCO Docs. ED/MD/33 Add. pp. 3–5; and ED-74/CONF.209/DR.71 (1974).
61. *Revised Recommendation*, op. cit., paras. 12, 21(a), 22, 24, 31, 35, 36(c), 64 and 92.
62. For attendance record, see UNESCO Doc. 18 C/25 (1974) Annex III.
63. *Revised Recommendation* op. cit., para. 5.
64. UNESCO Docs. ED/MD/28 (1973) Part C para. 5; and ED/MD/33 (1974) Annex III para. 5.
65. UNESCO Doc. ED-74/CONF.209/DR.31 (1974).
66. UNESCO Doc. ED/MD/28 (1973) Part C paras. 34(d), 36(c), 74(b) & 88.
67. UNESCO Doc. ED-74/CONF.209/DR.81 (1974).
68. *Revised Recommendation* op. cit., para. 36(d).
69. Ibid., para. 39(a).
70. Ibid., para. 76.
71. Ibid., para. 91.
72. See UNESCO Doc. ED-74/CONF.209/DR.125. (1974) and *Revised*

Recommendation op. cit., preamble, 2nd recital.

73. UNESCO Doc. ED-74/CONF.209/DR.23 (1974).
74. UNESCO Doc. ED-74/CONF.209/DR.112 (1974).
75. For attendance records, see UNESCO Docs. 18 C/25 (1974) Annex III, and 18 C/24 (1974) Annex III.
76. UNESCO Doc. 18 C/25 (1974) Annex I.
77. See UNESCO Doc. 18 C/25 (1974) Annex II.
78. UNESCO 18 C/*Reports*, p. 29.
79. UNESCO 18 C/*Proceedings* Part 2, pp. 275–6.
80. *Recommendation* on the Development of Adult Education (hereafter *Recommendation on Adult Ed.*), adopted by UNESCO 19 C/Res. 6.114 of 26 November 1976 (UNESCO 19 C/*Resolutions* Annex I at 3).
81. UNESCO Doc. 19 C/24 (1976) Annex II p. 1.
82. I am grateful to Mr Bertelsen for insights into the drafting process supplied during interview on 23 March 1983.
83. UNESCO Docs. ED/MD/40 (1976) Annex I, and ED/MD/40 Add. and Add. 2 (1976).
84. UNESCO Doc. ED/MD/40 (1976) Annex III.
85. See UNESCO Docs. ED/MD/37 (1975) Annex I, preamble, 3rd recital, and operative para. 2(b); and ED/MD/40 (1976) Annex III, preamble, 2nd recital.
86. See UNESCO Docs. ED/MD/40 Annex I; and ED/MD/40 Add. and Add. 2–5 (1976).
87. UNESCO Docs. ED-76/CONF.207/DR.1-275 (1976).
88. As notes 85–7 above.
89. Ibid.
90. Ibid.
91. UNESCO Docs. ED/MD/40 Annex I p. 29; ED/MD/40 Add., pp. 18, 23 and 27; and ED-76/CONF.207/DR.47 and 74 (1976).
92. UNESCO Docs. ED/MD/40 Add., e.g. pp. 5, 9–12, 21 and 30–3; and ED/MD/40 Add.5 p. 1 (1976).
93. See UNESCO Doc. ED/MD/40 (1976) Annex I, pp. 6, 19–21, 32, 35 and 45.
94. E.g. UNESCO Docs. ED-76/CONF.207/DR. 70, 71, 84, 86, 88, 100, 175, 177, 197, 253, 263 and 269 (1976).
95. UNESCO Doc. ED-76/CONF.207/DR.263 (1976).
96. UNESCO Doc. ED/MD/40 (1976) Annex I, pp. 7 and 40.
97. UNESCO Docs. ED-76/CONF.207/DR.1-275 (1976).
98. UNESCO Doc. ED-76/CONF.207/DR.88 (1976).
99. *Recommendation on Adult Ed.*, op. cit., para. 3(f).
100. UNESCO Doc. ED-76/CONF.207/DR.100 (1976).
101. *Recommendation on Adult Ed.*, op. cit., para. 3(h).
102. UNESCO Doc. ED-76/CONF.207/DR.35 (1976).
103. *Recommendation on Adult Ed.*, op. cit., para. 2(a).
104. UNESCO Doc. ED-76/CONF.207/DR.71 (1976).
105. *Recommendation on Adult Ed.*, op. cit., preamble, 6th to 12th recitals.
106. UNESCO Docs. ED-76/CONF.207/DR.54 and 109 (1976).
107. UNESCO Docs. ED/MD/40 (1976) Annex I p. 47, and ED-76/ CONF.207/DR.61 (1976).
108. UNESCO Doc. ED/MD/37 (1975) Annex I para. 2(g).

109. UNESCO Doc. 19 C/24 (1976) Annex I para. 2(j).
110. *Recommendation on Adult Ed.*, op. cit., para. 55(b).
111. UNESCO Doc. 19 C/PRG.II/DR.3 (1976).
112. UNESCO Doc. 19 C/24 (1976) Annex I para. 14(b).
113. UNESCO Doc. ED-76/CONF.207/DR.138 (1976).
114. *Recommendation on Adult Ed.*, op. cit., para. 14(b).
115. See UNESCO Docs ED-76/CONF.207/DR.32, 33, 42 and 66 (1976), and *Recommendation on Adult Ed.*, op. cit., paras. 11 and 25.
116. UNESCO Doc. ED/MD/40 (1976) Annex I p. 10.
117. UNESCO Doc. ED/MD/40 (1976) Annex III para. 19(i)
118. UNESCO Doc. ED-76/CONF.207/DR.133 (1976).
119. *Recommendation on Adult Ed.* op. cit., para. 9.
120. UNESCO Doc. 19 C/24 (1976) Annex I.
121. See UNESCO Doc. 19 C/24 (1976) Annex II p. 6.
122. UNESCO 19 C/*Proceedings* Part 2, p. 364, para. 4.9 and pp. 367–8 paras. 9.44 to 11.2.

8. Scrutiny of Textbooks in UNRWA/UNESCO Schools

1. The title of the relevant agenda item was 'Co-operation with the United Nations Relief and Works Agency (UNRWA)'. For background documents, draft resolutions, debates and decisions, see UNESCO Docs. 77 EX/34 (1967), 77 EX/DR.14, 17 and 18 (1976), 77 EX/SR.30 & 31 (3 November 1967) and 77 EX/Dec. 6.8 of same date (UNESCO 77 EX/*Decisions* at 31); 78 EX/16 and Add.1-2 (1968), 78 EX/SR.24, 25 and 27 (18–20 June 1968), 78 EX/DR.10 (1968) and 78 EX/Dec. 7.4 of 20 June 1968 (UNESCO 78 EX/*Decisions*); 81 EX/3 (1968), 81 EX/SR.3 (22 November 1968) and 81 EX/Dec. 8.1 of same date (UNESCO 81 EX/*Decisions* at 8); 82 EX/8 and Add. 1-3 (1969), 82 EX/DR.3, 5 and 6 rev. (1969), 82 EX/SR.12 to 14 & SR.16 (12–14 May 1969) and 82 EX/Dec.4.2.5 of 14 May 1969 (UNESCO 82 EX/*Decisions*); 83 EX/8 and Add. (1969), 83 EX/SR.21, 22 and 28 (7 and 10 October 1969) and 83 EX/Dec.4.2.3 of 10 October 1969 (UNESCO 83 EX/*Decisions* at 12); 84 EX/5 and Add. 1–2 (1970), 84 EX/DR.18 and 25 (1970), 84 EX/SR.27, 28 and 33 (17 and 19 June 1970) and 84 EX/Dec. 4.2.1 of 19 June 1970 (UNESCO 84 EX/*Decisions* at 15); 85 EX/4 (1970), 85 EX/DR.5 and 8–10 (1970), 85 EX/SR.14, 15 and 17 (6–7 October 1970) and 85 EX/Dec. 4.1.2 of 7 October 1970 (UNESCO 85 EX/*Decisions* at 9); 87 EX/9 and Add. 1–2 (1971), 87 EX/DR.1 & 2 (1971), 87 EX/SR.8 and 9 (11 May 1971) and 87 EX/Dec. 4.2.4 of same date (UNESCO 87 EX/*Decisions* at 15); and 88 EX/3 and Add. 1–4 (1971), 88 EX/DR. 5 and 7 (1971), 88 EX/SR.12, 13 and 15 (26–8 October 1971) and 88 EX/Dec. 4.1.1 of 28 October 1971 (UNESCO 88 EX/*Decisions* at 1).
2. For documentary background on the programme, see UNESCO Doc. 77 EX/34 (1967). For secondary accounts, see e.g. Edward H. Buehrig, *The UN and the Palestinian Refugees* (Bloomington: Indiana University Press, 1971); and David Forsythe, 'UNRWA, the Palestine Refugees, and World Politics: 1949–1969', *Int. Org.*, 25:1 (1971) pp. 26–45.

3. See UNESCO Doc. 77 EX/34 (1967) para. 12.
4. For text, see UNESCO Doc. 77 EX/34 (1967) Annex I.
5. Ibid., Art. 1(a).
6. See UNESCO Doc. 77 EX/SR.30 (1967) para. 69.3.
7. I am grateful to Mr. W. Mustakim of the UNESCO Education Sector for information concerning developments on the spot. For accounts of events by the Director-General of UNESCO and Commissioner-General for UNRWA, see UNESCO Docs. 77 EX/34 (1967) para. 7 and Annex IV p. 2, last paragraph; and 78 EX/16 Add. (1968) esp. p. 9. For an account by the Israeli Ministry of Foreign Affairs, see UNESCO Doc. 78 EX/16 (1968) para. 5.
8. UNESCO Doc. 77 EX/34 (1967) p. 3, and Annex II p. 2.
9. On this point see UNESCO Doc. 77 EX/34 (1967) para. 11.
10. See confidential Memorandum attached to *letter* of 17 June 1967 from Commissioner-General for UNRWA to Israeli Ambassador-at-large Michael Comay, UNESCO Doc. 77 EX/34 (1967) Annex II. I am grateful to Mr Mustakim, UNESCO Education Sector, for insights concerning the teaching-notes.
11. Confidential Memorandum cited in note 10 above; also UNESCO Doc. 77 EX/34 (1967) p. 2 and Annex IV.
12. See statement by Director-General in UNESCO Doc. 77 EX/34 (1967) paras. 11 and 14.
13. Ibid., pp. 2–3.
14. UNESCO Docs. 77 EX/34 (1967) p. 4 para. 13; and 77 EX/SR.30 (1967) paras. 69.1 to 69.7.
15. UNESCO Doc. 77 EX/Dec. 6.8 of 3 November 1967 (UNESCO 77 EX/ *Decisions* at 31).
16. Ibid., para. 3(a)–(c).
17. See UNESCO Doc. 77 EX/DR.14 (1967).
18. See UNESCO Doc. 77 EX/DR.18 (1967).
19. See *Notes-Verbales* of 11 January 1968 from the Director-General to the Arab host States and to Israel, in UNESCO Doc. 78 EX/16 (1968) esp. pp. 1–2.
20. UNESCO Doc. 78 EX/SR.24 (1968) para. 44.7.
21. For debates and decision, see UNESCO Docs. 78 EX/SR.24, 25 and 27 (1968) and 78 EX/Dec. 7.4 of 20 June 1968 (UNESCO 78 EX/*Decisions*).
22. For details of the Commission's membership, see UNESCO Doc. 81 EX/3 (1968) p. 1.
23. See UNESCO Docs. 82 EX/8 (1969) Annex I (First Report) and Annex II (Final Report).
24. I am grateful to Mr W. Mustakim of the UNESCO Education Sector for this information.
25. For debates on this issue, see UNESCO Docs. 83 EX/SR.21 and 22 (1969).
26. See e.g. UNESCO Doc. 78 EX/SR.25 (1968), statement by Mr Otetea, p. 5.
27. Ibid., statements by Mr Adeleye, para. 4.3, and Mr Dadie, para. 11.
28. UNESCO Doc. 77 EX/SR.31 (1967) para. 7.4, statement by Mr Avidor.
29. UNESCO Doc. 77 EX/SR.31 (1967), statements by Mr Tolba (Egypt),

paras. 3.1, 3.5 and 3.6, and Mr Dib (Lebanon), paras. 9.2 and 9.3.

30. For development of the arguments, see confidential Memorandum from the Commissioner-General for UNRWA cited in note 10 above.

31. For a table of contributions to UNRWA between 1950 and 1969, see Forsythe, 'UNRWA, the Palestine Refugees, and World Politics', op. cit., p. 39.

32. See confidential Memorandum from Commissioner-General for UNRWA cited in note 10 above, Annex II para. 8.

33. Ibid.

34. For the principal debates on the findings of the Commission of Outside Experts, see UNESCO Docs. 82 EX/8 (1969) para. 13, 82 EX/8 Add., 82 EX/SR.12 to 14 and SR.16 (12–14 May 1969), and 84 EX/5 (1970) Annex I.

35. UNESCO Docs. 78 EX/SR.24 (1968) para. 47.5; 82 EX/8 (1969) para. 11; 83 EX/SR.21 (1969) para. 4.1; and 84 EX/SR.28 (1970) para. 2.2.

36. For statements of the Israeli position, see e.g. *letter* of 20 July 1967 from Ambassador-at-large Comay to Commissioner-General for UNRWA, UNESCO Doc. 77 EX/34 (1967) Annex III; statements by Mr Avidor, in UNESCO Docs. 77 EX/SR.31 (1967) paras. 7.1 to 7.10 and 16.1 to 16.4; 78 EX/SR.24 (1968) paras. 47.1 to 47.9; and draft resolutions tabled by Israel, UNESCO Docs. 77 EX/DR.18 (1967) and 82 EX/DR.3 (1969).

37. See e.g. UNESCO Docs. 77 EX/34 (1967) Annex III, and 78 EX/16 (1968) pp. 2–3; and statements by Mr Avidor, UNESCO Docs. 78 EX/SR.24 (1968) paras. 47.2 and 47.8; 81 EX/SR.3 (1968); para. 5.1; and 82 EX/SR.12 (1969) para. 16.6.

38. UNESCO Doc. 83 EX/SR.21 (1969) para. 4.1.

39. See UNESCO Docs. 82 EX/8 Add. (1969) p. 2 para. 4(c), and 83 EX/DR.3 (1969) para. 3(c).

40. UNESCO Doc. 82 EX/SR.13 (1969), statements by Mr El-Khani (Syria) para. 5.4 and by Mr Dib (Lebanon) para. 10.11.

41. See e.g. UNESCO Doc. 78 EX/SR.24 (1968) para. 47.7; 81 EX/SR.3 (1968) para. 5.2; 82 EX/SR.12 (1969) para. 16.4; 83 EX/SR.21 (1969) para. 4.2; and 84 EX/SR.28 (1970) para. 2.12.

42. UNESCO Docs. 82 EX/8 Add. (1969) para. 3, and 84 EX/5 (1970) para. 24.

43. UNESCO Doc. 84 EX/SR.28 (1970) para. 2.15.

44. For statements of the Arab position, see e.g. *Note-Verbale* of 1 May 1968 from Syrian Minister of Education to Director-General, reproduced in UNESCO Doc. 78 EX/16 Add. (1968) pp. 2–7; *letters* of 11 and 12 October 1968 from the Permanent Delegates to UNESCO of Jordan, Egypt and Lebanon, to the Director-General, reproduced in UNESCO Doc. 81 EX/3 (1968) pp. 2–7; statements by Mr Yasin (Jordan) and Mr Hammad (Egypt) in UNESCO Doc. 78 EX/SR.25 (1968) paras. 1.1 to 1.9 and 2.1 to 2.7 resp.; by Mr Hammad (Egypt) in UNESCO Doc. 81 EX/SR.3 (1968) para. 2; and by Mr Salem (Jordan) in UNESCO Doc. 82 EX/SR.13 (1969) paras. 4.1 to 4.9. See also draft resolutions tabled by Arab members, UNESCO Docs. 77 EX/DR.14 (1967) and 82 EX/DR.5 (1969).

45. See UNESCO Docs. 78 EX/16 Add. (1968) pp. 4 and 6, and 84 EX/SR.28 (1970) para. 6.6.

46. UNESCO Docs. 78 EX/16 Add. (1968) p. 3, and 82 EX/SR.13 (1969), statement by Mr El-Khani (Syria), paras. 5.1 to 5.3 and 6.2.
47. See e.g. UNESCO Docs. 82 EX/SR.13 (1969) paras. 2.2, 6.3, 6.6, 7.9 and 10.13; 83 EX/SR.21 (1969) para. 8.1; and 84 EX/SR.28 (1970) para. 8.3.
48. See UNESCO Docs. 78 EX/16 Add. (1968) p. 5; 82 EX/8 (1969) p. 5; 78 EX/SR.25 (1968) paras. 1.7 and 2.6; 81 EX/SR.3 (1968) paras. 2 and 4.1; 82 EX/SR.13 (1969) paras. 4–7; and 84 EX/SR.28 (1970) para. 8.3.
49. UNESCO 9 C/Res. 7.81 of 30 November 1956 (UNESCO 9 C/*Resolutions* at 36).
50. UNESCO Doc. 82 EX/SR.13 (1969) para. 10.8.
51. See UNESCO Docs. 78 EX/16 Add. (1968) pp. 1–6, and 81 EX/3 (1968) p. 2 para. 5.
52. UNESCO Doc. 78 EX/SR.25 (1968) para. 13.1.
53. E.g. UNESCO Docs. 78 EX/SR.24 (1968) paras. 44.1 to 44.20, and 81 EX/SR.3 (1968) para. 1.3.
54. See e.g. UNESCO Doc. 85 EX/SR.15 (1970) para. 18.9.
55. UNESCO Doc. 77 EX/34 (1967) p. 4. See also UNESCO Docs. 77 EX/SR.30 (1967) para. 69.4, 82 EX/SR.12 (1969) para. 15.1, and 82 EX/SR.14 (1969) para. 7.1.
56. UNESCO Doc. 81 EX/SR.3 (1968) para. 1.2.
57. UNESCO Doc. 77 EX/SR.31 (1967), statement by Mr Wade, para. 22.2.
58. See e.g. statements by Messrs Dennery and Fernand-Laurent, UNESCO Docs. 77 EX/SR.31 (1967) paras. 6.1 to 6.2, 78 EX/SR.25 (1968) para. 14, and 82 EX/SR.14 (1969) paras. 1.1 to 1.5.
59. UNESCO Doc. 78 EX/SR.25 (1968), statements by Messrs Barbey and de Gorter, paras. 3.1, 3.2, 9 and 12; and UNESCO Doc. 84 EX/DR.25 (1970).
60. See e.g. UNESCO Docs. 77 EX/DR.17 (1967), 78 EX/DR.10 (1968), 82 EX/DR.6 rev. (1969) and 85 EX/DR.10 (1970).
61. See notably statements by Mr Prohme (USA), UNESCO Docs. 85 EX/SR.17 (1970) para. 42.1, and 88 EX/SR.13 (1971) para. 10.1.
62. See e.g. UNESCO Docs. 81 EX/3 (1968) pp. 3–4, 81 EX/SR.3 (1968) para. 4.2, and 82 EX/SR.13 (1969) para. 4.3.
63. See UNESCO Docs. 78 EX/16 Add. (1968) paras. 2, 8(1), 8(2,b) and 8(3); 78 EX/16 Add.2 (1968) pp. 1–3; 81 EX/3 (1968) paras. 5 and 8; and statements by Messrs Dib (Lebanon), Hammad (Egypt) and El-Khani (Syria) in UNESCO Docs. 77 EX/SR.31 (1967) para. 9.2, 81 EX/SR.3 (1968) paras. 2.6, 4.1 and 4.2, and 82 EX/SR.13 (1969) paras. 5.7 and 7.4.
64. UNESCO Doc. 77 EX/SR.30 (1967) para. 69.6.
65. UNESCO Docs. 85 EX/SR.15 (1970) para. 18.2, and 88 EX/SR.13 (1971) para. 21.3.
66. UNESCO Doc. 85 EX/SR.15 (1970) para. 18.9. (Translation from French original by this writer.)
67. UNESCO Doc. 84 EX/SR.28 (1970) para. 2.6.
68. UNESCO Doc. 82 EX/SR.12 (1969) para. 16.6.
69. See UNESCO Docs. 78 EX/16 (1968) pp. 2–4; 78 EX/SR.25 (1968) para. 1.8; 82 EX/8 Add.3 (1969) pp. 1–2; 82 EX/DR.5 (1969) point 8; and 82 EX/SR.13 (1969) paras. 4.3 and 6.3.
70. See e.g. UNESCO Docs. 77 EX/SR.31 (1967) para. 3.3; 82 EX/8 (1969)

para. 7; and 83 EX/SR.21 (1969) para. 8.1.
71. Jane Rosen, 'The Dilemma of Third World Reaction', *Guardian*, 14 January 1980.
72. See statements by Messrs Dennery, Fernand-Laurent, de Gorter, de Hoog, Prohme, Burgess and Mathieson, Miss Hersch and Miss Guiton, in UNESCO Docs. 84 EX/SR.28 (1970) paras. 16.2, 17.1, 18.1 and 20.4; 84 EX/SR.33 (1970) paras. 16.1 to 16.4, 33–5 and 38; 85 EX/SR.15 (1970) paras. 9, 11 and 13; 87 EX/SR.8 (1971) paras. 9.12, 14 and 17.1; 87 EX/SR.9 (1971) paras. 29 and 31; and 88 EX/SR.13 (1971) paras. 6.3, 10.3, 11.3 and 13.2. See also draft resolution tabled by the UK and US members, UNESCO Doc. 85 EX/DR.9 (1970).
73. See e.g. Forsythe, 'UNRWA, the Palestine Refugees and World Politics', op. cit., Buehrig, *The UN and the Palestinian Refugees*, op. cit., ch. VII; and David C. Gordon, *Self-Determination and History in the Thirld World* (Princeton University Press, 1971), pp. 85–8 and 114–5.
74. Sewell, *UNESCO and World Politics*, op. cit.
75. Hoggart, *An Idea and its Servants*, op. cit., pp. 75–81, 91, 188 and 194–5.
76. See review article by E. Buehrig, 'The Tribulations of UNESCO', *Int.Org.*, 30:4 (1976) 679–85; and René Maheu, 'Serving the Mind as a Force in History', *In the Minds of Men* (Paris: UNESCO, 1971) p. 311.
77. On this point see statements by Director-General, UNESCO Doc. 77 EX/34 (1967) p. 5 and Annex II p. 4; also *The Times Index*, [March–April 1968] p. 161.
78. See UNESCO *Press Reviews*, UNESCO Docs. COM/OPI PR 11–13 and 14–19 (1967).
79. Ibid.
80. See *The Times Index* [September–October 1967] p. 149; [November–December 1967] p. 143; [January–February 1968]; [March–April 1968] p. 161; and [1974] p. 108.
81. The *New York Times Index* [1967] p.739, and [1974] pp. 706–7.

9. Regulation of Science and Culture

1. *Recommendation* on the Status of Scientific Researchers, adopted by UNESCO 18 C/Res. 40 of 20 November 1974 (UNESCO 18 C/*Resolutions* at 169).
2. Ibid., esp. preamble, 6th to 8th recitals, and operative paras. 1(e), 4, 8, 11(b), 13–14, 16 and 17.
3. See 'Resolution on the nonpolitical tradition of ICSU' adopted by the ICSU Executive Committee in October 1966, reproduced in ICSU, Standing Committee on the Free Circulation of Scientists, *Advice to Organisers of International Scientific Meetings 1983/84*, Appendix III.
4. See e.g. UNESCO Doc. 16 C/22 (1970).
5. See e.g. ICSU, Report of the Committee on Science and Social Relations, *Proceedings* of the 5th General Assembly, Annex IV (Cambridge University Press, 1950); *Safeguard of the Pursuit of Science* (Paris: ICSU, February 1982); F. W. G. Baker, *The International Council of Scientific Unions: A Brief Survey* (Paris: ICSU, 1982) esp.pp. 26–9; and World

Federation of Scientific Workers, 'Declaration on the Rights of Scientific Workers', *Scientific World* (1969:4) pp. 23–5.

6. I am grateful to Mr Brian Goddard, UNESCO Science Policy Division, for information on the genesis of the Recommendation supplied during interviews on 22 March and 27 April 1983. For documentary background, see UNESCO Doc. 17 C/21 (1972) esp. pp. 1–2 and Annex II pp. 1–6; also UNESCO 15 C/Res. 2.141 of 19 November 1968 (UNESCO 15 C/*Resolutions* at 34) and 17 C/Res. 2.122 of 15–16 November 1972 (UNESCO 17 C/*Resolutions* at 39).

7. Ibid.

8. UNESCO Doc. SC/MD/35 (1973) esp. paras. 28, 42–4, 53, 56–63 and 75–7.

9. UNESCO Docs. SC/MD/41 Annex I pp. 20–2 and 26–7; and SC/MD/41 Add. 1 pp. 1–11 and 14–16 (1974).

10. See UNESCO Docs. SC/MD/41 Annex I pp. 6–19 and 27–9; and SC/MD/41 Add. 1 pp. 11–14. See also UNESCO Doc. 18 C/26 Part B (1974).

11. UNESCO Doc. SC/MD/41 (1974) Annex I para. 5.

12. See e.g. UNESCO 15 C/*Resolutions* Annex II (Reports) esp. paras. 574–5; and UNESCO Docs. SC-74/CONF.233/DR.39 rev. (1974), 18 C/SC/DR.4 (1974) and 18 C/26 (1974) para. 24.

13. UNESCO Doc. 18 C/SC/DR.4 (1974).

14. Compare UNESCO Doc. 18 C/26 (1974) Annex I para. 4, with *Recommendation* on the status of Scientific Researchers, note 1 above, para. 4.

15. Information from interview with Mr Brian Goddard on 22 March 1983.

16. UNESCO Doc. SC/MD/41 (1974) Annex III.

17. UNESCO Doc. SC/MD/41 (1974) Annex I and Add. 1.

18. UNESCO Docs. SC-74/CONF.233/DR.1-157 (1974). (Note that nos. 154–7 inclusive were allocated but that draft resolutions carrying those numbers were on file neither in UNESCO Archives nor in the programme department concerned.)

19. UNESCO Doc. 18 C/26 (1974) Part A.

20. Compare esp. ibid. paras. 14, 35 and 37 (and same photographs in the final text) with UNESCO Doc. SC/MD/41 (1974) Annex III paras. 14, 36 and 38, and with UNESCO Doc. SC/MD/35 (1973) paras. 26–8.

21. Ibid.

22. Ibid.

23. UNESCO 18 C/*Reports*, p. 56–60.

24. UNESCO 18 C/*Proceedings* Part 2, pp. 343–5.

25. *Recommendation* on participation by the people at large in cultural life and their contribution to it (hereafter *Recommendation on participation . . .*) adopted on 26 November 1976 (UNESCO 19 C/*Resolutions* Annex I at 29).

26. Ibid., para. 4(o).

27. Ibid., para. 14(h).

28. Ibid., para. 18(j).

29. UNESCO Doc. SHC-76/CONF.208/DR.107 (1976).

30. *Recommendation on participation . . .* op. cit., preamble, 23rd recital.

31. UNESCO Doc. SHC-76/CONF.208/DR.127 (1976).

32. *Recommendation on participation . . .* op. cit., para. 11.

33. For background reports and Secretariat drafts, see UNESCO Docs. 18 C/31 and Annex (1974); SHC/MD/28 (1975) Annex esp. paras. 3(p), 8(g), 14(b) and (j); and 19 C/27 (1976) Annex I para. 18(j).
34. See e.g. concerning para. 3(p), UNESCO Docs. SHC-76/CONF.208/DR.26, 32, 71, 73 and 91; concerning para. 8(g), Docs. SHC-76/CONF.208/DR.11, 19, 35, 59, 74, 115, 125 and 133; concerning para. 14(b), Docs. SHC-76/CONF.208/DR.15, 21, 38, 61, 149 and 151; and concerning para. 14(j), Doc. SHC-76/CONF.208/DR.149 (1976). See also UNESCO Docs. SHC/MD/31 Annex I pp. 5-10 and 15-17, and SHC/MD/31 Add. 1 pp. 3-6 (1976).
35. UNESCO Docs. SHC-76/CONF.208/DR.1-349 (1976).
36. On this point see UNESCO Doc. 19 C/27 (1976) Annex II para. 23.
37. SHC-76/CONF.208/DR.1, 48-9 and 161 (1976); 19 C/PRG.II/DR.8 and 17 (1976); and UNESCO 19 C/*Proceedings* Part 2, pp. 393-402.
38. See UNESCO Doc. SHC/MD/31 (1976) Annex I p. 17; and UNESCO 19 C/*Proceedings* Part 2, p. 400 para. 122, and p. 402 para. 134.
39. UNESCO 19 C/*Proceedings* Part 2, pp. 393-402.
40. Ibid.
41. See UNESCO Doc. SHC/MD/31 (1976) Annex I pp. 1-2, 4-6, 11, and 14-15, and UNESCO 19 C/*Proceedings* Part 2, p. 399.
42. UNESCO Docs. SHC/MD/31 Annex I pp. 11-14; SHC/MD/31 Add. 2 pp. 18-19; SHC-76/CONF.208/DR.33, 42, 47, 51, 55-6, 62-8, 75, 77, 81-3, 107 and 109-11 (1976); and UNESCO 19 C/*Proceedings* Part 2, pp. 393-402.
43. For a list of IFTC affiliates, see *Yearbook of International Organisations* [1981], entry A 2054.
44. Information provided during interview on 23 March 1983 by Mrs Vallet and confirmed by telephone by Mr Botbol, both of UNESCO Cultural Policies Division; and during interview with Mr Flipo, IFTC, on 28 April 1983.
45. Interview with Mrs Vallet, UNESCO Cultural Policies Division, on 23 March 1983.
46. UNESCO 19 C/*Proceedings* Part 2, pp. 393-402.
47. *Recommendation* concerning the Status of the Artist, adopted on 27 October 1980 (UNESCO 21 C/*Resolutions* Annex I at 147).
48. See UNESCO Docs. 99 EX/12 (1976), 99 EX/SR.34 (26 May 1976) paras. 46-55, and 99 EX/Dec. 5.4.2. of same date (UNESCO 99 EX/*Decisions*); 19 C/Res. 4.132 of 26 November 1976 (UNESCO 19 C/*Resolutions*, at 52); UNESCO 19 C/*Proceedings* Part 2, p. 371, para. 24.26; and p. 381, paras. 61.3 to 61.4; UNESCO 20 C/*Reports*, paras. 248 and 583-98; 20 C/*Proceedings*, pp. 1057-8, paras. 49.2 to 53.1; and UNESCO 20 C/Res. 4/3.6/3 of 28 November 1978 (UNESCO 20 C/*Resolutions* at 90).
49. Ibid. Also UNESCO Docs. CC/MD/44 (1980) Annex I pp. 1-2; CC/MD/44 Add. 1 pp. 7-13; and CC/MD/44 Add.2 pp. 9-12.
50. I am indebted to Mr Alexandre Blokh for information on this stage of proceedings.
51. See e.g. UNESCO Doc. CC-77/CONF.615/COL.6 (undated), statements by Messrs Thompson, p. 19, and Yllanes Gaxiola, e.g. pp. 57-8.
52. See UNESCO Doc. CC/MD/43 (1979) p. 6.

53. See e.g. UNESCO Docs. CC-77/CONF.615/COL.6 (undated); OIT/
UNESCO/RECA/5 (undated); and summary thereof in UNESCO Doc.
20 C/35 (1978) Annex pp. 8–11; also UNESCO Doc. CC/MD/43 (1979)
pp. 6–8; and staff report by Mr A. Blokh, *Memo* CC/MD/1002.29 of 26
September 1977, in UNESCO File 707 A 102 Part I (made available to this
writer by the programme department concerned).

54. UNESCO Doc. CC/MD/44 (1980) Annex I p. 6.

55. UNESCO Docs. CC/MD/44 Add. 1 p. 13, and CC/MD/44 Add. 2 pp. 7–12
(1980).

56. UNESCO Docs. CC/MD/44 Add. 1 pp. 23–4; and CC-80/CONF.211/
DR.48–9 (1980).

57. UNESCO Doc. CC/MD/43 (1979) Annex.

58. See amendments proposed to preamble, 12th to 15th paragraphs, and to
operative paras. 3F, 4B, 7A & 8B of the preliminary draft cited in note 57
above, in UNESCO Docs. CC/MD/44 Annex I pp. 1–2; CC/MD/44 Add.
1 pp. 9–12, 16–20 and 24–5; CC/MD/44 Add. 2 pp. 1–6 and 8; and CC-
80/CONF.211/DR.3, 6–8, 12, 27, 36, 60, 68 and 73 (1980).

59. See comments on and proposed amendments to para. 6E of preliminary
draft cited in note 57 above, in UNESCO Docs. CC/MD/44 Add. 1 pp. 11,
20 and 25; CC/MD/44 Add. 2 pp. 4–5 and 11; and CC-80/CONF.211/
DR.10, 61, 71 and 81 (1980).

60. See UNESCO Docs. CC/MD/44 Add. 1 p. 22; CC/MD/44 Add. 2 p. 9; CC/
MD/44 Add.3 pp. 1–3; and CC-80/CONF.211/DR.24–5, 44–6, 52 and
62–5 (1980).

61. See replies to a questionnaire analysed in UNESCO Doc. CC-77/
CONF.615/COL.1 Ref. (undated); summary of results of meetings and
studies concerning art and the Third World in UNESCO Doc. CC/MD/43
(1979) pp. 5–7; UNESCO Docs. CC-80/CONF.211/DR.13–15, 31–2,
39–43, 54–6, 66, 74 and 77; UNESCO Doc. 20 C/PRG.IV/DR.5 (1978);
and UNESCO 21 C/*Reports*, para. 522.

62. Interview with Mr A Blokh on 28 April 1983.

63. Ibid., and UNESCO *Register of Cards Issued to Journalists, 2.4.76–
27.5.81* (held by UNESCO Press Room), p. 59.

64. UNESCO Docs. CC-80/CONF.211/DR.1–84 (1980). Note that nos. 82–3
are missing from the UNESCO Archives collection.

65. See UNESCO Doc. 21 C/28 (1980) Annex. Compare preamble, 12th and
15th recitals, and operative paras. 3B, 3F, 4B and 6E of the latter with the
Secretariat draft, UNESCO Doc. CC/MD/44 (1980) Annex III, preamble, 7th and 15th recitals, and operative paras. 3C, 3G, 4B and 6E.

66. See UNESCO Doc. 21 C/98 (1980) p. 2.

67. See UNESCO Doc. 21 C/PRG.IV/DR.5 (1980).

68. UNESCO 21 C/*Reports*, paras. 513–23; and UNESCO 21 C/*Proceedings*,
pp. 1360–1 paras. 66.4 to 70.2.

10. 'Information' Outcomes in 'Race' Contexts

1. For detailed comparison, see e.g. Louis Henkin (ed.), *The International
Bill of Rights* (New York: Columbia University Press, 1981).

2. *International Covenant* on Civil and Political Rights (herafter 'ICCPR') adopted by UN GA Res. 2200A (XXI) of 16 December 1966 (UN GAOR 21 Supp.16 at 49).
3. For debates, see UN GAOR 16(I), C.3, 1070–84 mtg (11–26 October 1961) pp. 55–123; and report UN Doc. A/5000 and Annex (UN GAOR 16(I) Annexes, Agenda item 35).
4. For debate in the Sub-Commission, see UN Docs. E/CN.4/Sub.2/SR.68 and 69 (3 October 1951) pp. 7–15 and pp. 4–5 resp.; for report, see UN Doc. E/CN.4/641 (1951) para. 43 Annex II Res. V. (Art. 20 was discussed at this stage as Art. 26.)
5. See UN Doc. E/CN.4/SR.174 (28 April 1950) pp. 5–14; UN GAOR 9, C.3, 568 mtg (1 November 1954) pp. 123–8; *Observations by Governments*, UN Doc. A/2910 (1955) esp. Add. 1 p. 13, and Add. 3; and UN GAOR 16(I), C.3, 1083 mtg (26 October 1961) pp. 121–3.
6. UN Doc. E/2573 (1954) Annex I B, Art.26; also in UN Doc. A/2929 (1955) p. 185. For summary of debate in Commission on Human Rights, ibid., pp. 185–7. (Art. 20 was discussed at this stage as Art. 26.)
7. UN Doc. A/C.3/L.933 (1961).
8. UN GAOR 16(I), C.3, 1083–4 mtg (26 October 1961) esp. p. 121; and *YUN* [1961] p. 295.
9. Ibid.
10. UN GAOR 21, C.3, 1455–6 mtg (12 December 1966) pp. 476–86.
11. UN GAOR 21, Plen 1495–6 mtg (16 December 1966).
12. *Multilateral Treaties* . . . op. cit., pp. 120–8.
13. Ibid., pp. 123–7.
14. Ibid., pp. 118–19.
15. On this point see Buergenthal & Torney, *International Human Rights and International Education*, op. cit., ch. 5, esp. pp. 86–92.
16. UN GAOR 21, C.3, 1455 mtg (12 December 1966) pp. 447–8 esp. para. 36; and Plen 1496 mtg (16 December 1966) pp. 10–12.
17. See 'Message from the President of the United States transmitting Four Treaties pertaining to Human Rights to the Senate', 23 February 1978, cited in K. H. Partsch, 'Freedom of Conscience and Expression; Political Freedoms', in Henkin, *The International Bill of Rights*, op. cit.
18. See *Multilateral Treaties* . . . op. cit., pp. 118–19.
19. On this point see UN Doc. A/34/40 (UN GAOR 34 Supp.40) para. 414.
20. *Multilateral Treaties* . . . op. cit., pp. 114–16.
21. *International Convention* on the Elimination of All Forms of Racial Discrimination (hereafter Race Convention) adopted by UN GA Res. 2106 (XX) of 21 December 1965 (UN GAOR 20 Supp.14 at 47).
22. Ibid., Art. 4(a) and (b).
23. See UN GAOR 20,C.3, 1315–16 mtg (22 October 1965) pp. 133 and 137; and UN Doc. E/CN.4/SR.794 (3 March 1964) p. 11.
24. For debates on Art 4 in Sub-Commission, see UN Docs. E/CN.4/Sub.2/ SR.417 (21 January 1964) pp. 9–11; SR.418 and 420 (21–2 January 1964); SR. 422 (23 January 1964) pp. 9–15; and SR.428 (29 January 1964) p. 4; and report, UN Doc. E/CN.4/873 (1964) p. 47. For debates in Commission on Human Rights, see UN Docs. E/CN.4/SR.790 (28 February 1964) p. 6 to SR.796 (4 March 1964) p. 6; and detailed account in UN Doc. E/3873,

ch.XI, DR.I, Annex, paras. 144–8 (UN GAOR 37 Supp.8). For debate in Social Committee of ECOSOC, see UN Docs. E/AC.7/SR.490 to SR.493 (16–20 July 1964) and report, E/3952 and Corr.1 (1964) pp. 2 and 7–11 (UN GAOR 37 Annexes, Agenda item 27); in ECOSOC plenary, UN ESCOR 37, Plen 1338 mtg (30 July 1964) pp. 167–72, and ESC Res. 1015B(XXXVII) of same date (UN ESCOR 37 Supp.1 at 3); and in 3rd Committee of the General Assembly, UN GAOR 20, C.3, 1315–18 mtg (22–5 October 1965).

25. See UN GAOR 20, C.3, 1318 mtg (25 October 1965) p. 152; and US draft resolution, UN Doc. E/CN.4/Sub.2/L.308 (1964).
26. See note 37 below.
27. See UN Doc. E/3873 op. cit., ch. XI, DR.I, Annex.
28. See UN Docs. E/AC.7/SR.490 and 491, op. cit., p.15 and pp. 5 and 8 resp.
29. For composition of the Commission on Human Rights in 1964, see *YUN* [1964] p.612.
30. UN Doc. E/CN.4/873, op. cit., p.47 Art. 4; for debate in Sub-Commission, see note 24 above.
31. See Roster of the United Nations in *YUN* [1965] Appendix I.
32. UN Doc. A/C.3/L.1225 (1965).
33. UN Doc. A/C.3/L.1220 (1965).
34. UN GAOR 20, C.3, 1315–18 mtg (22–5 October 1965).
35. Ibid., 1318 mtg, pp. 133, 149 and 151.
36. Ibid., pp. 150–2.
37. UN Doc. A/L.480 (1965) (UN GAOR 20 Annexes, Agenda item 58, at 40).
38. UN GAOR 20, Plen 1406 mtg (21 December 1965) p. 7.
39. See UN GAOR 20, C.3, 1316 mtg, e.g. statements by Nigeria and Mauritania, p. 140.
40. Race Convention, note 21 above, Art. 4.
41. UN Doc. A/C.3/L,1245 (1965).
42. UN GAOR 20, C.3 1315 mtg (22 October 1965) p. 135.
43. UN Doc. A/C.3/L,1250 (1965).
44. UN GAOR 20, C.3, 1318 mtg (25 October 1965) p. 150.
45. Ibid., p. 151.
46. UN Doc. A/L.479 (1965) (UN GAOR 20 Annexes, Agenda item 58, at 40).
47. UN GAOR 20, C.3, 1368 mtg (8 December 1965).
48. UN GAOR 20, Plen 1406 mtg (21 December 1965) pp. 6–7.
49. Ibid., p. 6.
50. Ibid., pp. 11 and 13.
51. Ibid., pp. 6–7.
52. *Multilateral Treaties* . . . op. cit., pp. 96–106.
53. Ibid., declarations by Australia, Belgium, France and the United Kingdom.
54. See R. B. Lillich and F. C. Newman (eds.), *International Human Rights: Problems of Law and Policy* (Boston: Little Brown, 1979) p. 166.
55. See UN Doc. E/CN.4/Sub.2/SR.420 and 422, note 24 above, statements by Mr Capotorti (Italy) pp. 7–8 and p. 11 resp.; UN Doc. E/CN.4/SR.792, note 24 above, statement by Mr Sperduti (Italy) pp. 13–15; and UN GAOR 20, C.3, 1318 mtg (25 October 1965), statement by Israel, p. 151.

56. *International Convention* on the Suppression and Punishment of the Crime of *Apartheid* (hereafter *Apartheid* Convention) adopted by UN GA Res. 3068 (XXVIII) of 15 November 1973 (UN GAOR 28 Supp.30 at 75).

57. For background reports, see UN Docs A/9022 (1973) paras. 122–4, and A/9095 & Annex (1973) (both UN GAOR 28 Supp.22). For debates, see UN GAOR 28, C.3, 2002–8 mtg (19–26 October 1973) and Plen 2185 mtg (15 November 1973).

58. UN GAOR 28, C.3, 2008 mtg (26 October 1973) pp. 164–70.

59. For votes, ibid., pp. 162–3, and Plen 2185 mtg (15 November 1973) paras. 12–47.

60. UN Doc. A/C.3/L.2026 (1973).

61. UN GAOR 28, C.3, 2008 mtg (26 October 1973) p. 162.

62. *Multilateral Treaties. . .*, note 12 above, pp. 138–40.

63. *Declaration* on Race and Racial Prejudice (hereafter Race Declaration) adopted by UNESCO 20 C/Res. 3/1.1/2 of 27 November 1978 (UNESCO 20 C/*Resolutions* at 61).

64. For background to the Race Declaration see UNESCO Docs 18 C/35 (1974), SHC/MD/33 (1976), SS-77/CONF.201/1 (1977), 20 C/18 and Add. (1978).

65. UNESCO Docs SS-78/CONF.201/9 (1978), also reproduced as Doc. 20 C/18 (1978).

66. For report of the meeting see UNESCO Doc. SS-78/CONF.201/6 (1978) also available as Doc. 20 C/18 Add. (1978) pp. 3–12.

67. For attendance records, see UNESCO Doc. SS- 78/CONF. 201/6 (1978) Annex III, and UNESCO 20 C/*Proceedings*, pp. 25–90.

68. Ibid.

69. Race Declaration, note 63 above, Arts 5–7.

70. UNESCO Docs SS-78/CONF.201/DR.18, 19, 22, 59, 65, 67, 78–80 and 83–4 (1978).

71. See UNESCO Doc. 19 C/95 (1976) Annex II.

72. Ibid.; and UNESCO 19 C/Res. 3.173 of 22 November 1976 (UNESCO 19 C/*Resolutions* at 44).

73. See UNESCO Doc. 20 C/18 Add. (1978) paras. 66–8; UNESCO 20 C/*Reports*, para. 330; and UNESCO 20 C/*Proceedings*, pp. 1039–40 paras. 57.1 to 57.4.

74. See UNESCO 20 C/18 (1978) Annex esp. pp. 4–7.

75. For statement on this point, see UNESCO 20 C/*Reports*, para. 342. The record does not indicate the source of the statement but according to this writer's notes the speaker was the UK delegate.

76. UNESCO 20 C/*Reports*, p. 106 para. 328; and UNESCO C/*Proceedings*, p. 1039, paras. 54.129 to 54.131.

77. On this point, see UNESCO Doc. 19 C/95 (1976) p. 9.

78. See *The Times Index* [November–December 1965] p. 226; [November–December 1966] p. 211; and [November–December 1973] p. 232; and the *New York Times Index* [1965] pp. 995–1003; [1966] pp. 1197–203; and [1973] pp. 2400–4.

79. See *The Times Index* [1978] p. 393; and the *New York Times Index* [1978] p. 343.

Bibliography

1. PRIMARY SOURCES

A. United Nations and UNESCO Debates: bibliographical note

Our research was based chiefly on debates within the United Nations and UNESCO. Given the number of debates examined, the bibliographical cumbersomeness of the sources involved, and constraints of space, a bibliography of these particular primary sources cannot be supplied here.* Instead, the present note provides a key to document symbols and details of the way in which references were constructed.

1. Key to document symbols

All UN and UNESCO documents carry numbers which serve as the basic retrieval mechanism. Document numbers include a symbol identifying the organ to which a document pertains. Listed below are the symbols of the documents consulted and the names of the organs concerned:

A. *United Nations General Assembly and subordinate organs*

A/	General Assembly, plenary
A/AC.42/	Committee on the Draft Convention on Freedom of Information (1951)
A/AC.76/	Ad hoc Political Committee (1954)
A/BUR/	General Committee
A/C.1/	First Committee
A/C.3/	Third Committee
A/SPC/	Special Political Committee
†GA	General Assembly
†GAOR	General Asembly Official Records

B. *United Nations Economic and Social Council and subordinate organs*

E/	Economic and Social Council, plenary
E/AC.7/	Social Committee

---

* For a detailed bibliography of the UN and UNESCO primary sources consulted, see C. Wells, *The 'Politicisation' of United Nations Specialised Agencies? The UN, UNESCO and the Politics of Knowledge, 1945–82* (doctoral thesis for the University of Oxford, deposited with the Bodleian Library in Oxford and with the Archives Section of UNESCO Headquarters in Paris).

† These are not document symbols but standard abbreviations.

254

E/AC.34/	*Ad hoc* Committee on the Organisation and Operation of the Council and its Commissions
E/CN.4/	Commission on Human Rights
E/CN.4/Sub.1/	Sub-Commission on Freedom of Information and of the Press (1947–52)
E/CN.4/Sub.2/	Sub-Commission on Prevention of Discrimination and Protection of Minorities
E/CONF.6/	United Nations Conference on Freedom of Information (1948)
E/CONF.6/C.4/	Ibid., Fourth Commission
*ESC	Economic and Social Council
*ESCOR	Economic and Social Council Official Records

C. UNESCO *General Conference and subordinate organs*

C/	General Conference, plenary
C/C2/	Second Commission
C/COM/	Programme Commission (Communication)
C/ED/	Programme Commission (Education)
C/PLEN/	Plenary
C/PRG/	Programme and Budget Commission
C/PRG.II/	Programme Commission II
C/PRG.III/	Programme Commission III
C/PRG.IV/	Programme Commission IV
C/SC/	Programme Commission (Natural Sciences)
*C/Records	Records of the General Conference

D. UNESCO *Executive Board and subordinate organs*

EX/	Executive Board
EX/CP/	Programme Committee

E. UNESCO *Founding Conference*

ECO/CONF./	Conference for the Establishment of UNESCO (1945)
ECO/CONF./ Com.I/	First Commission

F. UNESCO *Preparatory Commission*

UNESCO/ Prep. Comm./	UNESCO Preparatory Commission (1945–6)

* These are not document symbols but standard abbreviations.

G. UNESCO Meetings held outside the framework of the General Conference

COM-74/CONF.616/	Meeting of Experts on a draft Declaration concerning the Role of the Mass Media (Paris, UNESCO House, 11–15 March 1974)
SC-74/CONF.233/	Special Committee of Governmental Experts to Examine a Draft Recommendation on the Status of Scientific Research Workers (Paris, UNESCO House, 23–30 April 1974)
ED-74/CONF.208/	Special Committee of Governmental Experts to Examine a Draft Recommendation concerning Education for International Understanding, Co-operation and Peace and Education relating to Human Rights and Fundamental Freedoms (Paris, UNESCO House, 29 April–8 May 1974)
ED-74/CONF.209/	Special Committee of Governmental Experts to Prepare a draft text of a Revised Recommendation concerning Technical and Vocational Education (Paris, UNESCO House, 13–22 May 1974)
COM-75/CONF.201/	Intergovernmental Meeting of Experts to Prepare a Draft Declaration on Fundamental Principles governing the Use of the Mass Media in Strengthening Peace and International Understanding and in Combating War Propaganda, Racism and *Apartheid* (Paris, UNESCO House, 15–22 December 1975)
SHC-76/CONF.208/	Special Committee of Governmental Experts to Examine a Draft Recommendation on Action to Ensure that the People at Large have Free, Democratic Access to Culture and Participate actively in the Cultural Life of Society (Paris, UNESCO House, 5–14 April 1976)
ED-76/CONF.207/	Special Committee of Governmental Experts to Prepare a Draft Recommendation on the Development of Adult Education (Paris, UNESCO House, 2–12 June 1976)
COM-76/LACCOM/	Intergovernmental Conference on Communication Policies in Latin America and the Caribbean (San José, Costa Rica, 12–21 July 1976)
CC-77/CONF.615/	Joint ILO/UNESCO meeting of experts on the Status of the Artist (Geneva, ILO Headquarters, 29 August–2 September 1977)
SS-78/CONF.201/	Meeting of Government Representatives to Prepare a Draft Declaration on Race and Racial Prejudice (Paris, UNESCO House, 13–20 March 1978)
CC-80/CONF.211/	Special Committee of Governmental Experts to Prepare a Draft Recommendation on the Status of the Artist (Paris, UNESCO House, 25 February–7 March 1980).

The UN records series GAOR and ESCOR are followed, and the UNESCO records series C/ and EX/ are preceded by a sessional running number in Arab numerals and where relevant by a part-session number in Roman numerals. The UNESCO records series C/ and EX/, and all the other symbols listed above may be completed by a running number alone, as in the case of reports and working papers; or they may be followed by any of the abbreviations listed below indicating other types of document, these abbreviations in turn being completed by a running number:

Dec. Decision
DR. Draft Resolution
L. Limited (used in the UN for draft resolutions)
P.V. Provisional Verbatim Record
Res. Resolution
RES. Resolution
SR. Summary Record.

Examples:

UNESCO Doc. 78 EX/Dec. 7.4	UNESCO Executive Board, 78th Session, Decision 7.4.
UNESCO Doc. 19 C/ PRG.II/DR.8	UNESCO General Conference, 19th Session, Programme Commission II, draft resolution 8.
UN Doc. E/CN.4/Sub.1/123	United Nations, Economic and Social Council, Commission on Human Rights, Sub-Commission on Freedom of Information and of the Press, document 123.
UN Doc. E/AC.7/SR.66	United Nations, Economic and Social Council, Social Committee, Summary Record of the 66th meeting.

The abbreviations GA and ESC are used only in connection with resolutions, in the following form:

ESC Resolution 414(IX)	Economic and Social Council Resolution 414 (Ninth Session). (Here, sessional running number is given in Roman not Arab numerals).

Finally, it should be noted that Doc.ECO/CONF./29 comprises the proceedings of the Conference for the establishment of UNESCO.

2. Construction of references to UN and UNESCO primary sources

Generally speaking we have followed standard practice in our referencing system. Where more than one method is in common usage we have chosen the most concise.

Since we are dealing with the records of two organisations, all references are preceded by an indication as to whether the item in question emanates from the UN or from UNESCO.

The four main types of source cited are the following:

a) records of debates;
b) reports or other documents, usually prepared by the Secretariats, and serving as bases for discussion;
c) draft resolutions or amendments submitted by Member States before or during debate;
d) outcomes in the form of decisions or resolutions.

References to items in each of the above categories are constructed as shown below.

A. Records of debate

For UN debates, references indicate the records series, session (and if relevant part-session) number, organ, meeting number and date, and page or paragraph if any.

Example:

UN GAOR 2, C.1, 79–86   United Nations *General Assembly Official*
mtg (22–7 October 1947),   *Records*, Second Session, First Commit-
p. 179   tee, 79th–86th meetings (22–7 October
   1947), p. 179.

UN ESCOR 11, Plen 405 mtg   United Nations *Economic and Social*
(9 August 1950), para. 12   *Council Official Records*, Eleventh Session, Plenary, 405th meeting (9 August
   1950), para. 12.

For UNESCO General Conference debates, references indicate the session number, the record series, the volume concerned (Proceedings, Reports or Resolutions), and where relevant the page or paragraph.

Example:

UNESCO 2   UNESCO *General Conference Records*,
C/*Proceedings*, p. 84   Second Session, *Proceedings*, p. 84.

For summary records of debates in bodies other than the plenary and first Committee of the General Assembly or the plenary of the Economic and Social Council within the UN, and in bodies other than the plenary of the General Conference within UNESCO, references give the document number, the number and date of the meeting, and the page or paragraph if any.

Example:

UN Doc. E/CN.4/Sub.1/ SR.67 (14 June 1949), p. 20	United Nations, Economic and Social Council, Commission on Human Rights, Sub-Commission on Freedom of Information and of the Press, Summary Record of the 67th meeting (14 June 1949), p. 20.
UNESCO Doc. 104 EX/ SR.22 (31 May 1978), para. 14	UNESCO, Executive Board, 104th Session, Summary Record of the 22nd meeting (31 May 1978), para. 14.

B. Reports and other documents serving as bases for discussion

References give the document number, year of publication, and page or paragraph if any. Where relevant, they also indicate the form in which the document was subsequently published: UN documents may be issued as annexes to official records, with a separate fascicle of annexes for each agenda item, or as supplements (Supp.) to the records.

Examples:

UN Doc. A/9022 (1973) (UN GAOR 28 Supp.22 at 5).
UN Doc. E/2427 (1953) (UN ESCOR 17 Annexes, agenda item 12 at 1)
UNESCO Doc. 17 C/76 (1974), p. 3

C. Draft resolutions and amendments submitted by Member States

References give the document number, year of publication, and where relevant the form in which the document was subsequently issued.

Examples:

UN Doc. A/C.3/L.252 (1952) (UN GAOR 7 Annexes, Agenda item 29 at 28)
UNESCO Doc. ED-76/CONF.207/DR.33 (1976)

D. Decisions and resolutions

References give the document number, date of adoption, details of publication in the records of the body concerned, and where relevant the page or paragraph.

Examples:

UN GA Res. 2448(XXIII) of 19 December 1968 (UN GAOR 23 Supp.1 at 52)
UN ESC Res. 414(IX) of 18 September 1951 (UN ESCOR 13 Supp.1 at 80)
UNESCO 15 C/Res. 1.271 of 19 November 1968 (UNESCO 15 C/*Resolutions*, at 26)
UNESCO 77 EX/Dec. 6.8 of 3 November 1967 (UNESCO Doc. 77 EX/Decisions at 31)

To conclude, the following two points should be noted. First, for items in categories b, c and d above, titles are given only exceptionally where the author judged it necessary or enlightening to do so.

Secondly, it is not standard practice when referring to UNESCO General Conference proceedings to indicate the number and date of meetings, nor is it necessary for retrieval purposes to give the year in which the particular session of the General Conference was held or the year in which the particular volume of the Records was published. But for the sake of completeness we close this note with a list showing the date of each session of the General Conference up to 1983.

Dates of sessions of the General Conference of UNESCO:

Conference for the establishment of UNESCO	1–16 Nov. 1945
General Conference:	
1st Session (1 C), Paris	20 Nov.–10 Dec. 1946
2nd Session (2 C), Mexico City	6 Nov.–3 Dec. 1947
3rd Session (3 C), Beirut	17 Nov.–11 Dec. 1948
4th Session (4 C), Paris	19 Sept.–5 Oct. 1949
5th Session (5 C), Florence	22 May–17 June 1950
6th Session (6 C), Paris	18 June–11 July 1951
7th Session (7 C), Paris	12 Nov.–11 Dec. 1952
8th Session (8 C), Montevideo	12 Nov.–10 Dec. 1954
9th Session (9 C), New Delhi	5 Nov.–5 Dec. 1956
10th Session (10 C), Paris	4 Nov.–5 Dec. 1958
11th Session (11 C), Paris	14 Nov–15 Dec. 1960
12th Session (12 C), Paris	9 Nov.–12 Dec. 1962
13th Session (13 C), Paris	20 Oct–20 Nov. 1964
14th Session (14 C), Paris	25 Oct.–30 Nov. 1966
15th Session (15 C), Paris	15 Oct.–20 Nov. 1968
16th Session (16 C), Paris	12 Oct.–14 Nov. 1970
17th Session (17 C), Paris	17 Oct.–21 Nov. 1972
18th Session (18 C), Paris	18 Oct.–23 Nov. 1974
19th Session (19 C), Nairobi	26 Oct.–30 Nov. 1976
20th Session (20 C), Paris	24 Oct.–28 Nov. 1978
21st Session (21 C), Belgrade	23 Sept.–28 Oct. 1980
22nd Session (22 C), Paris	25 Oct.–26 Nov. 1983.

B.   Other United Nations Sources

1.   Constitutional texts

Charter of the United Nations and *Statutes* of the International Court of Justice. Adopted on 26 June 1945. UN Document DPI/511–175 (2–80).

2.   Reference works published by the Secretariat

Multilateral Treaties Deposited with the Secretary-General: Status as at 31 December 1982 (UN Document ST/LEG/SER.E/2, 1983).
Yearbook of the United Nations [1946] to [1982].
For Fundamental Freedoms (New York: UN, 1948), Chapter VIII.
These Rights and Freedoms (New York: UN, 1950), Chapter VI.

C.   Other UNESCO Sources

1.   Constitutional texts

Constitution of the United Nations Educational, Scientific and Cultural Organization. Adopted on 16 November 1945. *UNTS* 4 at 275.
Agreement between the United Nations and the United Nations Educational, Scientific and Cultural Organization. Approved by the General Conference on 14 December 1946. Reproduced in *Manual of the General Conference* (Paris: UNESCO, 1984 revised edition, at 115).
International Programme for the Development of Communication: *Collection of Basic Texts*, UNESCO Doc. CC-81/WS/34 (1981).

2.   Documents of the International Commission for the Study of Communication Problems (ICSCP)

The World of News Agencies, ICSCP Doc. 11 (undated).
News Agencies Multilateral Co-operation, ICSCP Doc. 12 (undated).
Monographies (I), ICSCP Doc. 13 (undated).
Monographies (II), ICSCP Doc. 15 (undated).
Infrastructures of News Collection and Dissemination in the World, ICSCP Doc. 19 (undated).
Bogdan Osolnik, *Aims and Approaches to a New International Communication Order*, ICSCP Doc. 32 (undated).
Many Voices, One World: Towards a new, more just and more efficient world information and communication order (Paris: UNESCO, 1980).

3.   Other UNESCO documents and publications in the field of mass communication

Mass Media in Developing Countries: A UNESCO Report to the United Nations (Reports and Papers in Mass Communication No. 33, 1961).
Television Traffic: A One-Way Street? (Reports and Papers in Mass Communication No. 70, 1974).
Cross-Cultural Broadcasting (Reports and Papers in Mass Communication No. 77, 1976).
Varis, Tapio, *The Impact of Transnational Corporations on Communication*, UNESCO Doc. SHC-76/CONF.635/7 (1976).
Gritti, Jules, *La Réunion sur la Protection des Journalistes, Paris, UNESCO, 16–18 février 1981: Analyse des Contenus de Presse*, UNESCO Doc. OPI-81/WS/11 (1981).

4.   Signed articles in UNESCO periodicals and publications

Behrstock, Julian, 'In defence of Unesco', *Opinion: UNESCO Staff Association Journal* (Feb.–March 1980) pp. 48–50.
Gjesdal, Tor, 'The Right to Information', *The UNESCO Chronicle*, 6 (November 1960) pp. 420–7.
Harley, William G., 'The Mass Media and Society: An American Viewpoint', *The UNESCO Courier* (April 1977) pp. 28–31.
Maheu, René, 'Quel peut être notre rôle dans un débat politique?', *Le Courrier de L'UNESCO* (June 1948) pp. 7–8.
Maheu, René, 'Serving the Mind as a force in History', *In the Minds of Men* (Paris: UNESCO, 1971), pp. 281–319.
Najar, Ridha, 'A Voice from the Third World: Towards a "New World Order of Information"', *The UNESCO Courier* (April 1977) pp. 21–3.
Zasursky, Y. N. and Kashlev, Y. I., 'The Mass Media and Society: A Soviet Viewpoint', *The UNESCO Courier* (April 1977) pp. 24–7.

5.   UNESCO Publications in the education field

A Handbook for the Improvement of Textbooks and Teaching Materials (Paris: UNESCO Publication No. 368, 1949).
Towards World Understanding Series, Nos. I–IX (1949–52).
Bibby, Cyril, *Race, Prejudice and Education* (Paris: UNESCO, 1959).

6.   UNESCO Press Releases, Press Reviews and Registers of cards issued to journalists

Press Reviews compiled by the Office of Public Information were previously held by the Press Room; at the time of research they were available from the Private Office of the Director-General. Registers of cards issued to journalists attending UNESCO meetings are held by the Press Room.

7. Speeches by the Director-General

Address by Mr René Maheu, Director-General of the United Nations Educational, Scientific and Cultural Organization at the opening of the International Conference of States on Distribution of Programme-Carrying Signals transmitted by Satellite, Brussels, 6 May 1974, UNESCO Doc. DG/74/4 (1974).

Consensus in International Organizations: Address by Mr Amadou-Mahtar M'Bow, Director-General of the United Nations Educational, Scientific and Cultural Organization, to the International Diplomatic Academy, Paris, 21 March 1978; UNESCO Doc. DG/78/01 (1978).

8. UNESCO correspondence files

Central Registry File 327.6 371.214A 182/064(44) "49" on International Understanding: Teaching; Schools; Programme; Recommendation. (This file incorporates papers from earlier files Nos. 327.400.841.1 and 327.437.008.41 "49" 1.)

Central Registry File 001 A 3/82 "66" Parts I to V on the Free Flow of Educational, Scientific and Cultural Material: UNESCO Agreements.

File 659.3:323.1 INT on the Mass Media Declaration (file made available by Mr Hifzi Topuz, UNESCO Mass Communications Sector).

File 707 A 102 Part I on the Recommendation on the Status of the Artist (file available from the Cultural Development Division).

D. Other Primary Sources

1. League of Nations

International Convention concerning the Use of Broadcasting in the Cause of Peace (Geneva, 1936). *LNTS* No. 4.319, v.186, at 302.

2. United States Congress

Senate, Select Committee to Study Governmental Operations with respect to Intelligence Activities. *Hearings*, Volume 7: Covert Action. 94th Congress, 1st Session, 1975.

3. United Kingdom, House of Lords

Parliamentary Debates, Volume 426. 1 February 1982.

4. United Kingdom, House of Commons

Parliamentary Debates, Volume 29. 20 October 1982.

5. United Kingdom Public Record Office

Files bearing upon UN and UNESCO debates on freedom of information in the postwar era:

a) Foreign Office files

FO 924/299–304; FO 924/598; FO 924/642; FO 371/72774–8; FO 371/78894–908; FO 371/88722–3; FO 371/88776–7; FO 371/88909; FO 371/95832–6; FO 371/95885; and FO 371/101423–5.

b) Cabinet Office files

CAB 134/388–9; CAB 134/396–9; CAB 134/404–12; CAB 134/422–6; and CAB 134/973.

6. Newspapers and newspaper indexes

The Financial Times; *Guardian*; *International Herald Tribune*; *Le Monde*; *New York Times*; *New York Times Index*; *The Sunday Times*; *The Times*; *The Times Index*.

2. SECONDARY SOURCES

Armstrong, John, 'The Soviet Attitude toward UNESCO', *International Organisation*, 8:2 (May 1954) pp. 217–33.

Association Franco-arabe de juristes, *L'UNESCO et Israël: ce qui s'est réellement passé* (Paris: Imp. Inter Compos, undated).

Baker, F. W. G., *The International Council of Scientific Unions: A Brief Survey* (Paris: ICSU, January 1982).

Baldwin, David A., 'The International Bank in Political Perspective', *World Politics*, 18:1 (October 1965) pp. 68–81.

Binder, Carroll, 'Freedom of Information and the United Nations', *International Organisation*, 6:2 (May 1952) pp. 210–26.

Breed, Warren, *The Self-Guiding Society* (New York: Free Press Paperback, 1971).

Buehrig, Edward H., *The UN and the Palestinian Refugees* (Bloomington: Indiana University Press, 1971).

Buehrig, Edward H., 'The Tribulations of UNESCO', *International Organization*, 30:4 (Autumn 1976) pp. 679–85.

Buergenthal, Thomas and Judith Torney, *International Human Rights and International Education* (Washington, D.C.: US National Commission for UNESCO, Department of State, 1976).

Buzan, Barry, 'Negotiating by Consensus: Developments in Technique at the United Nations Conference on the Law of the Sea', *American Journal of International Law*, 75:2 (April 1981) pp. 324–48.

Claude, Inis Jr., 'The Nature and Status of the Sub-Commission on Prevention of Discrimination and Protection of Minorities', *International Organisation*, 5 (1951) pp. 300–12.

Claude, Inis Jr., *Swords into Plowshares* (New York: Random House, 1956).

Cohn, Theodore, 'Politics in the World Bank Group: the Question of Loans to the Asian Giants', *International Organisation*, 28:3 (Summer 1974) pp. 561–71.

Cox, Robert W. and H. Jacobson, (eds), *The Anatomy of Influence* (New Haven: Yale University Press, 1973).

Dag Hammarskjöld Foundation, *Report for 1975: What Now? Another Development* (Uppsala, 1975).

Development Dialogue, 1976:2 and 1977:1 (Uppsala: Dag Hammarskjöld Foundation).

Dexter, Byron, 'Unesco Faces Two Worlds', *Foreign Affairs*, 25:3 (April 1947) pp. 388–407.

Dexter, Byron, 'Yardstick for UNESCO', *Foreign Affairs*, 28:1 (1949) pp. 56–67.

Eban, Abba, 'Israel, Anti-Semitism and the United Nations', *Jerusalem Quarterly*, 1 (Fall 1976) pp. 110–20.

Evans, Harold, 'The Half Free Press', *The Freedom of the Press*, The Granada Guildhall Lectures (London: Hart-Davis MacGibbon, 1974).

Forsythe, David, 'UNRWA, the Palestine Refugees, and World Politics: 1949–1969', *International Organisation*, 25:1 (Winter 1971) pp. 26–45.

Garbo, Gunnar, 'Freedom of the Press: Media Structure and Control', *Bulletin of Peace Proposals*, 8:3 (1977) pp. 233–5.

Gimbel, John, *A German Community under American Occupation* (Stanford: Stanford University Press, 1961), Chapter 13.

Gordon, David C., *Self-Determination and History in the Third World* (Princeton, N.J.: Princeton Univeristy Press, 1971).

Heacock, Roger, *UNESCO and the Media* (Geneva: Institut Universitaire de Hautes Etudes Internationales, Etudes et Travaux 15, 1977).

Henkin, Louis (ed.), *The International Bill of Rights* (New York: Columbia University Press, 1981).

Hirsch, Fred and David Gordon, *Newspaper Money* (London: Hutchinson, 1975).

Hoch, Paul, *The Newspaper Game* (London: Calder & Boyers, 1974).

Hoggart, Richard, *An Idea and its Servants: UNESCO from within* (London: Chatto & Windus, 1978).

Hoggart, Richard, *The Mass Media: A New Colonialism?* (London: 8th STC Communication Lecture, 1978).

International Council of Scientific Unions, Report of the Committee on Science and Social Relations, *Proceedings* of the 5th General Assembly, Annex IV (Cambridge University Press, 1950).

International Council of Scientific Unions, Standing Committee on the Free Circulation of Scientists, *Advice to Organisers of International Scientific Meetings*, Appendix III (Paris: ICSU Secretariat, 1983–4).

International Council of Scientific Unions, *Safeguard of the Pursuit of Science* (Paris: ICSU, February 1982).

International Press Institute, *Government Pressures on the Press* (Zurich: IPI, 1955).

Katz, Jacob, 'Zionism vs. Anti-Semitism', *Commentary*, 67:4 (April 1979) pp. 46–52.

Kay, David A., 'On the Reform of International Institutions: A Comment', *International Organisation*, 30:3 (Summer 1976) pp. 533–8.

Kay, David A. (ed.), *The Changing United Nations: Options for the United States* (New York: Academy of Political Science, 1977).

Korey, William, 'UNESCO and Israel', *Midstream: A Monthly Jewish Review* (February 1975) pp. 7–17.

Laves, Walter H. C. and Charles A. Thomson, *UNESCO: Purpose, Problems, Prospects* (Bloomington: Indiana University Press, 1957).

Legum, Colin and John Cornwell, *A Free and Balanced Flow: Report of the 20th-Century Task Force on the International Flow of News* (Massachusetts: Lexington Books, 1978).

Lewis, Bernard, 'The Anti-Zionist Resolution', *Foreign Affairs*, 55:1 (October 1976) pp. 54–64.

Lillich, Richard B. and Frank C. Newman, *International Human Rights: Problems of Law and Policy* (Boston: Little Brown, 1979).

Miliband, Ralph, *The State in Capitalist Society* (London: Quartet Books, 1973).

Mill, John Stuart, 'On Liberty of Thought and Discussion', *On Liberty* (Harmondsworth: Penguin, 1978).

Mitrany, David, *A Working Peace System* (Chicago: Quadrangle Books, 1966).

Morawiecki, Wojciech, 'Institutional and Political Conditions of Participation of Socialist States in International Organisations: A Polish View', *International Organisation*, 22:2 (Spring 1968) pp. 494–507.

Moynihan, Daniel P., 'The US in Opposition', *Commentary*, 59:3 (March 1975) pp. 31–44.

Mylonas, Denis, *La Genèse de l'UNESCO* (Brussels: Bruylant, 1976).

Ploman, Edward W., *International Law Governing Communications and Information: A Collection of Basic Documents* (London: Frances Pinter, 1982).

Poulouse, T. T., 'India as an Anomalous International Person', *British Yearbook of International Law*, 44 (1970) pp. 201–12.

Raskin, A. H., *Report on News Coverage of Belgrade UNESCO Conference* (New York: The National News Council, March 1981).

Richter, Jim and L. S. Harms (eds), *Evolving Perspectives on the Right to Communicate* (Honolulu: East-West Center, 1977).

Righter, Rosemary, *IPI – The Undivided Word: A History of the International Press Institute 1951–1976* (Zurich: IPI, 1976).

Righter, Rosemary, *Whose News? The Press, Politics and the Third World* (London: Burnett Books, 1978).

Righter, Rosemary, 'Newsflow International', *The Political Quarterly*, 5:3 (July–September 1979) pp. 302–15.

Roach, Colleen, *The Reaction of the French Press to the Mass Media Declaration* (University of Paris, typescript, March 1979).

Roach, Colleen, 'French Press Coverage of the Belgrade UNESCO Conference', *Journal of Communication* (Fall 1981) pp. 175–87.

Rosenblum, Mort A., 'Reporting from the Third World', *Foreign Affairs*, 55 (July 1977) pp. 815–35.

Sathyamurthy, T. V., *The Politics of International Cooperation: Contrasting Conceptions of UNESCO* (Geneva: Librairie Droz, 1964).

Schiller, Herbert, *Mass Communications and American Empire* (New York: Augustus M. Kelly, 1969).

Schiller, Herbert, 'Libre Circulation de l'Information et Domination Mondiale', *Le Monde Diplomatique* (September 1975) p. 18.

Schramm, Wilbur, *Mass Media and National Development* (Paris: UNESCO, 1964).

Schramm, Wilbur, *Responsibility in Mass Communication* (New York: Harper, 1967).

Sewell, James P., *UNESCO and World Politics* (Princeton, N.J.: Princeton University Press, 1975).

Shuster, George N., *UNESCO: Assessment and Promise* (New York: Harper & Row, 1963).

Smith, Anthony, *The Politics of Information* (London: Macmillan Press, 1978).

St. John, Jeffrey, 'The Third World and the Free Enterprise Press', *Policy Review* 5 (Summer 1978) pp. 59–70.

Stairs, Denis, 'The press and foreign policy in Canada', *International Journal*, 31:2 (Spring 1976) pp. 223–43.

Steed, Henry Wickham, *The Press* (London: Penguin, 1938).

Sussman, Leonard R., *Mass Media and the Third World Challenge*; The Washington Papers (Washington D.C.: Center for Strategic and International Studies, Georgetown University, 1977).

Thomas, Jean, *U.N.E.S.C.O.* (Paris: Gallimard, 1962).

Tucker, Robert, *The Inequality of Nations* (Oxford: Martin Robertson, 1977).

Tunstall, Jeremy, *The Media are American* (New York: Columbia University Press, 1977).

Weiss, Thomas G. and Robert S. Jordan, *The World Food Conference and Global Problem-Solving* (New York: Praeger Publishers, 1976).

Williams, Francis, *Press, Parliament and People* (London: Heinemann, 1946).

Williams, Francis, *The Right to Know: The Rise of the World Press* (Longmans, Green, 1969).

Williams, Raymond, *The Long Revolution* (London: Chatto & Windus, 1961).

Williams, Raymond, *Communications* (London: Chatto & Windus, 1966).

Williams, Raymond, *Television Technology and Cultural Form* (London: Fontana/Collins, 1974).

Wiltse, Charles M., *The Jeffersonian Tradition in American Democracy* (University of North Carolina Press, 1935).

World Federation of Scientific Workers, 'Declaration on the Rights of Scientific Workers', *Scientific World* (1969:4) pp. 23–5.

Yearbook of International Organisations [1981].

Zink, Harold, *The US in Germany, 1944–1955* (Princeton, N.J.: van Nostrand, 1957), Chapter 13.

Index

Notes: 1. Most references are to the United Nations, unless otherwise stated. 2. Organisations and groups are indexed under their full names. For explanations of abbreviations and acronyms, *see* pages xv–xviii. 3. Sub-entries are in alphabetical order except where chronological order is significant.